THE CHURCH IN PRE-REFORMATION SOCIETY

F. R. H. Du Boulay

THE CHURCH
IN
PRE-REFORMATION SOCIETY

Essays in Honour of F. R. H. Du Boulay

EDITED BY

CAROLINE M. BARRON AND CHRISTOPHER HARPER-BILL

THE BOYDELL PRESS

© Contributors 1985

First published 1985 by The Boydell Press
an imprint of Boydell & Brewer Ltd
PO Box 9, Woodbridge, Suffolk IP12 3DF and
51 Washington Street, Dover, New Hampshire 03820, USA

ISBN 0–85115–421–2

British Library Cataloguing in Publication Data

The Church in pre-Reformation society: essays in honour
of F. R. H. Du Boulay.
1. Church and the world   2. England—Church history
3. Church history—Middle Ages, 600–1500
I. Barron, Caroline M.   II. Harper-Bill, Christopher
III. Du Boulay, F. R. H.
261.1′0942   BR750

ISBN 0–85115–421–2

Library of Congress Cataloging in Publication Data

The Church in pre-Reformation society.
  Bibliography: p.
  Includes index.
  1. Europe—Church history—Middle Ages, 600–1500
  —Addresses, essays, lectures.   2. Church history
  —Middle Ages, 600–1500—Addresses, essays, lectures.
  3. Middle Ages—Addresses, essays, lectures.
  4. Du Boulay, F. R. H.—Addresses, essays, lectures.
  I. Du Boulay, F. R. H.   II. Barron, Caroline M.
  III. Harper-Bill, Christopher.
  BR252.C55 1985   270.5   85–16624

ISBN 0–85115–421–2

Printed and bound in Great Britain by
Short Run Press Ltd, Exeter

*The editors wish to acknowledge with gratitude a grant
towards the costs of publication of this volume
from the late Miss Isobel Thornley's Bequest
to the University of London.*

CONTENTS

F. R. H. Du Boulay
An Appreciation

These essays by the pupils, colleagues and friends of Robin Houssemayne Du Boulay are both the acknowledgement of an intellectual debt and a mark of deep affection. It is usual to preface a *Festschrift* with some biographical information about the scholar whom the volume is designed to honour. Such details are of interest primarily to other scholars. For those who are not in the trade, the following brief outline will perhaps suffice. Robin Du Boulay is one of that generation of medievalists whose education was interrupted, and whose historical training was begun, by the experience of soldiering in the Second World War. After five years of war service, he returned to Balliol and graduated with a First in History in 1947. The same year he took up a post as Assistant Lecturer at Bedford College in the University of London, and there he remained for the rest of his teaching career. He was appointed successively Lecturer, Reader, and in 1960 Professor, of Medieval History, a post he held until his retirement in 1982. From 1976 to 1980 he was head of the Bedford History Department.

This sparse chronicle conveys neither the quality of his contribution to the Bedford Department nor the scale of his achievement as a scholar. It was, I think, his singular gift as a teacher that he enabled his pupils to enter the minds of medieval people and to feel the influence of the lives of men and women of the remote past. For undergraduates a tutorial with Robin was an unforgettable experience. Over the years his pupils and his writings did much to get the Department widely known and acknowledged as a flourishing centre of medieval studies. Some notion of the breadth of his scholarly interests is indicated by the range of studies in this volume. His first and most abiding interest has been with medieval Kent, on which he is the leading authority. He came to it through his early work on the register of Archbishop Thomas Bourgchier. In his definitive study of *The Lordship of Canterbury*, which was published in 1966, he himself has described the process by which, as he studied the archbishop's letters, he gradually became aware of a great but shadowy army of clerks, stewards, bailiffs and lawyers, who administered the temporalities of the see, and found himself drawn inexorably into the denes and folds and sulungs of the Kentish Weald. But if he made Kent his native heath, he did not stay there. His *Age of Ambition*, which appeared in 1970, was a brilliant survey of the English social scene in the later Middle Ages, in which he threw down a challenge to the waning myth of economic decline. From there he moved to the study of the sources for the history of medieval Germany, which preoccupied him in the last decade of his university career and which bore fruit in his important book on *Germany in the Later Middle Ages*.

This is not the place to attempt an appraisal of Robin's *oeuvre*, which gained him the accolade of a Fellowship of the British Academy. In any case, it is far from finished. Here, in introducing a celebratory volume, I would rather record the intellectual inspiration of his company, which I have been privileged to enjoy for over thirty years; the good years – at the time hardly recognised for what they were – when we argued and talked History together and much else in the common room of St John's Hall; the literary confessions we exchanged when we walked on the South Downs above Plumstead; his quick sympathy, and the scintillating wit that had us all convulsed with laughter. Such things hardly bear repeating when cold. But they are memories that will stay with us always. Beyond the word spinning and the changes of mood, one always sensed a deeper conviction, something too serious to be alluded to except in jest, a desperately held belief that, despite the awfulness of the human condition, in the end all shall be well and all manner of thing shall be well.

Bedford College, 1985   C. H. LAWRENCE

INTRODUCTION

The economics of publishing nowadays necessitate the selection of a theme when soliciting essays for a celebratory volume. The unfortunate consequence is that many who are eager to contribute are excluded because their current work does not fall within the scope of the *Festschrift*. This honorand will know that the collection is offered, with affection and respect, by a circle far wider than those whose papers are here included. It may, even so, be thought that this volume covers a wide variety of topics within the chosen theme, and this is a reflection of Robin Du Boulay's own catholic historical interests, and the influence which he has exerted through his teaching and publications.

The involvement of the *ecclesia Anglicana* in the great debate which absorbed the intellectual energy of western Christendom for three-quarters of a century after 1378 was treated by F. R. H. Du B. as a central strand in his essay on the English church and the Papacy in the fifteenth century,[1] and is here reflected in the translation by Professor Dunstan of the important address of Jean Gerson, probably delivered to the English delegation proceeding to Pisa, in which he argued that canonical objections to the convening of a council other than by papal authority were outweighed by the dictates of *epieikeia*, that higher form of justice which transcends the letter of the law. Dr Harvey engages in a detailed examination of the views on the relationship of pope and council of John Whethamstede, abbot of St Albans, and finds him to be a conciliarist, if a somewhat confused one, in general convinced by the decrees of the councils and by historical arguments, although rejecting the validity of the deposition by the council of Basel of Eugenius IV.

It is particularly appropriate that Professor Logan should present in this volume his study of a formulary book which supplements the material available for the study of the pontificate of Archbishop Thomas Bourgchier, whose register was edited by F. R. H. Du B. In particular, this source extends our knowledge of the operation of the archbishop's court of Audience,

---

[1] 'The Fifteenth Century', *The English Church and the Papacy in the Middle Ages*, ed. C. H. Lawrence, 1965, 195–242.

standing at the summit of ecclesiastical jurisdiction within the realm, for which so little documentation has survived. A lesser ecclesiastical court stands at the centre of Miss Kettle's paper on the relationship between the cathedral and lay communities in fifteenth-century Lichfield. Despite his determination to preserve the isolation of the close and yet to intrude into many aspects of the life of the city, Dean Heywood is shown to have exercised his authority in a sympathetic and humane manner, and to have manifested concern for the spiritual welfare of those subject to his peculiar jurisdiction. Once more a church court is exonerated from the charges which have frequently been brought against such institutions.[2]

Three papers are concerned with the monastic Order in the century before the Dissolution. Dr Hare, following the trail blazed by the investigator of the lordship of Canterbury, illustrates the continued demesne farming of many houses until late in the fifteenth century, characterised particularly by the maintenance of sheep flocks. He suggests that the southern monasteries responded flexibly to changing economic circumstances, maintained their initiative and investment, and only in the 1490s were finally transformed into rentiers. This gradual shift did, however, increase the dependence of the religious upon their lay neighbours, on whom they relied increasingly for the supply of food and for the administration of their estates. This reliance is probably one of the factors leading to mounting, and frequently justified, dissatisfaction with conventual diet, discussed in a paper which, it is hoped, may reflect F. R. H. Du B.'s consistent sympathetic interest in the vagaries of ordinary human behaviour. Dr Dunning's detailed study of the Cistercian abbey of Cleeve emphasises the economic difficulties of the house, caused by the maintenance of hospitality and corrodians, the exploitation of the community's assets by laypeople, especially the kin of the abbot, but most interestingly, and perhaps surprisingly, by the steady rate of recruitment to the cloister which over-taxed conventual resources. Despite the scruples of Henry VIII's commissioner, however, there seems to have been little manifestation of popular regret at the dissolution of this monastery.

In recent years there has been a shift away from concentration on ecclesiastical institutions towards a consideration of the religious climate of late medieval England. F. R. H. Du B. himself led the way in his treatment of 'The Apparatus of Religion',[3] in which he rejected the myth of decline and decay, stagnation and superstition, renouncing the folly of judging the increasing number of literate layfolk of the fifteenth century by the standards of spiritual giants such as St Bernard, and emphasising that one should take 'pride in modest but widespread advance, expecting something more of the children then being born and put to school'.[4] The educational achievement of

---

[2] For a recent treatment of similar courts, see Sandra Brown, *The Medieval Courts of York Minster Peculiar* (Borthwick Papers lxvi), York 1984.

[3] *An Age of Ambition*, 1970, 143–59.

[4] *An Age of Ambition*, 144.

the age, and particularly the contribution of the Lancastrian bishops, is here surveyed by Professor Rosenthal, who concludes that even if only half the episcopate were moved to become founders or benefactors of educational establishments, yet their efforts contributed greatly to noteworthy expansion of opportunity. Their main investment was, of course, in the training of young men destined for, or already members of the clerical order, but it is certain that some who never entered the priesthood also benefited, either directly or indirectly.

The religious attitudes of the laity are considered in several essays in this volume. At the highest level of the royal court, Miss Crawford examines the role of queens-consort and the mothers of kings as potential leaders of religious fashion, and finds in three generations of royal ladies an intense devotion far from stereotyped in its manifestations. Dr Hicks's survey of the Hungerford foundations leads him to propose important modifications to the received view of the availability of licences to alienate in mortmain and of the number of intercessory institutions in early Tudor England. He records lavish benefactions of a conventional kind, directed no longer towards the monasteries but to secular chantries and hospitals, and most significantly, he detects a disinclination to make any spiritual investment in those foundations established by ancestors, or even to implement their bequests, but rather a desire to found anew for the benefit of the soul of the donor himself. It seems that, just as the English gentleman was becoming divorced in his religious life from the mass of the population, so he abandoned any great concern for the salvation of his own progenitors.[5] The study by Professor Jack of the lordship of Dyffryn Clwyd, which examines the religious manifestations characteristic of the intermingling of races in a Marcher lordship and the interaction of episcopal and seignorial courts, concentrates upon the career of Edmund, earl of Kent, whose religiosity led him to an interesting if unsuccessful experiment in monastic foundation, to the usurpation of the moral jurisdiction of the church courts and to the encouragement of a programme of ecclesiastical rebuilding and ornamentation throughout his lordship.

At a lower social level, the current preoccupation with religious associations of laypeople is reflected in Dr Barron's study of parish fraternities in medieval London. Few in number before the mid-fourteenth century, they multiplied dramatically in the wake of the Black Death, a reflection of the desire for decent burial and concerted prayer for the dead. Their membership was predominantly artisan, and within them women played a significant role. This paper supports the assertion by Professor Scarisbrick of the importance of guilds and lay fraternities in the pre-Reformation church, but diverges from his interpretation in seeing, as does Dr Tanner in his study of Norwich, a strong element of continuity in the vitality of parish life,

---

[5] See Colin Richmond, 'Religion and the Fifteenth-Century English Gentleman', *Church, Politics and Patronage*, 193–208.

expressed before 1548 in participation in such fraternities, and in the Elizabethan age by the endowment of Puritan lectureships.[6]

As an epilogue to these investigations of the church and religion in late medieval England, Mrs Russell emphasises the crucial part which Mary Tudor hoped that the University of Oxford would play in her plans for the restoration of traditional religion, and recounts her efforts to strengthen the university through the exercise of patronage and by financial support, and by quieting fears of the misappropriation of academic possessions. Her endeavours were posthumously rewarded by the adherence to the old faith of many *alumni* of Marian Oxford. In the wider context, Mary is dissociated from the strident new brand of Tridentine Catholicism. She sought to re-establish in England, through the encouragement of preaching and education, the old pattern of religious belief and practice destroyed by her father and by her brother's ministers, and was not deterred from this intention by any novel ideas emanating from Rome.[7]

Finally, two papers on the ecclesiastical affairs of the Germanic world reflect Robin Du Boulay's migration, in the most recent phase of his academic career, from the farms of Kent to the largely uncharted territory of late medieval German politics and social organisation. Like several of the contributors on English themes, Dr Rady emphasises the importance of guilds and fraternities in late medieval Buda, and shows how, in addition to their religious, philanthropic and commercial functions, they served either as agents of German domination or as channels of Hungarian resentment. He reveals also how the German stranglehold on the formal ecclesiastical organisation of the city was broken only in the wake of the rebellion of 1439, which resulted in a more equitable political settlement. Dr Burleigh, concentrating on the career of the forceful Bishop Franz of Ermland and the lay reaction to his attempts to secure the untrammelled judicial supremacy of the German Order, finds no reason to doubt that violent anticlericalism, the very existence of which in England has recently been questioned,[8] was endemic in Prussian society. and suggests that the explanation lies not in any structural weakness in society or lack of strong governance, but in the vociferously aggressive clericalism by which the Estates were confronted.

It is impossible that any common argument can emerge from so diverse a collection of essays, although many of the studies do suggest that the late medieval church was far from moribund, and that the Reformation grew out of the vitality of fifteenth-century religion. It is hoped that they will all in

---

[6] Scarisbrick, *Reformation*, 19–39; N. P. Tanner, *The Church in Late Medieval Norwich, 1370–1532*, Toronto 1984, 73–82, 170–71.
[7] See Christopher Haigh, 'From Monopoly to Minority: Catholicism in Early Modern England', *TRHS* 5th series xxxi, 1981, 129–47; 'The Continuity of Catholicism in the English Reformation', *P & P* xciii, 1981, 37–69.
[8] Christopher Haigh, 'Anticlericalism and the English Reformation', *History* n.s. lxviii, 1983, 391–407.

various ways illuminate some corner of the social and ecclesiastical history of the period. Most of all, however, the contributors would wish that their papers might give some pleasure to a scholar who has been in the vanguard of the exploration and exploitation of the sources for the history of the later middle ages.

Lady Day, 1985   C.H-B.

In the interval between conceiving and realising this volume of essays, I became Dean of Arts of a college which was merging with another academic institution. The result of this has been that Christopher has borne the brunt of the editorial work, and the achievement of the volume is largely his. I am immensely grateful to him for all that he has done.

C.M.B.

ABBREVIATIONS

AgHR	*Agricultural History Review*
Anc. Deeds	*Descriptive Catalogue of Ancient Deeds*, 6 vols., 1890–1915.
Arch. Cant.	*Archaeologia Cantiana*
Benedictine Chapters	*Documents Illustrative of the General and Provincial Chapters of the English Black Monks 1215–1540*, ed. W. A. Pantin (Camden Society, 3rd series xlv, xlvii, liv), 1931–37.
BIHR	*Bulletin of the Institute of Historical Research*
BJRL	*Bulletin of the John Rylands Library*
BL	British Library
Blythe's Visitations	*Bishop Geoffrey Blythe's Visitations, c. 1515–1525*, ed. P. Heath (Staffordshire Record Society, 4th series vii), 1973.
BRUC	A. B. Emden, *Biographical Register of the University of Cambridge to 1500*, Cambridge 1963.
BRUO	A. B. Emden, *Biographical Register of the University of Oxford to 1500*, Oxford 1957–59.
BRUO 1501–40	A. B. Emden, *Biographical Register of the University of Oxford, A.D. 1501–1540*, Oxford 1974.
CAP	*Collectanea Anglo-Premonstratensia*, ed. F. A. Gasquet (Camden Society, 3rd series vi, x, xii), 1904–6.
CCR	*Calendar of Close Rolls*, 67 vols., 1902 etc.
CPL	*Calendar of Entries in the Papal Registers relating to Great Britain . . .*, 15 vols., 1901 etc.

CPR	*Calendar of Patent Rolls*, 60 vols., 1901 etc.
CSP Dom.	*Calendar of State Papers, Domestic*
CYS	Canterbury and York Society
D&C	Dean and Chapter
EcHR	*Economic History Review*
EETS	Early English Text Society
EHR	*English Historical Review*
Ep. Ac. Ox.	*Epistolae Academicae Oxonienses*, ed. H. Anstey (OHS xxxv–vi), 1898.
Fasti 1300–1541	*John Le Neve, Fasti Ecclesiae Anglicanae 1300–1541*, ed. J. M. Horn, B. Jones and H. P. F. King, 1962–67.
HBC	*Handbook of British Chronology*, ed. F. M. Powicke and E. B. Fryde, 2nd edn, 1961.
HJ	*Historical Journal*
HMCR	*Reports of the Historical Manuscripts Commission*
HMSO	Her Majesty's Stationery Office
JEH	*Journal of Ecclesiastical History*
JMH	*Journal of Medieval History*
Linc. Vis. 1420–49	*Visitations of Religious Houses in the Diocese of Lincoln, 1420–49*, ed. A. Hamilton Thompson (LRS vii, xiv, xxi, and CYS xvii, xxiv, xxxiii), 1914–29.
Linc. Vis. 1517–31	*Visitations in the Diocese of Lincoln 1517–31*, ed. A. Hamilton Thompson (LRS xxxiii, xxxv, xxxvii), 1940–47.
LJRO	Lichfield Joint Record Office
LP	*Letters and Papers, Foreign and Domestic, of the Reign of Henry VIII, 1509–47*, 21 vols., 1862–1920.
LRS	Lincoln Record Society
Monasticon	*Monasticon Anglicanum* of William Dugdale, ed. J. Caley *et al.*, 6 vols. in 8 parts, 1817–30.
MRH	D. Knowles and R. N. Hadcock, *Medieval Religious Houses, England and Wales*, 2nd edn, 1971.

9

Norwich Vis.	*Visitations of the Diocese of Norwich, A.D. 1492–1532,* ed. A. Jessopp (Camden Society, n.s. xliii), 1888.
n.s.	new series
OHS	Oxford Historical Society
o.s.	old series
PCC	Prerogative Court of Canterbury
PG	*Patrologia Graeca,* ed. J. P. Migne, 221 vols., Paris 1841–64.
P & P	*Past and Present*
PPC	*Proceedings and Ordinances of the Privy Council of England,* ed. N. H. Nicolas, 1834.
PRO	Public Record Office, London
Reg.	Register (followed by bishop's name)
Reg. Bekynton	*Register of Thomas Bekynton, bishop of Bath and Wells 1443–65,* ed. H. C. Maxwell-Lyte (SRS xlix, l), 1934–35.
Reg. Bourgchier	*Registrum Thome Bourgchier Cantuariensis Archiepiscopi 1454–86,* ed. F. R. H. Du Boulay (CYS liv), 1956.
Reg. Chichele	*Register of Henry Chichele, Archbishop of Canterbury 1414–43,* ed. E. F. Jacob (CYS xlii, xlv–vii), 1937–47.
Reg. Hallum	*Register of Robert Hallum, Bishop of Salisbury 1407–17,* ed. J. M. Horn (CYS lxii), 1982.
Reg. King	*Registers of Oliver King and Hadrian de Castello, bishops of Bath and Wells 1496–1503 and 1503–18,* ed. H. C. Maxwell-Lyte (SRS liv), 1939.
Reg. Myllyng	*Registrum Thome Myllyng episcopi Herefordensis 1474–92,* ed. A. T. Bannister (CYS xxvi), 1920.
Reg. Stillington	*Registers of Robert Stillington and Richard Fox, bishops of Bath and Wells 1466–91 and 1492–4,* ed. H. C. Maxwell-Lyte (SRS lii), 1937.
RO	Record Office
Rot. Parl.	*Rotuli Parliamentorum: the Rolls of Parliament,* 6 vols and index, 1783–1832.

RS	Rolls Series, 99 vols, 1858–97.
RSB	*The Rule of St Benedict*, ed. J. McCann, 1952.
SAC	*Sussex Archaeological Collections*
SCH	*Studies in Church History*
Som. Med. Wills, *1383–1500* and *1531–58*	*Somerset Medieval Wills 1383–1500* and *1531–58*, ed. F. W. Weaver (SRS xvi, xxi), 1901–5.
SRO	Somerset Record Office
SRS	Somerset Record Society
Test. Vet.	Testamenta Vetusta, ed. N. H. Nicolas, 2 vols., 1826.
TRHS	*Transactions of the Royal Historical Society*
VCH	*Victoria County History*
VE	*Valor Ecclesiasticus temp. Henry VIII, auctoritate regia institutus*, ed. J. Caley and J. Hunter, 6 vols., 1810–34.
WAM	*Wiltshire Archaeological Magazine*
WRO	Wiltshire Record Office
YAJ	*Yorkshire Archaeological Journal*

SHORTENED TITLES

The following abbreviated titles are used for frequently cited works.

Church, Politics and Patronage	*The Church, Politics and Patronage in the Fifteenth Century*, ed. R. B. Dobson, Gloucester 1984.
Griffiths, *Henry VI*	R. A. Griffiths, *The Reign of Henry VI*, 1981.
Knowles, *RO*	D. Knowles, *The Religious Orders in England*, 3 vols., Cambridge 1948–59.
Pfaff, *Feasts*	R. W. Pfaff, *New Liturgical Feasts in Later Medieval England*, Oxford 1970.
Scarisbrick, *Reformation*	J. J. Scarisbrick, *The Reformation and the English People*, Oxford 1984.

Weiss, *Humanism* R. Weiss, *Humanism in England in the Fifteenth Century*, Oxford 1957.

Wilkins, *Concilia* *Concilia Magnae Brittaniae et Hiberniae* . . . *446–1718*, ed. D. Wilkins, 4 vols., 1737.

Unless otherwise stated, the place of publication of all works cited is London.

The Parish Fraternities of Medieval London

CAROLINE M. BARRON

By the beginning of the sixteenth century medieval London comprised 107 parishes within the City's jurisdiction, and a further ten lay in the suburbs. Within these parishes, but by no means evenly distributed throughout the parish network, there were a host of lesser groupings known as parish fraternities or guilds. These were voluntary associations of men and women linked together to provide mutual charitable help and communal prayers for living and dead members. Between 1350 and 1550 there are references to between 150 and 200 of these associations within the parishes of London, both inside the walls and outside in the suburbs, if it is proper to describe Westminster and Southwark in this way.[1]

The parish guilds of medieval London received a fair amount of scholarly attention at the beginning of this century, but then languished for a time.[2] Recently, however, historians have been concerned to explore the nature of popular piety in England in the century before the Reformation. Heresy has always provoked attention, but the ordinary religion of ordinary people is more elusive. Several historians, in particular Dr J. A. F. Thomson, Dr Susan Brigden and Professor J. Scarisbrick have been exploring the character of parish life in England in the fifteenth century. All three have emphasised the importance of parish fraternities as suggestive of the vitality of Christian faith and practice, and of the neighbourly and social obligations which bound the parish community together.[3] It is surely likely that it is in their

---

[1] C. L. Kingsford, *Prejudice and Promise in Fifteenth Century England*, Oxford 1925, 141, noted that he had identified 160 parish fraternities in London but gave no sources. I have identified 176 London parish fraternities, but some of these rapidly developed into trade guilds and there must be many others whose existence is not revealed by the chance survival of the evidence for which see below pp. 18–23.

[2] See George Unwin, *The Guilds and Companies of London*, 1911, esp. chap. ix; H. F. Westlake, *The Parish Guilds of Medieval England*, 1919; L. Toulmin Smith, *English Gilds* (EETS, 1870).

[3] J. A. F. Thomson, 'Clergy and Laity in London 1376–1531' (unpublished Oxford D.Phil. thesis 1960), chap. ii; Scarisbrick, *Reformation*, chap. ii; Susan Brigden, 'Religion and Social Obligation in Early Sixteenth-century London', *P & P* ciii, 1984, 67–112.

13

voluntary associations that medieval men and women most truly expressed their priorities and preoccupations.

The size of London's population ensured that there was a degree of specialisation of purpose in the hundreds of different associations within the city: the larger the population, the greater the degree of specialisation. It is therefore possible to distinguish more clearly than elsewhere different kinds of associations or groupings for different purposes. Interestingly, and for our purpose helpfully, the government of London was not carried on by a guild, as at York or Coventry. The old Anglo-Saxon cnichtengild of London was already disintegrating by the twelfth century and in its place emerged government by Aldermen, each representing a territorial unit of the city. By the fourteenth century, although the aldermen took an oath and wore a common livery, they had no religious association and came from a variety of trades. The Common Council was, by the fifteenth century, also composed of ward representatives and did not even wear a common livery. So, as early as the thirteenth century, the government of London had outgrown its guild structure and, even at the local level, it was not the parish fraternities which were responsible for local government. The citizens met together in the wardmotes to elect their beadles and ward officers and to present offenders and offences.[4] Because they lacked this governing role parish guilds in London were more spontaneous, and more voluntary, than elsewhere. It was not necessary to join them to get to the top or to exercise power.

The link between the parish fraternities and the trade guilds is, however, less easily severed. Every craft association in London, as elsewhere, had at its core a fraternity or religious brotherhood dedicated to the worship and promotion of a particular saint. But it is important to try to eliminate craft associations from this study because their purposes were different and, to some extent, their membership was not entirely voluntary. By the fifteenth century it is possible to separate true parish fraternities from craft guilds, but it is not so easy in the fourteenth century when this distinction was only just beginning to develop with the explosion of the guild movement as a whole. It is clear that in many cases a guild began as a neighbourhood fraternity but then, perhaps because men following the same craft tended to live in the same area, these parish associations developed into trade fraternities and then, later, into trade or craft companies. For example, the guild of Corpus Christi in the church of All Hallows, Bread Street, was first referred to in the wills of a mercer and a salter in 1349. But later most of the bequests to the guild were from salters and in 1454 Thomas Beaumond, a salter, bequeathed land to the fraternity on which a hall called 'Salters' Hall' was in course of being built. By 1483 the chapel of the Corpus Christi guild in All Hallows

---

[4] For a discussion of the structure of London government in the fifteenth century see my thesis 'London and its relations with the Crown 1400–1450' (London Ph.D. thesis, 1970).

was known as the Salters' chapel.[5] In the same way the joiners seem, by the end of the fourteenth century, to have taken over the fraternity of St James in the church of St James Garlickhythe (although the fraternity return of 1388 gave no hint of such a craft association).[6] The poulterers took over the fraternity of Corpus Christi in the church of St Mildred Poultry and adopted the little chapel of St Mary Coneyhope in the parish as their own.[7] The butchers appear to have monopolised the guild dedicated to the Virgin Mary in St Leonard Eastcheap[8] and, among the great trading companies, the drapers took over the guild of the Virgin in St Mary le Bow[9] and the skinners dominated the Virgin's guild in St John Walbrook and also the Corpus Christi guild in the same church.[10]

The way in which this transformation from neighbourhood fraternity to trade fraternity took place is well illustrated in the case of the brewers. In 1342 a group of seven Londoners, including a chandler, a whitetawyer, an

[5] R. R. Sharpe, *Calendar of Wills enrolled in the Court of Husting*, 2 vols., 1859 (hereafter *HW*), i 547, 565–6; ii 533, 534, 535, 587.

[6] The fraternity ordinances of 1388 are printed in R. W. Chambers and Marjorie Daunt, *A Book of London English 1384–1425*, Oxford 1931, 44–7 (hereafter Chambers and Daunt). Bequests by joiners to the fraternity are recorded in the Archdeacon of London, Register of Wills, Guildhall Library, MS 9051/1 in 1398 fo. 13; 1405 fos. 13v–14; 1407 fos. 19–19v; 1412 fo. 15v. I am extremely grateful to Robert Wood who has read all the wills in the Archdeacons' Register (1393–1414) and most kindly provided me with references to bequests to fraternities and guilds. For the association of the joiners' company with the fraternity of St James Garlickhithe see also H. L. Phillips, *Annals of the Worshipful Company of Joiners*, 1915, 2.

[7] This fraternity was established in the chapel of the Blessed Virgin in Coneyhope lane in the parish of St Mildred Poultry. The first reference to the fraternity appears in the will of a helmet-maker in 1349, *HW* i 576 and there were bequests from smiths and armourers in 1394, 1399 and 1408, Guildhall Library MS 9051/1 1395 fo. 5v; 1398 fo. 20v; 1408 fo. 3v; bequests from poulterers are recorded in 1397, *HW* ii, 335 and Guildhall Library MS 9051/1 1397 fos. 7v–8. In 1441 John Hildy, poulterer, made a bequest to the guild of Corpus Christi in the chapel of St Mary de Conynghopelane *HW* i 501. See also *Anc. Deeds* A 7595, A11938. See also John Stow, *A Survey of London*, ed. C. L. Kingsford, 2 vols., Oxford 1908 (hereafter, Stow), i, 263; C. J. Kitching ed., *London and Middlesex Chantry Certificate 1548*, London Record Society 1980 (hereafter *Chantry*), 100.

[8] There are bequests from butchers, or their widows, to the fraternity of the Blessed Virgin in St Leonard Eastcheap recorded in 1383, 1389, 1422, 1434, 1442, *HW* ii, 257, 280, 433, 495, 563. The chantry return of 1548 mentions some of these bequests, but not the fraternity, *Chantry*, 31b.

[9] In 1361 certain good men of the drapers of Cornhill, and other good men and women had founded a fraternity dedicated to the Blessed Virgin in the Hospital of St Mary of Bethlehem outside Bishopsgate, PRO, C47/42/202. Bequests are recorded from a jeweller in 1364, a vintner in 1371 and a draper in 1380, *HW* ii, 90, 159, 218. But the drapers appear to have switched their allegiance from St Mary Bethlehem to the more central church of St Mary le Bow. A fraternity there, dedicated to the Virgin, first appears in 1361 and attracted pouchmakers and leather merchants, but by 1388 Robert Warwyk, a draper, made a bequest to the 'Common Box of the fraternity of St Mary established by the drapers in the church of St Mary le Bow', *HW* ii, 271. From this time onwards the Drapers monopolised the fraternity there, see A. H. Johnson, *History of the Worshipful Company of Drapers of London*, Oxford 1914, i, 110–11.

[10] Elspeth M. Veale, *The English Fur Trade in the Later Middle Ages*, Oxford 1966, 105–15; the earlier guild dedicated to the Virgin developed into the fraternity of the yeomanry and the Corpus Christi guild became the fraternity of the livery.

attorney at law and a brewer decided to repair a chapel in the church of All Hallows London Wall 'in honour of Jesus Christ who hanged on the Cross and of his mother and all saints'. They funded a taper to burn before the cross in the chapel. Then the first pestilence came and all the members of this small fraternity died except John Enefeld, a brewer, who 'assembled other good men of the brewers of London and persuaded them to maintain the light in the church'. At his death in 1361 John Enefeld bequeathed a tenement in West Smithfield to the fraternity, and in 1383 the four wardens of the guild (two of whom may be certainly identified as brewers) purchased a rent to help support the costs of a chaplain. The fact that this guild was developing into a craft guild is revealed by the tell-tale clause in the ordinances returned into Chancery in 1389: no member of the fraternity was to receive the servant of another member unless he left 'in a good manner' and with his master's good will. A further clause stipulated that if a member placed his son or daughter with another to learn the craft, then the brethren were to help to ensure that the terms of the indenture were carried out. Such clauses are never to be found amongst the ordinances of 'pure' parish fraternities and reveal that between 1342 and 1389 the original small fraternity founded simply to maintain a light before the Cross in a chapel in All Hallows church, had developed into the craft fraternity of the brewers.[11]

Not all the guild returns of 1388/9 make this distinction clear. For example neither the self-declared brotherhood of whitetawyers which met to honour the Virgin in the church of All Hallows London Wall, nor the pouchmakers who honoured the Virgin in the Hospital of Our Lady of Bethlehem outside Bishopsgate, included any craft clauses among their ordinances and, if they had not declared themselves to be associations of whitetawyers or pouch-makers, there would be no way of knowing this from their ordinances.[12] On the other hand, like the brewers, the curriers who met at Whitefriars, the carpenters (appropriately dedicated to St Joseph) who met at St Thomas of Acon and at St John at Halliwell and the glovers who met in the chapel of the new plague churchyard (later Charterhouse) all inserted craft clauses into their ordinances.[13] The glovers' ordinances are very detailed, the curriers'

---

[11] The fraternity return of 1389 is in two parts, PRO, C47/42/206 and 471.

[12] The return of the whitetawyers is PRO, C47/42/211 and that of the pouchmakers C47/46/464 which is also printed in Chambers and Daunt, 53–7.

[13] The return of the fraternity of the curriers is in the Bodleian Library, MS London and Middlesex Roll 3; the return of the carpenters is PRO, C47/46/465 and is also printed in Chambers and Daunt, 41–4; the glovers made a return in 1389 but no saint is specified nor place of meeting, PRO, C47/42/217. One of the fifteenth-century registers of the Commissary Court of London contains the enrolled ordinances of the fraternity of the craft of glovers, dated to 1354 when the fraternity met at Newchurchhawe (later Charterhouse). Although these ordinances may contain a core of fourteenth-century clauses, many of the ordinances are distinctly fifteenth century in character, see H. C. Coote, 'Ordinances of some secular guilds of London', *Transactions of the London and Middlesex Archaeological Society* (hereafter *TLMAS*) iv, 1871, 33–7.

quite brief and the carpenters merely enjoin that:

> if any brother go idle for default of work and another brother has work whereon he may worken his brother, and that work be such that his brother can work it, then shall he work his brother before any other thing, and give him as another man would take of him for the same work.[14]

But whereas this craft or trade regulation element was rare among the ordinances of 1388, even among self-confessedly craft associations, yet by the fifteenth century there was no longer any confusion between what was, and what was not, a craft guild. In the 1380s the difference was in the process of definition as groups of men drew up their ordinances for the first time.

If parish fraternities in London may be distinguished from governing groups and from trade or craft associations, they may also be distinguished from confraternities. Only one of the 150 or so London parish fraternities ever calls itself a confraternity, and that is the fraternity of the Holy Blood of Wilsnak established in 1491 in the church of the Austin Friars.[15] Their use of the word confraternity may reveal the European origins of the membership, since the word was frequently used on the continent. In Florence the word confraternity was used indiscriminately and meant simply fraternity or association.[16] In England, however, confraternity was used to mean 'association with', an outside group joined in some way, but not completely, to a larger body. In 1455 William Estfeld, a mercer and ex-mayor of London, bequeathed a cask of red Gascony wine, or its value, to St Alban's Abbey, the Priory Church at Canterbury, the Charterhouse at London, the Priory Church at Walsingham and to the Convent at Sopewell Hertfordshire, because he was a capitular brother of each of these houses.[17] The Priory of St Mary Overy in Southwark had an association of *confratres*, and the advent of printing seems to have stimulated the practice of confraternity in the religious houses of London.[18] Early in the sixteenth century the Carmelites, the Hospitals of St Mary Bethlehem, St Thomas of Acon and St Katharine

---

[14] Chambers and Daunt, 43. I have modernised the spelling.

[15] Coote, *TLMAS* iv, 1871, 65–9. There was another brotherhood dedicated to the Holy Blood of Wilsnak established in the Crutched Friary in 1459, *ibid*, 59–62. On this cult see Jonathan Sumption, *Pilgrimage*, 1975, chap. iv.

[16] See John S. Henderson, 'Piety and Charity in Late Medieval Florence' (unpublished London Ph.D. thesis, 1983) and see also his 'The flagellant movement and flagellant confraternities in central Italy 1260–1400', *SCH* xv, 1978, 147–60. I am very grateful to Dr Henderson for many helpful discussions about Florentine confraternities. See also Brian Pullan, *Rich and Poor in Renaissance Venice: the Social Institutions of a Catholic State*, Oxford 1971; Ronald F. E. Weissman, *Ritual Brotherhood in Renaissance Florence*, 1982.

[17] *HW* ii, 510.

[18] Membership lists of this confraternity survived as flyleaves of a Book of Hours, BL Additional MS 62105. I am most grateful to Dr Martha Carlin for drawing this manuscript to my attention. For letters of confraternity see Clark Maxwell, 'Some letters of Confraternity', *Archaeologia* lxxv, 1926, 19–60 and lxxix, 1929, 179–216.

by the Tower all advertised their confraternities through the medium of the printed word.[19] At St Katharine's a *confrater* made a single payment of ten shillings and four pence, or spread the sum over seven years, and in return received the usual prayers and also a room, bedding and food in old age.[20] Obviously the practices of confraternities must have influenced the practices of parish fraternities, but they were different kinds of associations. Whereas confraternities were organised by the religious houses to raise money from lay people for spiritual ends, parish fraternities were spontaneous and self-motivated associations and reveal a different aspect of lay piety.[21]

Of the 150 or so parish fraternities which are known to have existed in London only seven have left any records of their own. From Westminster there survive some accounts of the guild founded in the small hospital and chapel of St Mary Rounceval at Charing Cross and also a reasonably substantial run of accounts of the guild of Our Lady's Assumption in St Margaret's church.[22] The guild of the Assumption in St Margaret's church in Southwark also has a few accounts surviving among the parish records.[23] The Register book of the fraternity of St Charity and St John the Baptist survives as a much damaged Cotton manuscript in the British Museum[24] and there is a fine Bede book in the Guildhall library, which belonged to the

[19] *A Short Title Catalogue of books printed in England . . . 1475–1640*, comp. A. W. Pollard and G. R. Redgrave, 2nd edn 1976, 14077 c50–56a.

[20] The fraternity in the Hospital of St Katharine by the Tower made a return in 1389 and there are bequests recorded in 1378, 1386, PRO, C47/42/216, *HW* ii, 209, 268, 343. The fraternity appears to have been refounded and dedicated to St Barbara early in the sixteenth century. An account of the distinguished membership, headed by Henry VIII and Queen Katherine, and of the social benefits which could be derived from membership was printed in 1518 when Sir William Skevington was master, see *Short Title Catalogue*, 14077 c55a. It was probably this printed prospectus which Strype saw and incorporated into his *Survey of the Cities of London and Westminster*, 1720, i part 2, 6–7.

[21] It is interesting to note, however, that the advent of printing seems to have encouraged enterprising parish fraternities to offer associated membership to outsiders and thus to style themselves as confraternities, see the printed leaflets of the confraternities of St Ursula in St Lawrence Jewry, St George in Southwark and St Cornelius in Westminster, *Short Title Catalogue*, 14077 c59, 70 and Brigden, 'Religion and Social Obligation', fig. 2.

[22] The accounts for the guild of the Assumption survive for 1474–77, 1487–90, 1505–08, 1515–21, and for St Mary Rounceval for 1520–24, 1538–40, these are bound together in a single volume in the Westminster Abbey Muniment room. These accounts were used by Westlake (see n. 2) but have been most recently studied by Dr A. G. Rosser in 'Medieval Westminster: the vill and Urban community 1200–1540' (unpublished London Ph.D. thesis, 1984) and in his article 'The Essence of Medieval Urban Communities: the vill of Westminster 1200–1540', *TRHS* xxxiv (1984), 99–112.

[23] Accounts for 1495–97, 1533–34, Greater London RO, P92/SAV/5, 6, 14. There are also some miscellaneous receipts, etc., P92/SAV/23, 28, 29. For a discussion of the fraternities in Southwark see Martha Carlin, 'The Urban Development of Southwark c. 1200–1550' (unpublished University of Toronto thesis, 1983).

[24] BL MS Vitellius F xvi fos. 113–23. This fraternity was established in the Hospital of St Augustine Pappey in 1430 to care for poor and impotent priests, Stow, i, 146, 161; ii 293 and T. Hugo, 'The Hospital of Le Papey in the City of London', *TLMAS* v (1877), 183–221.

fraternity of parish clerks in the city dedicated to St Nicholas.[25] There are, in fact, only two London fraternities whose records survive as more than fragments. The register and accounts of the united guilds of the Holy Trinity and SS Fabian and Sebastian survive in a manuscript now at the British Museum. The register, compiled c. 1463 covers events from 1377 to the Dissolution of the Chantries, but most of the information, the rental and accounts, dates from the 1440s and 1450s.[26] The other substantial register is that of the guild of the Name of Jesus which met in the Shrouds beneath St Paul's Cathedral. This fraternity, which was originally founded in the middle of the fifteenth century, was reformed by John Colet when he was Dean of St Paul's. The manuscript, now in the Bodleian Library, records on the flyleaf that it was 'bought and ordained by Master John Colet, Anno 1507' and contains detailed ordinances, copies of letters patent, deeds and complete accounts from 1513 to 1534.[27]

The register of the parish church of St Peter Cornhill, compiled c. 1425–26, has copied into it the 1403 ordinances of the guild of St Peter in that church.[28] About thirty other London parishes have surviving records, either churchwardens' accounts or parish registers and cartularies, which date from before 1540 but none of them contains anything but incidental material relating to parish fraternities.[29] On occasion the guildwardens contributed sums of money to church expenses, or lent torches or burial cloths, but there are no guild accounts intermingled with those of the churchwardens. What seems to be clear is that the guild or fraternity wardens, like the light-wardens, kept their own separate accounts. The wardens of the guild of Our Lady and the Jesus Brotherhood in the church of St Dunstan in the East had their own boxes and, on occasion, paid sums over to the churchwardens.[30] When the parishioners of St Michael Cornhill drew up regulations in 1480 for the better ordering of the finances of the church, it was laid down that the churchwardens and the wardens of the brotherhoods were to bring in their

[25] Guildhall Library MS 4889 (usually on exhibition in the Museum of London). The Bede roll covers the years 1448–1523. The earliest reference to the guild is to be found in a bequest in 1406, Guildhall Library MS 9051/1 1406 fo. 8. The parish clerks tried, unsuccessfully, in 1548 to claim that they were a trade guild, see J. Christie, *Some account of the Parish Clerks*, 1893, and R. H. Adams, *Parish Clerks of London*, 1971.

[26] P. Basing, ed., *Parish Fraternity Register: Fraternity of the Holy Trinity and SS Fabian and Sebastian in the Parish of St Botolph without Aldersgate*, London Record Society 1982.

[27] Bodleian Library MS Tanner 221. Extracts from this volume were printed by W. Sparrow-Simpson, *Registrum Statutorum et Consuetudinem Ecclesiae Cathedralis Sancti Pauli Londinensis*, 1873, 435–62.

[28] Guildhall Library MS 4158 fos. 131–65. Long extracts were printed in *HMCR, Sixth Report, Appendix*, 1877, 411–14.

[29] For a list of Pre-Reformation churchwardens' accounts, see Guildhall Library, *Churchwardens Accounts of Parish Churches within the City of London, a handlist*, 2nd edn, 1969. For a list of London parish cartularies see A. G. Dyson, 'A Calendar of the Cartulary of the Parish Church of St Margaret Bridge Street', *Guildhall Studies in London History* i, 1974, 163–91, esp. 163 n. 4.

[30] Guildhall Library MS 4887, accounts of St Dunstan in the East 1497–1509, see fos. 7, 113, 123, 132.

accounts regularly.[31] Thomas Bentley, who wrote the history of his parish church of St Andrew Holborn in the 1580s clearly had access to the brotherhood rolls of the St Sythe guild and the guild of St John and St Christopher which are now lost.[32] Such examples might be multiplied. Almost none of this material now survives and much of our information about the London parish guilds must be tangential.

Royal covetousness provoked two important collections of evidence, one near the start of this survey and the other towards the end. The earlier collection of material is known as the guild returns of 1388–89; the later collection is the chantry certificates of 1546 and 1548. The earlier enquiry, initiated at the Cambridge Parliament of 1388 may have been prompted by fear as well as greed. The sheriffs were instructed to require all masters and keepers of guilds and fraternities, and also of misteries of artificers, to return into Chancery such licences as they had for the existence of the guild, together with any rules, forms of oaths, details of congregations, assemblies, liveries, privileges, lands and rents (whether within or without mortmain) and of any goods or chattels. In response to this demand some thirty-one religious and fourteen craft guilds in London brought in their rules, and details about their foundation and endowments, to Chancery early in 1389.[33] It is most unlikely that we have the complete corpus of such returns: many must have been lost or strayed from Chancery. Indeed four of the London returns are now to be found among the miscellaneous charters in the Bodleian Library.[34] It is likely that many guilds avoided making any sort of return. Certainly there are references to guilds which existed before 1388 and for which there are now no returns. It is likely that the Parliament of 1388 was anxious to ensure that land was not slipping into mortmain without the purchase of a licence (to compensate the king for lost services), but the MPs may also have been anxious to flush out dangerous secret societies, the kind of illicit secret associations which contemporaries believed lay behind the Great Rising of 1381.[35] Certainly London had spawned numbers of associations of discontented yeomen, journeymen and day labourers who tried to

---

[31] W. H. Overall, *Accounts of the Churchwardens of St. Michael Cornhill 1456–1608*, 1869, 200–206, 212.

[32] Caroline M. Barron and Jane Roscoe, 'The Medieval Parish Church of St. Andrew Holborn', *London Topographical Record* xxiv, 1980, 31–60.

[33] The London returns are listed in Westlake, *Parish Guilds*, 180–88. This list is not complete and additions have been made by transfers from Ancient Petitions etc., so it is necessary to consult the typescript list in the Round Room of the PRO. Many of the London returns are transcribed and translated in a manuscript volume in Guildhall Library MS 142. The six returns in English are printed by Chambers and Daunt, 40–60.

[34] Bodleian Library MS London and Middlesex Rolls, 2, 3, 4 a and b. These returns are in English and I intend to publish them in full elsewhere.

[35] For the background to the Cambridge Parliament see Anthony Tuck, 'The Cambridge Parliament of 1388', *EHR* lxxxiv, 1969, 225–43.

unite against the repressive regulations of the craft masters.[36] It is hardly surprising, therefore, that the guild returns are somewhat bland documents; the members of the guilds were anxious to stress their poverty and their piety. Although the returns may reflect the genuine purposes of the guilds, one must remember that the members themselves, and the scriveners who drafted the returns, were not unaware of the intentions and anxieties which lay behind the royal writs. The ambiguity of purpose in the responses of 1388 may have been intentional and several craft fraternities may have been anxious to appear simply as parish guilds. Yet in spite of these caveats the returns throw a good deal of welcome light on some associations of lesser men in the late fourteenth century; they tell us something, if not everything, about the reasons which led men to form themselves into associations in this way. The royal servants who read the returns rapidly drafted new legislation emerging in a statute in 1391 which brought land left to parish or other fraternities within the scope of the mortmain legislation.[37] But the guilds were not banned as seditious, which suggests that the dominant royal motive had been greed all along. Or perhaps the clerks believed in the innocence of the returns which they received?

At the end of the period the chantry returns of 1546 and 1548 throw some light on the most successful guilds, namely those which had acquired a landed endowment. Since it was land in which the king was interested, those guilds, by far the majority, which ran their finances on quarterage payments rather than income from rents, did not feature in the Chantry certificate for London and Middlesex. Only some twenty or so endowed London parish guilds are described in the Chantry certificate.[38]

The darkness between these two floodlights is illuminated somewhat by references to fraternities to be found in London wills. Indeed it is only from wills that we can learn of those evanescent fraternities which never became wealthy enough to maintain a permanent chaplain, never acquired any lands or rents and whose members probably gathered together informally to provide half-pennies to maintain a light before the altar of their chosen saint in their parish church. London is richly served with wills. The Hustings Court in which citizens enrolled their wills has a complete set of rolls surviving from the middle of the thirteenth century.[39] Those Londoners who were not citizens, and many who were, registered their wills either in the Archdeaconry or the Commissary Court; the Archdeaconry registers cover

---

[36] Between 1350 and 1417 the city records reveal the existence of yeomen or journeymen groupings among the shearmen, saddlers, skinners, spurriers, cordwainers and tailors, see H. T. Riley, ed., *Memorials of London and London Life*, 1868, 247–8, 250–51, 306–7, 495–6, 543, 609–12, 653; *Letter Book G*, ed. R. R. Sharpe, 1905, 143; *Calendar of Plea and Memoranda Rolls of the City of London 1364–81*, ed. A. H. Thomas, Cambridge 1929, 89, 264, 291–2. 291–2.

[37] 15 Richard II cap. 5, *Statutes at Large* i, 1769, 401–2.

[38] *Chantry*.

[39] *HW*.

only the years 1393 to 1415 whereas there are Commissary Court registers for the whole period.[40] The wills run into several thousands and it has only been possible to sample this rich source of material.

Some of the more prosperous London guilds sought the security of royal letters patent. Only two guilds, in the churches of St Magnus and St Botolph at Billingsgate saw the need to obtain such royal licences before the 1388 enquiry,[41] four other guilds purchased licences in 1392, 1397, 1400 and 1403,[42] but between 1440 and 1475 fourteen London guilds sought such licences.[43] In part this may have been provoked by further legislation in the 1430s,[44] but it may also reflect a flurry of reorganisation and reinvigoration which characterises London guild life in the mid-fifteenth century. At this time older, and not very well-organised guilds within the same church were amalgamated, as the two guilds in the church of St Botolph Aldersgate were amalgamated in 1446;[45] some guilds were simply reorganised and put on a more secure footing, like the St Sythe guild in St Andrew Holborn.[46] These reorganised guilds are, not surprisingly, those which make the strongest showing in the 1548 Chantry certificate. Unfortunately the Letters Patent reveal less about the purposes of these mid-fifteenth-century parish guilds than the earlier 1388 returns into Chancery; they concentrate on the legal *persona* of the guild and describe the right to wear a livery, have a seal and plead and be impleaded in the courts, but they reveal nothing about the guild ordinances beyond the fact that members were empowered to draft them,

---

[40] The Archdeacons' Register is now Guildhall Library MS 9051/1 (see n. 6 above). The Commissary Court Registers (1375–1548) are Guildhall Library MSS 9171/1–14 and contain thousands of wills which have not been read with an eye to parish fraternities although Dr Brigden has read the commissary wills for the period 1522–39, see her 'Religion and Social Obligation', 94 and n. 153.

[41] 1370, *CPR 1367–70*, 448; 1371, *CPR 1370–74*, 165.

[42] Fraternity of the Blessed Virgin in St Giles Cripplegate, 1392, *CPR 1391–96*, 43, 170; fraternity of St Katherine in St Mary Colechurch, 1400, *CPR 1399–1401*, 284; fraternity of St Michael in St Michael Cornhill, 1397, *ibid.* 202; fraternity of St Peter in St Peter Cornhill, 1403, *CPR 1401–05*, 206.

[43] Fraternity of the Virgin in St Dunstan in the West, 1440, *CPR 1436–41*, 447; fraternity of the Assumption in St Margaret Westminster, 1440, *ibid.* 448; fraternity of Rectors in St Benet Fink, 1441, *CPR 1441–46*, 4; fraternity of St Nicholas of the Parish Clerks of London, 1442, *ibid*, 51–2 (see also 1449, *CPR 1446–52*, 263; 1475, *CPR 1467–77*, 544), fraternity of the Virgin in St Giles Cripplegate, 1443, *CPR 1441–46*, 140–41; fraternity of St Sythe in St Andrew Holborn, *ibid.* 194–5; fraternity of the Virgin in All Hallows Barking, 1443, 1465, *LP 1509–1514*, 5242; *CPR 1461–67*, 428; fraternity of the Holy Trinity in St Botolph Aldersgate, 1446, *CPR 1441–46*, 451; fraternity of St Katherine in St Mary Colechurch, 1447, *CPR 1446–52*, 70; fraternity of Salutation of the Virgin in St Magnus, 1448, *ibid.*, 173–4; fraternity of the Virgin in St Margaret Southwark, 1449, *ibid.*, 264; fraternity of the Name of Jesus in St Paul's Cathedral, 1459, *CPR 1452–61*, 480; fraternity of the Holy Trinity in Leadenhall Chapel, 1466, *CPR 1461–67*, 516; fraternity of the Virgin in St Mary Rounceval, 1475, *CPR 1464–77*, 542.

[44] *Rotuli Parliamentorum*, 1832, iv, 507; R. R. Sharpe, ed., *Calendar of Letter Book K*, 1911, xli.

[45] The guilds which were amalgamated were those of the Holy Trinity (earliest reference 1374) and SS Fabian and Sebastian (earliest reference 1378), Basing, *Parish Fraternity Register*, xiii–xvi.

[46] Barron and Roscoe, *London Topographical Record*, 37.

and to elect wardens or masters. It is clear that the government was less afraid of secret societies than it had been in the fourteenth century.

The late fifteenth-century records of the commissary court of London and the registers of Bishop Fitzjames (1508–22) and Bishop Tunstall (1522–30) record the ordinances of some new fraternities which were established in the houses of the five orders of friars in London.[47] Some of these new fraternities were really craft associations, like the shearmen who met in the Austin Friars from 1454 and the fraternity of St Christopher of the waterbearers who met from 1497 in the same church. Some of these new guilds were fraternities of foreigners: the Germans who honoured the Holy Blood of Wilsnak met in 1459 at the Crutched Friars, and in 1491 at Austin Friars when their ordinances specify that 'noon shall not be received but if he be born beyond the sea'. The Dutchmen met to honour St Katherine from 1495 in the same church. But there were other fraternities which were neither craft associations, nor groupings of foreigners, who used the London friaries as their base. Oddly enough their ordinances are almost identical which may suggest that the fraternities were inspired, or encouraged, by the friars themselves.[48]

The chronological pattern of the foundation of parish fraternities may reveal something of the motives of those who formed them. Only five London fraternities appear to have been in existence before the Black Death of 1348–49, the earliest of these was the guild of St Katherine which was founded in 1339 to build a chapel in honour of the saint on the south side of St Mary Colechurch.[49] Five more fraternities were formed in the years 1349–50 and then a further seventy-four appear for the first time in the years 1350 to 1400. It might be argued that this rapid acceleration in the rate of foundation is more apparent than real and is merely the product of our source material, in that the guild returns of 1388/9 provide a good deal of information about recently founded fraternities. But the evidence of the wills enrolled in the Hustings Court shows that this cannot be the explanation. The wills go back to the mid-thirteenth century and yet there are no recorded bequests to fraternities until the decade 1340–50 after which the number of recorded bequests rises steeply throughout the later fourteenth century.

Why then this sudden popularity? Parish fraternities, whatever else they may have been, were essentially communal chantries. Those who were not rich enough to endow a personal chantry could, nevertheless contribute to the costs of a fraternity chaplain who would pray for all the members, both

[47] Coote, *TLMAS*, iv, 1871; Reg. of Bishop Fitzjames, Guildhall Library MS 9531/9 fo. 9v (fraternity of the Virgin in Austin Friars, 1509); fo. 27 (fraternity of the Virgin and St Barbara in Black Friars, 1511); fo. 142v (fraternity of the Virgin in Crutched Friars, 1521); Reg. of Bishop Tunstall, Guildhall Library MS 9531/10 fos. 32–32v (confirmation of the 1511 ordinances of the fraternity of the Virgin and St Barbara in Black Friars, 1522).

[48] Dr Brigden has suggested that the foundation of new fraternities based on the Friaries may reflect dissatisfaction with, or hostility to, parish life and the parish priests, 'Religion and Social Obligation', 95.

[49] See return of 1388, PRO, C47/41/199.

living and dead. Professor Kreider has discussed the pattern of chantry foundation in England and has demonstrated that the greatest number of foundations took place in the fourteenth century and that in most counties, including London and Middlesex, the greatest number of chantries were founded in the first half of the fourteenth century.[50] It seems clear that in London the foundation of personal, private chantries came first and was then followed by the foundation of communal fraternal chantries. Whereas at first only the rich could attempt to protect their souls in the afterlife, yet by the second half of the fourteenth century 'middling' Londoners had evolved a means of communal spiritual self-help which found expression in parish fraternities. There may also have been another factor: the shortage of labour following the Black Death led to a rise in wages and an improvement in the standard of living of wage-earners, including artisans and craftsmen. Out of their wages such men were now able to afford small amounts of quarterage to help to insure their souls.[51] The communal London parish fraternities, therefore, follow at a little distance the private chantries which inspired them.

The extent to which the Black Death itself may have inspired men to found chantries or fraternities has long been a matter of debate. Professor Kreider firmly rejects 'the hoary notion that the chantries were the response of piously petrified Englishmen to the terrors of the Black Death'.[52] But whereas Englishmen may not have been 'piously petrified' about the welfare of their souls, they may have been 'socially petrified' at the prospect of an indecent burial. When the house of Carthusians was established in 1371 on the site of the City's major plague cemetery to the north of St Bartholomew's a plaque was placed on the building. It recorded that the plague had reached London

> where people superabounded. So great a multitude eventually died there, that all the cemeteries of the aforesaid city were insufficient for the burial of the dead. For which reason very many were compelled to bury their dead in places unseemly and not hallowed or blessed; for some, it was said, cast the corpses into the river.[53]

It is not by chance that every set of London fraternity ordinances which has survived from the fourteenth century specifies in great detail the obligations which members have towards ensuring the decent burial of dead brothers and sisters; the collection of the body from outside London, the recitation of psalms, dirges and masses, the attendance at the funeral clothed in the livery

[50] Alan Kreider, *English Chantries: the road to Dissolution*, 1979, chap. iii, esp. figures 1, 2, and table 3:1.
[51] Quarterage payments ranged from as little as two pence in the guild at St Austin at Paul's Gate, PRO, C47/41/193, to as much as thirteen shillings and four pence a quarter in the guild of St Katherine at St Mary Colechurch, PRO, C47/41/199.
[52] Kreider, *English Chantries*, 86.
[53] William St John Hope, *The History of the London Charterhouse*, 1925, 7.

of the fraternity, the fines imposed for absence without reasonable excuse and the provision of a goodly number of candles and tapers around the corpse. The regulations about funerals and about intercessory prayers are the dominant components in the fourteenth-century ordinances. In London it would seem that it was the Black Death of 1348/9 which provided both the incentive and, indirectly, the means for the formation of parish fraternities.

But once the immediate terrors of the plague had receded (and plague remained an intermittent visitor to London throughout the fifteenth and sixteenth centuries) did the fraternities continue to attract members? The evidence suggests that they did. Whereas seventy-four parish fraternities appear for the first time in the fifty years between 1350 and 1400, in the next fifty years there were a further twenty-five, in the next fifty another twenty and in the years between 1500 and 1548 another thirty appear for the first time. These figures suggest a continuing popularity and the evidence from wills points in the same direction. Of the 1,383 wills enrolled in the Archdeaconry court between 1393 and 1415, just over 8 per cent record bequests to parish fraternities. In the 666 wills enrolled in the Commissary court between 1522 and 1538, 22 per cent of the testators remembered their parish fraternities.[54]

The available evidence suggests that parish fraternities did, indeed, continue to retain their hold upon the imagination and the purses of medieval Londoners. But were the fraternities of the later fifteenth and the sixteenth centuries answering the same needs as those of the earlier period? An answer to this question may be provided by comparing the guild ordinances of 1388/9 with those recorded in the later registers. The two groups of ordinances reveal certain common preoccupations. The fraternity feast remains, throughout the period, a constant and important event. Members were obliged to attend the feast and to contribute to its cost. It was on these occasions that the new masters would be chosen, the accounts read and audited and mass celebrated by the fraternity chaplain. Eating and praying together remained essential elements in fraternity associations. Another common theme throughout the period was the constant concern that all members of the fraternity should live at peace with one another. Law suits between members were to be avoided at all costs and agreed methods of arbitration were laid down. In the guild of the Assumption in the church of St Stephen Coleman Street disputes between brothers were to be taken to the two masters, who were to summon two other brothers, so that the four of them might 'strive to make peace without the interference of any stranger and without the need to go to the common law'.[55] It is impossible to know

---

[54] These figures are derived from the researches of Robert Wood and Dr Susan Brigden, see n. 6 and 40 above. Between 1539 and 1547 when the royal hostility to chantries and to the doctrine of purgatory became more apparent, the percentage drops to 8.5 per cent, information supplied by Dr Susan Brigden in a letter.

[55] Return of 1388, Bodleian Library MS London and Middlesex Roll 4b.

how far the masters of the parish fraternities did, in fact, exercise this equitable jurisdiction, but the provision of arbitration procedures remained a feature of guild ordinances. In the later guilds, however, there were more emphatic injunctions against brothers and sisters slandering each other, quarrelling or resisting the authority of the wardens. A reading of these later ordinances suggests that the members of fraternities were often unruly and headstrong and could be barely restrained from assaulting each other by the common rules of decent behaviour.[56]

Many historians, and in particular George Unwin, have emphasised the 'social security' aspect of fraternity associations. Certainly the declared intention to assist financially the sick and needy members of the fraternity remained a common characteristic of guild ordinances throughout the period. Virtually all the fourteenth-century fraternities aimed to care for the sick and indigent members at rates varying from eight to fourteen pence a week; in the later fifteenth century the rates had risen from twelve to twenty pence a week. The care of needy members was seen as both a social and a Christian duty, and some fraternities specified in great detail how this help was to be administered. But there are difficulties in tracking down the practice of these charitable functions. The references in the surviving fraternity accounts, admittedly not very numerous, are extremely slight. The guild of Our Lady's Assumption at Westminster maintained four cottages for poor people who also received six shillings and eight pence each a quarter, but it would appear that the beneficiaries were not themselves members of the guild.[57] In 1495–6 the wardens of Our Lady's guild in St Margaret's church in Southwark paid John Sent seven pence every Sunday for forty-nine weeks which amounted in all to £1 8s 7d, and in 1533–4 two men received £1 6s 8d and £1 from the guild wardens.[58] There is no record of charitable payments in the accounts of the guilds in St Botolph Aldersgate. On the other hand the Chantry returns of some of the London fraternities do suggest that considerable charitable help was being administered. The fraternity of the Blessed Virgin in the church of St Dunstan in the West was giving a total of £17 1s 4d to eleven poor people and the *Salve* guild in St Magnus spent nearly £20 on helping brothers and sisters who were in prison, blind, fallen into decay and poverty, or sick of the palsy.[59] Other guilds apart from that at St Magnus, recognised the victims of false imprisonment as worthy recipients

[56] See, for example, the injunctions against slander and drunken behaviour among the ordinances of the fraternity of Dutchmen founded in the Crutched Friars in 1495, Coote, *TLMAS* iv, 1871, 74.

[57] A. G. Rosser, thesis, 353–4.

[58] Greater London RO, P92/SAV/5; P92/SAV/14.

[59] *Chantry*, 20, 25. The fraternity of the Virgin in St Giles Cripplegate distributed just over nineteen pounds to sixteen poor householders and the fraternity of the Virgin in St Bride Fleet Street relieved seven poor people at a cost of eight pounds annually, *ibid.*, 18, 107.

of fraternal charity.[60] But the only recorded acts of charity of the great Jesus guild in St Paul's were the payments of £8 each year to four poor old men who acted as vergers in the guild chapel in the Shrouds beneath the Cathedral. Yet this guild had a recorded excess of income over expenditure of £201 in 1532.[61] The inference to be drawn from the surviving London guild accounts is that only a very small proportion of the fraternity income was spent on works of charity and that the bulk of the money was spent on the stipends of the fraternity priest and the clerk and in payments to the tallow chandler. This discrepancy between declared intention and surviving evidence remains somewhat baffling. It may be that the economics of the proposals had not been realistically costed. Members of the guild of the Virgin in the house of the Carmelite friars paid only three pence a quarter in dues and yet they could receive seven pence a week in sick pay, thus in two weeks they could receive more than they paid in a whole year.[62] Even though most ordinances stipulated membership for a period of years – usually five – before a new member might receive benefits, yet it is easy to see how rapidly the wardens might run out of funds. Since most of the guilds had quite small memberships it seems unlikely that they were able to afford the scale of health insurance schemes outlined so hopefully in their ordinances. But what may have happened is that the guild offered informal rather than formal help. The members of the guild of the Holy Blood of Wilsnak decided in their ordinances that

> when any brother or sister is sick, then shall every brother and sister give a half penny every week to the sustentation and keeping of the said sick.[63]

In this way the money was handed to the sick member but never passed formally through the guild accounts. Hence membership of a guild, throughout this 200-year period, may have provided some insurance against abject poverty, but the help was probably casual and informal rather than automatic and regulated. But if the parish fraternities of London remained consistent in some of their functions, yet it is clear that there were also significant changes of emphasis over the period. By the late fifteenth century the earlier concern for a decent burial has shrunk simply to one clause in twenty or thirty. This apears to be no longer a major preoccupation in fraternity association and, indeed, in the great Jesus fraternity at St Paul's, founded in 1459 and

---

[60] The fraternity in St James Garlickhythe ordained that if a member had been falsely imprisoned, and had been in the brotherhood seven years, then he was to receive fourteen pence a week while he was in prison, PRO, C47/41/191; Chambers and Daunt, 47; the guild of St Stephen in St Sepulchre Newgate also gave fourteen pence to members who were in prison, PRO, C47/42/207.

[61] Sparrow Simpson, *Registrum*, 458; Bodleian Library MS Tanner 221 fo. 126.

[62] PRO, C47/41/189.

[63] Coote, *TLMAS*, iv, 1871, 67, 68.

reorganised in 1504, the burial of members did not feature at all. In the same way intercessory prayers became much less prominent and the emphasis seems to have shifted towards this life, conviviality, decent living, processions and the celebration of saints' days. Again, whereas all the fourteenth-century fraternities hoped to provide lights or tapers to burn before the image of their saint in the parish church, none of the fifteenth- and sixteenth-century ordinances specify such devotions. Another change which is perhaps unexpected is a decline in the attachment to a common livery. In all but one of the fourteenth-century ordinances provision was made for the wearing of a common livery, if not a gown, then at least a common hood. But only two out of the six late fraternity ordinances are concerned to maintain this outward form of common association, although the mid-fifteenth century Letters Patent had all licensed the wearing of a livery. It is difficult to explain the declining popularity of liveries unless it was that the general governmental disapproval of the liveries worn by noble retinues was beginning to make an impression lower down the social scale. This comparison of the earlier ordinances with the later ones, however impressionistic, does suggest some interesting shifts in the religious and social preoccupations of ordinary Londoners. The continuing popularity of parish fraternities in London may owe something to their capacity to respond to changing needs and concerns.

The geographical distribution of parish fraternities in London may be instructive. It is striking that all but one of the sixteen extra-mural parish churches had a fraternity, and several had more than one.[64] Ten of these extra-mural parish fraternities were among the most prosperous and most securely established of all the London parish guilds on the eve of the dissolution of the Chantries.[65] The extra-mural parishes were extremely large (St Botolph Aldersgate had 1,100 communicants in 1548 and St Margaret's at Westminster had 2,500) and some of the parishioners may have been particularly eager to create a smaller unit with which they might identify. The guild membership may have included about one-tenth of the parishioners in these larger parishes.[66] It is also likely that in these large suburban parishes, some of which fell within the jurisdiction of the city and others did not, the parish fraternity came to play a quasi-governmental role as Dr Rosser has demonstrated in the case of the guild of the Virgin's Assumption

[64] The only extra-mural parish church which appears not to have had a fraternity is St Botolph Aldgate. St Olave's church in Southwark had five fraternities and St Margaret's in Westminster had eight.

[65] The guilds in St Botolph Bishopsgate, St Giles Cripplegate, St Botolph Aldersgate, St Sepulchre Newgate, St Andrew Holborn, St Bride Fleet Street, St Dunstan in the West, St Clement Danes, St Olave Southwark, St Margaret Southwark. The Westminster guilds at St Margaret's church and at St Mary Rounceval were also flourishing.

[66] The figures of communicants are derived from the Chantry certificate of 1548, *Chantry*, 48, 139. For estimates of guild membership see A. G. Rosser, thesis, 312–13 and Basing, *Parish Fraternity Register*, xiii, xxi–xxv.

at Westminster.[67] Five London parish fraternities are known to have maintained common halls and all of these lay outside the city walls. In the west the guild of the Virgin in St. Bride's Fleet Street had a hall by 1533 and the fraternity in St. Clement Danes built a hall in the churchyard where the parishioners assembled, which had rooms underneath which were let out to the poor rent free.[68] To the north the guild of the Holy Trinity in St Botolph Aldersgate built a fine hall in the 1490s and glazed the windows with painted glass and by the 1540s the neighbouring guild in the church of St. Giles Cripplegate had also acquired a common hall.[69] South of the river in the parish of St Olave, the guild dedicated to the Name of Jesus had a hall known as Jesus House from the time of its foundation in 1533.[70] It seems clear that these halls served as a focus for the life of the parish, as well as the guild, and when the fraternities were disendowed the parishes by various means continued to maintain the old fraternity halls as parish halls or rooms. So the impulses which were at work in parish communities before the 1540s and 1550s continued to shape the form of parish life after the Chantries were dissolved and the superstitious fraternities abolished.

The membership of the parish fraternities may reveal something of the needs to which they answered. Mrs Basing in her study of the Holy Trinity guild in St Botolph Aldersgate managed to identify about a third of the 667 known members of the fraternity; 119 of these were royal servants, lawyers, clergy or gentry and the remaining 124 belonged to London craft guilds or companies. The membership of so many who were not citizens is surprising but many of these may have become members when Henry IV stayed at the Priory of St Bartholomew in 1409.[71] But the vast majority of the London members of the guild belonged to the artisan crafts in the city, brewers, butchers, dyers, carpenters, smiths and tailors. Only one alderman belonged and there were very few members from the great mercantile companies. Many of the artisan members can be found acting as masters or wardens of their crafts.

The same membership pattern is reflected in the other parish fraternities. Although we have no other membership lists comparable with those of the guild at St Botolph Aldersgate, it is possible to collect together the names of *c.* 725 men and women who belonged to other parish fraternities during these

---

[67] Thesis, 315–16 and *TRHS*, 1984, 104.

[68] The earliest reference to the hall of the fraternity of the Virgin in St Bride Fleet Street occurs in the will of Thomas Threyne, gentleman, in 1533, see typescript list of references to St Bride's in Guildhall Library MS 6570A; further references to the hall in 1545 and 1547, *ibid*. In St Clement Danes there were parish rooms which may have belonged to the fraternity, but this is not clear, *Chantry*, 152.

[69] Basing, *Parish Fraternity Register* xvii–xix; the 'Comen Hall' of the guild of the Virgin in St Giles Cripplegate was sold in 1549, see *CPR 1547–48*, 294–5 and deeds of 1567 and 1710 relating to the later history of this hall are to be found in Guildhall Library, Additional MSS 632, 404.

[70] Carlin, thesis, 272.

[71] Basing, *Parish Fraternity Register* xxi–xxv.

years. Only sixty-three of these can be identified as members of the great overseas trading companies (skinners, grocers, mercers, vintners, fishmongers, goldsmiths and drapers) and of these, only nine were aldermen. It may be that the great merchants did not feel the need of either the spiritual or the social benefits offered by the parish fraternities. To answer their social needs the merchants had their exclusive club, the court of Aldermen, or their trade company. Life at Mercers' hall or Grocers' hall was far grander than anything which could be offered by a parish fraternity. To answer their spiritual needs these men could afford to endow permanent private chantries; they did not need the communal prayers of parish fraternity chaplains.[72] What seems clear is that the parish fraternity movement was, predominantly, a 'middle class' artisan movement and to such men the parish fraternity was often the centre of their social and spiritual world.[73]

There were, however, three fraternities which were distinctly more upper class; the guild of the Virgin in the church of All Hallows Barking which, after modest beginnings in the fourteenth century was reformed in the 1440s by a distinguished clutch of royal officials and London merchants and continued to serve as a social club for the wealthy aldermen/merchants of this newly-prosperous eastern part of the city.[74] The guild of the Name of Jesus, as refounded by John Colet in 1504, was also composed of distinguished aldermen, among whom the Mercers were conspicuous.[75] Lastly the fraternity dedicated to St Barbara at St Katharine's Hospital appears to have come into existence in the early sixteenth century and to have had a membership list headed by Henry VIII and Queen Katherine and including two dukes and their ladies, three earls and a collection of knights.[76] The connection of this guild with London seems to have been very slight.

The membership of London parish fraternities was not only predominantly artisan, it was also markedly feminine. All the guild ordinances which have survived specify sisters as well as brothers, except, perhaps, one.[77] It is clear

---

[72] The greater merchants of London may also have succumbed to that 'privatisation' of religious practice which Dr Colin Richmond has recently described in 'Religion and the fifteenth-century English Gentleman', in R. B. Dobson, ed., *Church Politics and Patronage*, 193–208.

[73] Chaucer observed that it was a haberdasher, a carpenter, a weaver, a dyer and a tapisser who were all clothed in the same livery 'of a solempne and a greet fraternitee', *Prologue to the Canterbury Tales*, lines 361–4.

[74] For this guild see *CPR 1461–67*, 428; *CPR 1467–77*, 46, 192; *LP 1509–1514*, 5242; *Chantry*, 47, 95; *CPR 1547–48*, 384; *CPR 1548–49*, 31, 64; *CPR 1549–51*, 409, 424–5; Stow i, 131. Bequests recorded in the Archdeacon's Register between 1394 and 1402 suggest that the members in the early years were quite modest people, Guildhall Library MS 9051/1.

[75] See n. 27 above.

[76] See n. 20 above. This grand fraternity, with its distinguished membership bears comparison with the guild of the Holy Trinity at Luton of which Edward IV and Queen Elizabeth Woodville were members and from which a very fine illuminated register survives (paper read to the Conference of the British Archaeological Association by Dr Jeremy Griffiths, April 1984).

[77] The exception was the guild of St Katherine founded in St Paul's Cathedral in 1352; sisters are not mentioned, but they may have been excluded, PRO, C47/41/200.

that women joined the fraternities on equal terms with men; they did not join solely in their capacity as wives. The ordinances of the guild of St Katherine in St Botolph Aldersgate specified that brothers should pay three pence quarterage 'and if he have a wife, and she will be a sister, then shall he pay six pence for them both in the quarter . . . and if a single woman come into the brotherhood, pay as a brother doth'. The ordinances of the guild of SS Fabian and Sebastian in the same church put it more stringently, 'And if a singlewoman come into the brotherhood she shall pay no less than a brother doth'.[78] Indeed the membership lists of the Holy Trinity fraternity in that church reveal the presence of many single women; eighteen entered the fraternity between 1377 and 1415.[79] To the accounts of the guild of the Virgin's Assumption in St Margaret's church in Southwark in 1495–6 is appended a list of fourteen 'new-made' brothers and sisters of the guild, including the parish priest, ten married couples, two single men and Alice Davy.[80] In this case a married couple paid a shilling entrance fee which was the same as a single person, but guilds varied in their practice.[81] In the Bede roll of the fraternity of St Nicholas (the parish clerks guild) those to be prayed for are listed in five categories, clerks, priests, secular brothers, secular sisters and dead brothers and sisters.[82] What is perhaps even more surprising is to find women listed alongside men as founders of a guild. In 1403 sisters are named with brothers as founders of the fraternity in St Peter Cornhill, sixteen brothers and three sisters who bore names which were different from those of the brothers and so were not, we may presume, wives.[83] In the same way sisters, together with brothers, petitioned for new letters patent in 1442 for the fraternity at St Augustine Pappey. In this case twenty-six brothers and eleven sisters joined together in the petition.[84] In 1448 when new letters patent were sought for the guild of *Salve Regina* in the church of St Magnus, the petition was presented by the four wardens, together with six named brothers and six named sisters.[85] There is no instance, however, of women holding office in a·London parish fraternity, but the fact that wives, single women and widows could all belong to fraternities

---

[78] Chambers and Daunt, 48, 51.

[79] Basing, *Parish Fraternity Register*, 5–18.

[80] Greater London RO, P92/SAV/5. The ordinances of the guild of the Virgin established in the Black Friars in 1511 specify that if a brother dies his wife may remain as a member provided that she pays her dues; if she remarries however, she may only remain if her new husband joins, Guildhall Library MS 9531/9 fo. 29.

[81] In the same way in some guilds husbands and wives together paid a set amount for the guild feast, but in the guild of St Peter Cornhill, men paid twelve pence for the feast and their wives paid eight pence, *HMCR Appendix to Sixth Report*, 413a. In the guild of the Virgin and St Barbara founded in the Black Friars in 1511, men paid fourpence for the feast and women paid twopence, Guildhall Library MS 9531/9 fos. 27v–28.

[82] Guildhall Library MS 4889 fo. 5 *et seq.*

[83] *HMCR Appendix to Sixth Report*, 412a.

[84] BL MS Cotton Vitellius F xvi fos. 114v–115.

[85] *CPR 1446–52*, 173–4; this petition was presented by the four wardens, six brothers and six sisters, only two of whom bore the same names as the men.

on equal terms with men, must have contributed considerably to their popularity.[86]

The dedications of the London parish fraternities reveal an expected pattern. The Virgin Mary rises head and halo above all the other saints, fifty-seven fraternities were dedicated to her, alone or in partnership. Next in popularity, but far behind the mother of Christ, was His supposed bride, St Katherine, the protectress of the dying, patron of young girls, students and craftsmen whose work was based on the wheel. Following St Katherine was St Anne, the mother of the Virgin. Twelve fraternities were dedicated to her. It is possible that there may have been secular reasons for choosing St Anne. In 1397 the parishioners of St Michael Cornhill petitioned the king to be allowed to form a guild in honour of St Anne to maintain a chaplain to pray for the king, the brothers and sisters of the guild and for the soul of the late Queen Anne (d. 1394). Perhaps they had a shrewd suspicion that their chances of obtaining the licence would be enhanced by an appropriate dedication. By 1491, when considerable water had flowed under the political bridges of England, the parishioners had wisely added St George to the original dedication.[87] In fact St George claimed eleven dedications, all but two in the years after 1450. Another saint who enjoyed some late popularity was St Christopher who attracted ten dedications in all. The Holy Trinity had eleven dedications and Corpus Christi seven. The most striking addition to the dedications in the fifteenth century is that of the Name of Jesus. The famous fraternity founded in St Paul's in 1459 was followed by others at St Dunstan in the East (1481), St Bride Fleet Street (1487). St Olave Southwark (1533) and St Michael Queenhythe (1544).[88] The fact that Londoners were attracted to the new cult of the name of Jesus suggests the vitality of their faith in the half century before the Reformation.[89]

More important, perhaps, than the choice of saints, was the selection of a fraternity chaplain. Only about twenty-five of the London fraternities had sufficient landed endowments out of which to pay the salary of a permanent

---

[86] There was only one London guild which was described as a 'sisterhood', that of St Anne in St Olave Southwark. A membership list names five women, but there are bequests recorded in the wills of men, see Carlin, thesis, 416, 519 n. 28.

[87] *CPR 1396–99*, 202. The connection of St Anne with St George is made in the will of Alice Hongreforth, *HW* ii, 608. The church had a guild dedicated to St Michael and the Virgin, and two other guilds, one dedicated to St Nicholas and St Katherine and the other to the Name of Jesus. By 1524 the pairings of saints had shifted and in the will of John Maidenhead, draper, the five guilds listed are the Jesus guild, the Virgin and St Anne, St Michael, St George and St Christopher and St Nicholas and St Anne, J. A. F. Thomson, thesis.

[88] *CPR 1452–61*, 480; 1481 will of Sir Bartholomew James, *HW* ii, 598 and Guildhall Library MS 4887; 1487, will of Robert Pykemere, citizen and cutler, Guildhall Library typescript MS 6570A; 1533, Carlin, thesis, 272; the 1544 subsidy for London refers to the brotherhood of Jesus and the Virgin in St Michael Queenhythe, PRO, E179/144/123 (I owe this reference to the kindness of Professor Robert Lang). In 1524 there appears also to have been a guild of Jesus in the church of St Michael Cornhill, see n. 87 above.

[89] On this new feast, see Pfaff, *Feasts*, esp. chap. iv.

chaplain. But there is no doubt that even from their modest fourteenth-century beginnings the desire to have their own chaplain was paramount in the minds of the members. The brothers and sisters of the guild of St Austin at Paul's Gate hoped to be able to afford a priest to maintain a chantry in the church, and to pray for the brothers and sisters of the guild and for all Christians. The 'little company' of the light of Corpus Christi in the church of St Giles hoped that if their chattels increased they would be able to afford a chaplain.[90] The more prosperous guild of the Virgin at the church of St Dunstan in the East had originally supported a chaplain 'every good man of the brotherhood and the parish' and a few others gave a sum towards this every year. But this proved unsatisfactory and unreliable so the brotherhood invested in property to provide a more reliable income.[91] Most fraternity priests were, however, maintained on a yearly *ad hoc* basis and depended for their salary on the ability of the wardens or masters of the guild to collect the quarterage payments. Most of these fraternity priests were, therefore, insecure; more than most of the clergy within the late medieval church, their livelihood depended upon the whim of lay people. If the brotherhood failed to hold together, or if its members disliked their chaplain, then his salary might not be forthcoming. May it not be that this element of control was attractive to lay men and women?

We know a little of how these London parish fraternity chaplains were selected. The guild of the Virgin in the church of St Giles Cripplegate had, by 1388, acquired sufficient lands to employ a perpetual fraternity chaplain who was to celebrate mass every day. The chaplain was to be chosen by the vicar of the church (if he were a member of the guild), the two wardens and twelve of the best men of the guild. The chaplain was to be provided with a house, he was to be attentive to all brothers and sisters, poor as well as rich, sick and healthy. The chaplain was not to be removed without reasonable cause and without the assent of the same group who had selected him.[92] The fraternity chaplain at St Peter Cornhill was also to be chosen by the parson of the church and the wardens of the guild. But his contract of employment specified that he could only be absent from his duties for forty days in the year, and he was to be fined a penny for each day's absence beyond the forty. If he was absent for more than twenty days beyond the specified forty he was to lose his job. If he turned out to be a notorious lecher ('which God forbid'), or night wanderer or tavern-goer, then he was to be warned by the parson and guild wardens. If the chaplain ignored this warning, and was convicted on the evidence of reliable witnesses, then he was to be dismissed by the parson in the presence of the wardens and parishioners. On the other hand if

---

[90] Return of guild of St Austin, PRO, C47/41/193; return of guild of the little company of the light of Corpus Christi, PRO, C47/46/469.
[91] PRO, C47/42/204.
[92] PRO, C47/42/205.

he became old and feeble, he was to continue to receive his salary until his death.[93] Although in this case the parson is involved in the choice and dismissal of the fraternity priest, yet in neither case can he act without the assent of the lay wardens of the fraternity.

No other guild ordinances specify in such detail the terms of employment of the fraternity priest. Dr Rosser has pointed out that the wardens of the guild of the Virgin's Assumption at St Margaret's Westminster, actually advertised for candidates for their fraternity priest in the early sixteenth century.[94] Even if the rector or vicar was involved in the selection of a fraternity chaplain (and this was doubtless a reasonable precaution since the two men would have to work together in the same church) yet it was the wardens who paid the salary and to whom, ultimately, the chaplain was answerable. The power to select the priest with whom you might be most frequently involved, to choose the kind of moral person you required, and to be able to dismiss incompetent or negligent chaplains, must have been powerful incentives for joining a fraternity. Lay involvement in the running of the parish church is not something that emerges with Protestantism, indeed it might be argued that the Reformation was but an extreme expression of that lay interest.

The parish fraternities of London were, above all, expressions of parish, neighbourly solidarity. With a few exceptions, most fraternities drew their membership from the parishes themselves. They are an expression of an active corporate parish life. If we accept that the existence of one or more fraternities within a parish is the sign of an active parish community before the Reformation it may be instructive to compare such parishes with those where, later in the sixteenth century, parishioners funded the salary of a lecturer to work alongside their rector or vicar. Between 1559 and 1581, twenty-six London parishes established lectureships.[95] All but six of these parishes had fraternities before the Dissolution. Or to look at the picture the other way round, before the Dissolution there were twenty-one active parishes in London (judged by the number of parish fraternities or the extent of landed endowment for them), of which eleven had established lectureships by 1581 and a further six by the end of the century.[96] Thus of the twenty-one

[93] *HMCR Appendix to Sixth Report*, 412–13.

[94] Rosser, thesis, 313 n. 3.

[95] Paul S. Seaver, *The Puritan Lectureships: the politics of Religious Dissent 1560–1662*, Stamford California 1970, list on pages 123–4 and Appendix D. Three of the parishes listed by Seaver, Christ Church Newgate, Holy Trinity Minories and St Helen Bishopsgate were not parishes before 1548. St Saviour Southwark took over St Margaret Southwark and so has been included. Those which established lectureships but had not had parish fraternities before 1548 were St Margaret Lothbury, St Mary Aldermanbury, St Michael Paternoster, St Martin Ironmonger Lane, St Martin Orgar and St Mary Aldermary.

[96] Seaver, Appendix D. The pre-1548 'active' parishes which do not appear on Seaver's list are St Botolph Billingsgate, St John Zachary, St George Southwark, St Margaret Westminster, St Michael Queenhythe and St Olave Southwark. All these had lectureships by 1654.

most vital parishes in London before 1548, all but four had established lectureships before the end of the century. There can be detected, therefore, a tradition of parish life and community effort which transcended the changes of doctrine.

Some of the London fraternities were, already before the Reformation, concerned to provide preaching. The guild of the Name of Jesus at St Paul's provided preachers at Paul's Cross and at St Mary Spittal.[97] The guild attached to the hospital of St Mary Rounceval also recruited preachers and the fraternity in the church of St Giles Cripplegate in 1548 was paying 3s 4d annually to a preacher.[98] By 1565 this same parish was employing the puritan Robert Crowley to preach every Sunday.[99] This, in itself, is an interesting instance of a continuity of practice within a single parish.

It would be a mistake to paint too rosy a picture of parish fraternities. Many of them cannot have been more than very fleeting associations. Geoffrey Bonere, a paternostermaker, had bequeathed tenements in Fleet Street in 1368 to the fraternity of St Hilda in the church of St Michael Le Querne. But by 1407 the guild no longer survived and the tenements had passed into eager private hands.[100] The guild in honour of the Conception of the Virgin which had been founded in the church of St Sepulchre at Newgate before 1349 by 'poor people of the parish' had disappeared by 1402 when the mayor held an enquiry to find out what had happened to tenements bequeathed to the fraternity.[101] The fraternity in the church of St Mary Woolnoth which had been bequeathed the tenement called the Cardinal's Hat by Simon Eyre in 1459, had disintegrated by 1492 when the tenement passed to the rector and churchwardens instead.[102] Even those fraternities which did not disintegrate, were not always well run. In the course of a visitation of the church of St Magnus in c. 1519 it was reported that, through the negligence of the churchwardens and the masters of the *Salve* guild, neither the priests, nor the clerks attended the mass of the Virgin and the parish clergy were generally negligent in their attendance. The visitors reported that in their view the masters of the *Salve* guild could well have rectified the situation if they had bestirred themselves.[103] Whether the guild priests ceased from frequenting taverns and from going fishing at the times of divine services is not clear, but the chantry return of 1548 describes a

[97] Sparrow Simpson, *Registrum*, 457.
[98] Rosser, thesis, 351; *Chantry*, 18.
[99] Seaver, 123.
[100] *HW* ii, 132; *CCR 1405–09*, 189–90, 334–35; *Calendar of Inquisitions Miscellaneous 1399–1422*, 158–9.
[101] The return of this little fraternity which claimed that it had no oaths, no livery, no goods and no chattels is PRO, C47/42/201. John de Shenefeld, a tanner, bequeathed tenements to the fraternity in 1349, *HW* i, 540–41, but the guild had dissolved by 1402, *Calendar of Inquisitions Miscellaneous 1399–1422*, 107–8.
[102] See the will of Sir Hugh Bryce, Alderman, *HW* ii, 600–601; Stow i, 205.
[103] [Richard Arnold], *The Customs of London, otherwise called Arnold's Chronicle*, 1811, 273–8.

comparatively well organised guild in which the two priests received £16 between them and nearly £20 was distributed in poor relief.[104] But the visitors' report reveals that not all laymen could live up to the responsibilities for which some craved.

It would, of course, be wrong to suggest that parish fraternities were the only expression of parish vitality; parish halls were built by parishioners at Hackney and at St Clement Danes and the returns of 1548 make it clear that several parishes made some sort of provision for the poor.[105] Thrice weekly lectureships had been endowed by James Finche at Whittington College and at St Leonard Foster Lane the parishioners subscribed for an additional priest to help the rector 'of devotion and good will at their own charge'.[106] The churchwardens' accounts of St Dunstan in the West, St Mary Magdalen Milk Street, St Andrew Hubbard and St Stephen Walbrook all reveal that the wages of the parish clerk depended upon collections made in the parish.[107] At St Stephen's in 1507 the names of the contributors and the amounts of their contributions are all recorded.[108] The rebuilding of parish churches such as St Margaret's at Westminster, St Andrew Undershaft and St Giles Cripplegate is a further indication of parish cohesion and vitality.[109]

This study of the London parish fraternities may have revealed something of the preoccupations of medieval men and women. It has demonstrated both the fragility, and the adaptability, of the guild structure. Fraternities which were first formed to secure decent burial and sufficient prayers for their members, evolved over two hundred years into organisations to focus the parish will, to build halls, to administer poor relief, to provide sermons and, above all to allow lay men and women a say in the quality and character of the religious services offered to them. The increasing vitality of parish fraternities in London in the early sixteenth century may demonstrate, not so much an increasing commitment to the doctrines of what was to become 'the old faith' but, rather, a rising tide of lay participation in religion fed, in its turn by rising prosperity and increasing literacy. Perhaps we concern ourselves too much with changes of doctrine. When the Reformers, and the Counter-Reformers had trampled across the parishes of England, lay men and women sprang up once more like trodden grass, and found in parish vestries and lectureships and the administration of the Elizabethan Poor

[104] *Chantry*, 25.
[105] *Chantry*, 151, 152.
[106] *Chantry*, 216, 65; see also the will of William Jarden, tailor, who endowed an annual sermon at St Margaret's Westminster so that a scholar from Queen's College Oxford might come once a year to preach the word of God, Rosser, *TRHS*, 1984, 110.
[107] All the accounts are in Guildhall Library, St Dunstan in the West MS 2968; St Mary Magdalen Milk Street, MS 2596/1; St Andrew Hubbard, MS 1279; St Stephen Walbrook, MS 593.
[108] Guildhall Library MS 593 fo. 6.
[109] St Margaret Westminster was rebuilt between 1487 and 1523, Rosser, thesis, 283–97; St Andrew Undershaft between 1520 and 1532; St Giles Cripplegate between 1545 and 1550, Nikolaus Pevsner, *London: the Cities of London and Westminster*, 2nd edn, 1962, 136, 145.

Law, adapted solutions for old needs. Perhaps we may look for the seed bed of the English Reformation, not in Lollardy, nor in anti-clericalism, but in the vitality of the parish community.

Bedford College, London

Anticlericalism in Fifteenth-Century Prussia: the Clerical Contribution Reconsidered

MICHAEL BURLEIGH

In late medieval Germany, the higher clergy were mainly noblemen. Unremarkably enough, this meant that they behaved like noblemen. Sometimes, this resulted in their indulgence in violence worthy of the most overwrought Jacobean tragedy. As for the laity, they were not much better. They were contemptuous of the 'peaceful behaviour of which the Christian clergy had . . . been special guardians' and this manifested itself in 'widespread practical rejection of clerical immunity' which, it has been argued, was the specific identity of German anticlericalism.[1] Looked at in this way, anticlericalism becomes merely an aspect of a society peculiarly prone to violence; 'clericalism' as a contributory factor has apparently been ruled out. However, the intensity of the former seems directly related to the intensity of the latter.[2] It would be difficult, for example, to write about the *Kulturkampf* without reference to the creation of the confessional Centre Party or the extreme conservatism of Pope Pius IX. So what was the clerical contribution to late medieval German anticlericalism? How did the clergy's claims to a privileged relationship with God, power to impose spiritual sanctions, separate standing at law, membership of an international institution and, last but not least, their deployment of these claims in pursuit of local political goals, affect their relations with the laity? In fifteenth-century Prussia these questions derived added force from the fact that government was in the hands of a clerico-military oligarchy. The only exception to the unitary rule of the German Order was the bishopric of Ermland which, as a physical

[1] F. R. H. Du Boulay, *Germany in the Later Middle Ages*, 1983, 202.
[2] R. Rémond, 'Anticlericalism: Some Reflections by Way of Introduction', *European Studies Review* xiii, 1983, 123.

immunity ruled for many years by a champion of clerical judicial privilege, has some bearing on these problems.

We must first situate the bishopric within a broader Prussian framework. The bishopric of Ermland encompassed parts of the native Prussian territories of Warmia, Pogesania, Natangia and Barten.[3] Within this large area lordship was subject to division. While two-thirds of the see were absorbed into the network of German Order commanderies, the bishops enjoyed comprehensive seignorial powers in the remainder. In 1260 this fraction was subdivided in the ratio 2:1 to provide for a cathedral Chapter of sixteen canons who subsequently resided in Frauenburg.[4] The seven episcopal and three capitular *Kammerämter* formed a wedge-shaped territory both in terms of the diocese and the *Ordensstaat* as a whole; narrow on the coast of the Frisches Haff at Braunsberg, extensive in the interior between Allenstein and Rössel. The lordship of the bishops was co-ordinate with rather than subordinate to that of the Knights. Defence of the diocese was entrusted to advocates who were invariably knights of the Order; there was a high degree of collaboration between the Order and the bishops in the drafting of legislative ordinances, and finally, members of the Chapter sometimes served the Grand Masters as envoys, chaplains and secretaries.[5] By contrast, the cathedral Chapter of Frauenburg represented something of an anomaly. Unlike the Chapters of Kulm, Pomesania and Samland, the learned canons of Frauenburg (from 1384 members were obliged to have spent a minimum of three years at university) were unincorporated. This meant that they were not subject to the obedience of the Grand Masters and that their number was not replenished from the ranks of the Order's own priest-brothers. Both this, and the contiguous nature of the lordship, gave the bishopric of Ermland something of the character of a state within a state.[6]

In the fifteenth century, there were two attempts by the Order to substitute clientage for relative autonomy. The first resulted from political miscalculation on the part of Bishop Heinrich IV (1401–15). His precipitate flight following the defeat of the Order at Tannenberg in 1410 ensured that he was

---

[3] M. Töppen, *Historisch-comparative Geographie von Preussen*, Gotha 1858, 125–30.
[4] V. Röhrich, 'Die Kolonisation des Ermlandes', *Zeitschrift für die Geschichte und Altertumskunde Ermlands* xii, 1899, 613–14.
[5] For the advocates see R. Wenskus, 'Das Ordensland Preussen als Territorialstaat des 14. Jahrhunderts', *Der Deutsche Territorialstaat im 14. Jahrhundert*, ed. H. Patze for the *Konstanzer Arbeitskreis für mittelalterliche Geschichte* i, Sigmaringen 1970, 354; for the legislative ordinances see *Akten der Ständetage Preussens* (hereafter *ASP*), ed. M. Töppen, Leipzig 1874–86, nos. 363–6, pp. 469–77; 487, pp. 625–30; 2, nos. 244, pp. 361f; 383, pp. 617f; for members of the Chapter as servants of the Order see H. Boockmann, *Laurentius Blumenau, Fürstlicher Rat-Jurist-Humanist (ca. 1415–1484)* (*Göttinger Bausteine zur Geschichtswissenschaft*, ed. H. Heimpel, R. Nurnberger, H. Roos, G. Schnath, P. Schramm, R. Wenskus, R. Wittram), Göttingen 1965, 37, p. 116.
[6] On the educational background of the Chapter see G. Matern, *Die kirchlichen Verhältnisse in Ermland während des späten Mittelalters*, Paderborn 1953, 75–6; for the status of the Chapter see K. E. Murawski, *Zwischen Tannenberg und Thorn* (*Göttinger Bausteine zur Geschichtswissenschaft*, ed. Heimpel et al.), Göttingen 1953, 10 and 11, p. 182.

numbered among those regarded by the Order as traitors.[7] For the next four years Heinrich IV was obliged to stalk the peripheries of Prussia in search of testimonials absolving him from the charge of conspiring with the Poles.[8] Since the Order considered the strategic value of the see to be too great to be left in such uncertain hands, the Order's proctor in Rome was given the task of securing the election of a more reliable candidate to the 'vacant' see.[9] In the meantime, Grand Master Plauen took over the administration of the bishopric. He made use of the episcopal residence and made himself at home, so to speak, with transports of wine from his own cellars in Marienburg. He also directed the bishop's revenues into the Order's coffers and granted lands to favoured servants.[10] This despoliation continued for three years until mounting external pressure resulted in the return of the wandering Heinrich. In 1454 an admittedly partial source estimated that three years of administration by the Knights had cost the bishop 25,000*m* in lost revenues.[11]

The autonomy of the bishopric came under renewed attack in the mid-1440s. Grand Master Konrad von Erlichshausen's initial concern was to tap the source of patronage represented by the Chapter on behalf of one of his secretaries.[12] In this endeavour he got both rather more and rather less than he had bargained for. More because in July 1447 Nicholas V granted the Order the right of nomination to two major prebends; less because the papal grant took no account of the Order's attempts to revise the early history of the see. Employing revisionist arguments similar to those it had already used against its lay subjects, the Order maintained that the first bishop of Ermland had been a member of the Order, that the Order had created both the bishopric and the Chapter from lands it had conquered and that therefore the bishopric was merely a fief.[13] Not surprisingly, the Chapter was prepared to go to considerable lengths to combat these claims. Two senior canons, including the chronicler Plastwich, made the journey to Rome. They came armed with the requisite weapons for a curial duel. Writing in 1463, Plastwich calculated that the dispute had cost the Chapter 1,000 Hungarian *Gulden*.[14] They also claimed to have a 'concordat' in which a past Grand Master had formally relinquished any right to interfere in the affairs of the

[7] H. Schmauch, 'Ermland und der Deutschorden während der Regierung des Bischofs Heinrich IV Heilsberg (1401–1415)', *Zeitschrift für die Geschichte und Altertumskunde Ermlands* xxii, 1926, 471f.

[8] *Monumenta Historiae Warmiensis*, II. Abteil. *Scriptores rerum Warmiensi*, ed. C. P. Woelky, Braunsberg 1866–89, i, 83, n. 70.

[9] *Die Berichte der Generalprokuratoren des Deutschen Ordens an der Kurie*, ed. H. Koeppen, Göttingen 1960, ii, no. 75, p. 156.

[10] Schmauch, 'Ermland und der Deutschorden', 476–8.

[11] *ASP* iv, no. 235, p. 355.

[12] Boockmann, *Laurentius Blumenau*, 117f.

[13] Murawski, *Zwischen Tannenberg und Thorn*, 183; for the Order's use of revisionist arguments against secular opponents see M. Burleigh, 'History, Privilege and Conspiracy Theories in mid-fifteenth Century Prussia', *European History Quarterly* xiv, 1984, 388–91.

[14] *Scriptores rerum Warmiensi*, 89.

Chapter. With considerable relief, the three officials of the Order deputed to scour the archives in search of this elusive document could only find charters related to boundary disputes.[15] In the end, however, the superior resources of the Order took effect. In 1449 the pope confirmed his earlier grant of the right to nominate two senior canons. The Chapter had expended its money in vain.

That the Order abandoned this aspect of its *Inkorporationspolitik* in 1453 by voluntarily relinquishing the rights it had acquired in the late 1440s was a belated tribute to the political services of bishop Franz of Ermland who had become an indispensable ally in the Order's struggle with its Prussian opponents.[16] Inevitably, relations between the bishop, Chapter and their subjects were a microcosm of relations between rulers and ruled in Prussia at large. In a fifteenth-century context, this meant that they were universally bad.

To begin with, in 1440 the peasants of the capitular *Kammeramt* of Mehlsack decided to down tools. In 1411 the Chapter had commuted the task of floating logs down the Passarge from Allenstein for use in the seignorial ovens into an annual rent of $9\frac{1}{2}m$.[17] However, what was given with one hand was soon taken back with the other. The peasants found themselves obliged to transport honey and clay over inordinate distances and to help with fishing. As the resulting dispute could be settled by neither the parties concerned nor through the arbitration of the bishop, it was decided to refer the conflict to the council of Braunsberg and, through their mediation, to the recently established territorial court of appeal.[18] The first, and apparently last, judgement of this court was passed in June 1441.[19] Its effects were nugatory since many of the peasants chose to ignore it while in January 1442 the bishop resorted to the more drastic expedient of seizing over forty of the peasants involved and consigning them to a dispersed network of seignorial gaols.[20]

Acceptance by the clergy of lay arbitration in a dispute with peasants did not mean that relations between the lordship and the classes represented in the Estates were cordial. As in Prussia as a whole, conflict centred on the question of appellate jurisdictions. For a decade the Estates had called for the creation of a 'mixed' court of appeal for the resolution of questions of privilege and cases involving both the Order and the clergy at large. Although in 1440 the Order finally conceded the issue, there was nothing to

---

[15] Geheimes Staatsarchiv, West Berlin, *Ordensbriefarchiv, Regesta historico-diplomatica Ordinis S. Mariae Theutonicorum 1198–1525*, prepared by E. Joachim and edited by W. Hubatsch, Göttingen 1948–50, i (2), no. 11161.

[16] Murawski, *Zwischen Tannenberg und Thorn*, 184.

[17] V. Röhrich, 'Ein Bauernaufruhr im Ermlande (1440–1442)', *Königliches Gymnasium zu Rössel. Bericht über das Schuljahr Ostern 1893/94*, Rössel 1894, ii.

[18] For the progress of the dispute see *ASP* ii, no. 261, p. 398f.

[19] *ASP* ii, no. 227, pp. 348–50.

[20] Röhrich, 'Ein Bauernaufruhr', xii–xiii; *ASP* ii, no. 260, p. 397.

guarantee that the court we have already encountered would not prove to be evanescent. As a result, in March 1440 a number of noblemen and the representatives of the major towns joined together to form the Prussian League. The main clause of the charter of foundation unilaterally outlined a system of appeals that effectively mediatised the position of the Grand Master (and, by implication, the prelates), and gave the last word in any dispute to bodies summoned by the Estates. Ominously, the Leaguers added that acts of interference against the course of justice that they had outlined would 'not go unrevenged'.[21]

The Hanseatic town of Braunsberg was among the original signatories of the charter of the League and shortly it was followed by the knights and smaller towns of the see.[22] Like storm clouds massing on the horizon, the twin issues of clerical privilege and the desire of the Estates to territorialise jurisdiction came rolling towards the see. In May 1440 the Diet of Elbing decreed that henceforth the town council of Braunsberg should serve as a court of appeal within Ermland but that matters it could not resolve should be referred to 'the lords of Culm', or in other words the League.[23] In the summer of 1444 the townsmen asked the League for assistance in the event of an attack upon them by the bishop with whom they were in perpetual dispute over the demarcation of their respective jurisdictions as well as the bishop's efforts to drag them through remote and costly ecclesiastical courts.[24] Soon, the problems of the Braunsbergers and the more general issue of the clergy's resort to the nexus of church courts regularly figured among the grievances of the Estates.[25]

These local difficulties as well as aggressively clerical attitudes acquired through the higher study of canon law in Leipzig and Prague, contributed to Bishop Franz's decision to mount a general assault on the legality of the League. In April 1446 he astonished the Diet of Elbing with a characteristic outburst in which he denounced the League as being 'against all spiritual and natural law'. It was his duty – for the episcopal conscience was in turmoil – to lead his flock away from error. Almost in passing he alluded to ordinances issued by Frederick II (1220), Charles IV (1356), Honorius III and the Second Lateran Council, whose combined effect would have been to outlaw and hence destroy everyone involved with the League. His ensuing

[21] *ASP* ii, no. 108, pp. 173–4; on the League see M. Biskup, 'Der preussische Bund 1440–1454 – Genesis, Tätigkeit und Bedeutung in der Geschichte Preussens und Polens', in K. Fritze *et al.*, eds., *Hansische Studien* iii, Weimar 1975, 214f, and M. Burleigh, *Prussian Society and the German Order: an aristocratic corporation in crisis c. 1410–66*, Cambridge 1984, 147–57.

[22] For Braunsberg's membership see *ASP* ii, no. 108, p. 175; for the knights and smaller towns (of which there were twelve) see *ASP* ii, no. 119, pp. 179–80.

[23] *ASP* ii, no. 148, p. 214.

[24] *ASP* ii, no. 369, p. 601.

[25] *ASP* ii, nos. 369, p. 601; 377, p. 609; iii, nos. 33, p. 65; 42, p. 77; 63, p. 120, and 68, pp. 140 and 154.

offer to cover the costs of an examination of the legality of the charter either by the Curia or 'other learned people' did nothing to lessen the blow.[26] His speech ensured the undying enmity of the Estates towards the bishop. In June, after further angry exchanges, the Estates declared that they wished the bishop of Ermland would 'stay at home'.[27] In July even the Grand Master (who while knowing in advance of the bishop's intention to speak had expected something more solicitudinous in tone), was moved to send one of his officers to the prelate asking him to desist from his 'persecution' of the League.[28]

Following the death of Konrad von Erlichshausen in 1449, Franz moved from the wings to centre stage. From 1450, until the outbreak of civil war in 1454, Franz was part of a ruling trio responsible for the conduct of the Order's affairs. The consequences of his closer involvement were two-fold. First, it meant the adoption by the Order of his shrill insistence upon the privileges of the clergy and, secondly, the use of spiritual sanctions and higher authority to crush internal dissent.

The first development can be seen in the records of the Diet held in Elbing in April 1450. The meeting began on a fractious note when the Estates demanded the exclusion from the Diet of the Grand Master's *ménage* of academic jurists and Bishop Franz.[29] Three days later the Diet reassembled to consider the creation of a permanent court of appeal. Having answered affirmatively to the question of whether they wanted the Grand Master and his subordinates to be subject to such a court, the Estates were told that:

> the lord Grand Master and his Order and all of the brothers of the Order were privileged and exempted by the Holy See and the Emperor. That they were only answerable to the Holy Father, the Pope, and were only justiciable in the court of the Holy Father, the Pope, without any intermediate jurisdiction. Neither the Emperor, the King of the Romans, cardinals, patriarchs, archbishops, bishops nor any spiritual or lay judge, except the Holy Father, the Pope, and the Apostolic See could judge them.

The officers added pointedly that 'it would be a very strange thing that they should now be the justiciables of their subjects in the towns of Culm and Thorn'. The Estates were questioned further as to whether they thought that the clergy should be subject to the court of appeal. They answered affirmatively, adding 'because the clergy are so litigious and always want to cite our people to Rome and out of the country'.[30]

---

[26] *ASP* ii, no. 432, p. 693. For the penalties contained in these coercive ordinances see E. Lüdicke, 'Der Rechtskampf des deutschen Ordens gegen den Bund der preussischen Stände 1440–53', *Altpreussische Forschungen* xii (1935), 20–22.

[27] *ASP* ii, no. 440, p. 710.

[28] *ASP* ii, no. 467, p. 735.

[29] *ASP* iii, no. 69, p. 159.

[30] *ASP* iii, no. 69, pp. 164–5.

Fears that the Order was preparing to use higher authority to attack the League had been expressed as early as 1448. In that year a knight of the Culmerland had warned a gathering in Thorn that the Order's proctors in Rome were working to acquire papal documents whose effect would be to destroy the League. When told that he was deluding himself, the knight replied: 'delusion or not, they are already in chests'.[31] Two years later, the Grand Master informed the Diet of the imminent arrival of a papal legate, the Portuguese bishop Louis Perez. When pressed to expand on the subject, Ludwig claimed to have no knowledge beyond what was contained in the letters informing him of the legation, which, he said, was at the instigation of the pope.[32] This was an outright falsehood. In reality, the Order's proctors had received instructions to engineer the legation for the express purpose of destroying the League. The ways in which this was to be done were carefully outlined in a secret memorandum which bore the unmistakable authorship of the bishop of Ermland. The latter was careful to credit the officers of the Order with some independence of mind by suggesting that they might 'pick out whatever they regarded as being good and agreeable'.[33] The memorandum covered all eventualities. One scenario began with the announcement by the Grand Master of the legate's impending arrival. A number of representatives of the Estates would be summoned before the Grand Master's council where his officers and the prelates would adopt various tactical positions. The bishops would voice the most 'curialist' line, whose effect would be to throw the Estates back on the mercies of the Grand Master who would deliver them from the threat posed by the legate in return for their abrogation of the League. If this plan failed, there was another to cover the legate's visit. The pretence that he had come to investigate the Order as well as the League would be maintained. A meeting would take place in which the legate would scrutinise the charter of the League for anything incompatible with clerical privileges. He might make a speech, outlining the dire penalties awaiting those who interfered with the liberties of the Church, but ending on a note of reconciliation after the Grand Master had interceded on behalf of his aberrant subjects. Throughout, the memorandum recommended the use of the papal connection to block local concessions to the Estates.[34]

The legate's opening contact with the Estates was at a Diet in December 1450. The Grand Master stressed that both the Order and the Estates were accused in the legate's letters of commission. It proved easier for the former to exculpate themselves than the latter. With unremarkable facility, the

[31] *ASP* iii, no. 50, p. 88.
[32] *ASP* iii, nos. 78, pp. 185–6; 79, pp. 186–8. The Grand Master's exact words were 'No, he knew nothing more than what lay in the letters which they (the Estates) had heard read (*neyn, her wuste nicht andirs, denne als im brieffe, den sie hatten gehort lesen, stunde*).
[33] Lüdicke, 'Der Rechtskampf', 32.
[34] Lüdicke, 'Der Rechtskampf', 35.

Order cleared itself of the charge that misgovernment was responsible for the creation of the League. The legate was duly overjoyed:

> raising his hands to heaven praising and thanking God that he had found such obedient sons and brothers as the lord Grand Master, his officers, the Order and also the lord prelates . . . and would also thank them before the most Holy Father, the Pope.[35]

He employed a different tone in his dealings with the Estates. Tired of their procedural delays, and despite his declared willingness to court martyrdom in the service of the pope, unwilling to remain through the winter in a land riddled with pestilence, the legate had little patience with the arguments put forward by the League. In January 1451 he informed the Diet:

> You wish to judge those who with five words have the power to bring the only Son of God down from heaven. . . . You ask me to excuse you before our Holy Father, the Pope. How can I excuse you? . . . I find you in error and not obedient sons and therefore many souls stand in danger and must be damned.[36]

His intransigence, allied with regular denunciations from the Prussian pulpits induced a spirit of compromise in the Estates.[37] They asked the Grand Master to intercede on their behalf. The Grand Master assured them that he would work as truly on their behalf 'as if the matter were our own'. In a profound sense, the matter was undoubtedly 'his own' and, not least to the astonishment of the legate, the visit was brought to an end.[38]

One immediate result of the legation was increased animosity towards Bishop Franz in particular and the clergy in general. Although some historians have sought to qualify the concept of anticlericalism out of existence, like most prejudices it is obviously impervious to reason, and operates partly by attaching the supposed failings of individuals onto groups and *vice versa*. In this case, one can follow the flow of anticlerical sentiment, beginning with certain individuals and ending in a flood tide of generalised anticlerical abuse. In 1451 members of the League told Franz: 'lord bishop of Heilsberg, this trouble comes from you. The entire country feels bitterly towards you.'[39] As for the legate, at least one member of the Estates felt moved to say that he should have stayed at home in Portugal where there were enough unbelievers, Jews and religious deviants to occupy his attentions.[40]

---

[35] *ASP* iii, no. 85, p. 225.
[36] *ASP* iii, no. 91, p. 249.
[37] *ASP* iii, no. 91, p. 251.
[38] *ASP* iii, no. 91, p. 252.
[39] *ASP* iii, no. 91, pp. 244–5; see also the letter dated 7 December 1450 from the *Vogt* of Leipe to the Grand Master in which he remarked '*Item mir hat ein gut freunt gesagt, das sy ew. gn. und dem hern bischof von Heylsperg schult geben, das der legat ins lant kumen sey*'. For the letter see *ASP* iii, no. 82, p. 192.
[40] *ASP* iii, no. 85, p. 213.

The Order's subsequent attempts to belabour the League with papal bulls, imperial and princely letters were equally laid at the bishop's door.[41] Hardly bothering to deny the charge, Franz casually remarked that 'what he had done, he had done because of the Braunsbergers'.[42] Presently, these accusations were translated into threats of violence against the clergy at large. In a letter dated 21 October 1452, the *Vogt* of Roggenhausen described words spoken during a Diet held in the Culmerland. The Estates had decided that in the event of their being excommunicated, for refusing to abandon the League, 'they will attack the bishops and will punish them both physically and through their property, since they hold no one else responsible other than the spirituality'.[43] The town councillors of Elbing were more forthright: 'let's take hold of the priests by the scruff of the neck', they said, 'and throw them from the council chambers'.[44]

However one chooses to characterise these outbursts, it is clear that both the political activities of Bishop Franz and the use of external ecclesiastical authorities to coerce the League were widely resented in Prussia. In the mind of Tilman vom Wege, a leader of the League, the role of the Church as an ideologically legitimising force on behalf of an unjust regime was closely connected with the decision to throw off the lordship of the Order. In a letter to the council of Thorn dated 30 March 1453, Tilman said

> with the advice of the jurists I will bring our grievances before the Emperor, how our lord threatens us with spiritual laws. I hope to do that on the Feast Days when his grace (the Emperor) will be resting. Also I am of a mind to say to his grace that if his grace will not protect us from the violence and various threats which our lords commit daily . . . so we must find a lord who will protect us.[45]

In Ermland, the Estates were well placed to understand the essential hollowness of these strident statements of clerical immunity that we have been considering. In February 1454 the Estates of Ermland informed the Diet in Thorn that the Chapter of Frauenburg had made common cause with

---

[41] *ASP* iii, no. 141, p. 329; for the letters see no. 109, p. 282 (Margrave Hans of Brandenburg); 112, p. 283 (Archbishop of Cologne); 115, p. 284 (Margrave Friedrich of Brandenburg); 118, pp. 285–7 (King Frederick III); 113, p. 283 (Pope Nicholas V). For the reactions of the Estates see *ASP* iii, no. 174, pp. 393–5. The letters of Margrave Hans and the Archbishop of Cologne have been examined comparatively by E. Maschke in his 'Nikolaus von Kues und der Deutsche Orden', reprinted in *Domus Hospitalis Theutonicorum. Europäische Verbindungslinien der Deutschordensgeschichte. Gesammelte Aufsätze aus den Jahren 1931–1963. Quellen und Studien zur Geschichte des Deutschen Ordens*, ed. K. Wieser and U. Arnold, Bonn-Bad Godesberg 1970, x, 205–7. Although the Grand Master claimed to know nothing about the letters, they were based on a common draft, which originated from the chancellory of the German Master. The letters are therefore a manifestation of the Order's penchant for 'spontaneous' external involvement in Prussian affairs. See Maschke, 'Nikolaus von Kues', 127–31.

[42] *ASP* iii, no. 141, p. 329.

[43] *ASP* iii, no. 246, p. 495.

[44] *Scriptores rerum Prussicarum. Die Geschichtsquellen der Preussischen Vorzeit bis zum Untergange der Ordensherrschaft*, ed. T. Hirsch, M. Töppen, E. Strehlke, Leipzig 1861–74, iv, 97.

[45] *ASP* iii, no. 371, p. 624.

the League.[46] A few days later, the knights and townsmen of the bishopric renounced their allegiance to Bishop Franz. Their letter of defiance sheds some light on the actions of both themselves and the Chapter. They accused the bishop of failing to consult either the Estates or his Chapter before embarking on his persecution of the League. In what was perhaps a thoroughly conscious reference to the exchanges of 1446, they said that had they been consulted, they would have advised the bishop 'to stay at home'. His predecessors had risked life and limb in defence of the liberties of the see. They could still remember the days when the Order

> had driven a bishop of Ermland out of the country, and had taken over all of his lands, towns and castles, and stole whatever they had found in the houses and held the bishopric by *force majeur* for three years[47]

They added that Bishop Franz had said nothing about the losses sustained during the long exile of Heinrich IV and had failed to press the Order for compensation. Had the Estates been better informed of the Order's recent dealings with the clergy in other parts of their far-flung territories, they might have paused to reflect that Bishop Heinrich IV had escaped rather lightly. For the Order's extended definition of clerical privilege could accommodate the disappearance under the ice of Lake Liva of a sixteen-man delegation from the bishops of Livonia in 1428 and in the following year a grim conspiracy to murder the bishop of Ösel. Ironically enough, the victims were merely availing themselves of the clerical connection by pressing charges against the Order for interfering with clerical liberties and oppressing the Livonian Church.[48] The causes of anticlericalism in late medieval Prussia lay less in some generalised propensity to violence in a society lacking strong monarchical government – for the Order ruled with an iron hand and private violence was rapidly extinguished – but rather where the causes of anticlericalism have traditionally been found. It was a consequence of aggressive clericalism rather than a structural fault in German society.

New College, Oxford

---

[46] *ASP* iv, no. 208, p. 330. For the Chapter's adhesion to the League see no. 199, p. 324 and for their fortunes in the resulting Thirteen Years War see W. Brüning, 'Die Stellung des Bistums Ermland zum Deutschen Orden im dreizehnjährigen Städtekriege', *Altpreussische Monatsschrift* xxxii (1895), 23f.

[47] *ASP* iv, no. 235, pp. 354–6.

[48] For the background to the murders in Livonia see C. A. Lückerath, *Paul von Rusdorf, Hochmeister des Deutschen Ordens 1422–1441. Quellen und Studien zur Geschichte des Deutschen Ordens*, ed. K. Wieser, Bonn-Bad Godesberg 1969, xv, 104–9, and for the plot to kill the bishop of Ösel see *Die Berichte der Generalprokuratoren*, iv (1), no. 45, pp. 95–7.

The Piety of Late Medieval English Queens

ANNE CRAWFORD

What significance, if any, did the piety of their queens hold for Englishmen in the second half of the fifteenth century? Did it matter how this piety expressed itself? The answer to both questions is perhaps 'more than might be supposed'. The queens were leaders of domestic society and their characters and interests could substantially modify the tone of the court set by the king. While it was unlikely that a queen would initiate any totally new mode of pious expression, how she chose to perform, or neglect, her pious and charitable duties would influence other leaders of society. She would therefore both reflect the trends of her time and be responsible for the spread of those she favoured. Since her chaplains or chancellors might well be future bishops, whether she favoured scholars or administrators might affect a whole diocese. In this context, considerable significance may be given to the fact that with the exception of the first queen with whom we are concerned, Margaret of Anjou, the queens were English by birth and upbringing and thus brought no foreign influences to their husband's court. Elizabeth Woodville, Anne Nevill and Elizabeth of York rarely, if ever, set foot outside England and they were the first English queens since the Conquest.

Margaret of Anjou found on her arrival in England in 1445 that the queen's traditional leading role in pious and charitable affairs had already been usurped by her husband. Nothing to which she could hope to aspire in these fields would be anything other than a pale shadow of Henry VI's achievements, but there is no evidence to show that Margaret was anything more than conventionally pious. In the last few years of her life, when all her family were dead and she herself stripped of all her worldly possessions by Louis XI, her biographer describes her as finding solace not so much in religion as in reading. Her favourite book was written by Chastellain at her own request and described the sufferings of princes and nobles like

Charles VII and her own father King Réné.[1] Her only major charitable foundation was educational rather than religious. In 1448 she petitioned the king for permission to emulate him and found a college at Cambridge, where there was 'no collage founded by eny quene of Englond hidertoward'.[2] In fact Cambridge already boasted two foundations by women, Clare and Pembroke Colleges. The inspiration for the act did not belong to Margaret, for she had been approached by Andrew Docket, principal of St Bernard's College, recently re-endowed by Henry VI, but overshadowed by his great, new foundation of King's. Docket desired his college to be renamed the Queens' College of St Margaret and St Bernard. The king granted his consort a licence to found her college on 30 March 1448 and to endow it with lands to the value of £200 p.a.[3] However, Margaret's interest in her college did not extend to seeing it adequately endowed, with the result that it might well have foundered without the patronage of her successor as queen, her former lady-in-waiting, Elizabeth Woodville. The first evidence of her interest came only a few months after she was openly acknowledged as Edward IV's queen. On 25 March 1465, Andrew Docket and the fellows of Queens' College were granted a licence to acquire the land to the value of £200 p.a. which they had not so far succeeded in obtaining, and the college is described as being under the patronage of Elizabeth, queen of England.[4]

If Queen Margaret's charitable benefactions were slight, her influence on the episcopal bench was arguably greater than that of any other medieval queen consort. No fewer than four members of her household became bishops. Promotions to episcopal sees from the royal household were by no means uncommon, but they usually came from the king's rather than the queen's household. If nothing else, the clerics concerned had proved their administrative capabilities, and Margaret's promotions were talented men, though not necessarily noted for their spiritual qualities. Walter Lyhert had become the queen's confessor on her marriage and was advanced to the see of Norwich only a few months later. This may have owed more to the patronage of the duke of Suffolk than the new young queen, but there is little doubt of Margaret's influence in the promotion of her chancellor to the diocese of Coventry and Lichfield and then to the archdiocese of York in 1452. William Booth was in fact the only common lawyer among the fifteenth-century bishops. His brother, Lawrence, who succeeded him as the queen's chancellor, was soon appointed Dean of St Paul's. In 1457, when the princely see of Durham fell vacant, the queen most pressingly recommended him to the pope, despite the king's previous nomination of his own physician, John Arundel. Calixtus III appointed the queen's nominee. Arundel, probably

[1] The title of Chastellain's treatise was *Temple de la ruine de quelques nobles malheureux*; see J. J. Bagley, *Margaret of Anjou, Queen of England*, 1948, 239.
[2] W. G. Searle, *History of the Queen's College . . ., 1446–1560*, Cambridge 1867, 15.
[3] *CPR 1446–52*, 143–4.
[4] *CPR 1461–67*, 495.

this time with Margaret's backing, received the see of Chichester two years later. John Hals, one of the queen's chaplains since her marriage, was her candidate for Exeter in 1456, but during the duke of York's second protectorate the queen's influence was no longer paramount and she had to wait until 1459 when her second bid on his behalf brought him the see of Coventry and Lichfield.[5]

Margaret's assiduousness in promoting the interests of her servants, be it to offices, fees, grants, or rich marriages is well documented. There is nothing in her correspondence to indicate that she saw ecclesiastical appointments in any different light to those for the laity.[6] Her letters to clerics, even the archbishop of Canterbury, do not differ in tone, and the episcopate was seen as little more than a suitable reward for her abler clerics. If her piety went deeper than the gift of a gold tablet set with pearls, sapphires and rubies (and worth £29) to the shrine of our Lady of Walsingham, when she was hoping for an heir, then there is very little evidence for it.[7]

Unlike Margaret's husband, the saintly Henry VI, his successor, Edward IV, was noted neither for his piety nor his love of learning. His sole educational foundation was a lectureship in divinity at Oxford and his building programme, extensive as it was, was almost entirely secular.[8] His passion was collecting books, particularly Burgundian manuscripts, and his patronage of Caxton, a protégé of his sister Margaret, duchess of Burgundy, was never more than nominal. His queen, Elizabeth Woodville, however, seems to have been rather more interested in learning than he. She seems to have tempered to some extent the very chill Yorkist wind that blew upon the Lancastrian foundation of Eton and her patronage of Queens' College, Cambridge, has already been mentioned.[9] One of Caxton's earliest printed works, *A Boke of the Hoole Lyf of Jason*, was presented by him to the young Prince of Wales with the king's permission and 'by the supportacion of oure most redoubted liege lady, most excellent princesse, the Quene'.[10] Unlike those of her predecessor, none of Elizabeth's household clerics found their way on to the episcopal bench.

Many of Elizabeth's actions show her to have been grasping and totally lacking in scruple where her family was concerned, and it would be easy to dismiss her as completely worldly in her attitudes. Yet there are much less well-known indications of a piety that went beyond the purely conventional. She founded the chapel of St Erasmus in Westminster Abbey and received papal permission to enter Carthusian houses which were royal foundations,

[5] Griffiths, *Henry VI*, 258, 348, 757, 777.
[6] *Letters of Queen Margaret of Anjou*, ed. Cecil Munro (Camden Society lxxxvi), 1863.
[7] A. R. Myers, 'The Jewels of Queen Margaret of Anjou', *BJRL* xlii, 1959, 113–31.
[8] The most notable exception was St George's Chapel, Windsor; see Charles Ross, *Edward IV*, 1974, 270, 275.
[9] Ross, *Edward IV*, 269.
[10] D. MacGibbon, *Elizabeth Woodville*, 1938, 208.

provided she obtained the priors' consent. Papal letters also confirm her devotion to the feast of the Visitation of the Blessed Virgin and her particular support of the Austin friars at Hungtingdon.[11] She also chose to end her days in religious surroundings, not with the Carthusians, but in the Cluniac abbey of Bermondsey. The reasons for this retirement are not entirely clear. It used to be supposed that she was deprived of her lands and despatched to a convent by Henry VII for complicity in the Lambert Simnel affair, but this is not an argument that bears any scrutiny. Failing health and a desire to simplify her affairs by surrendering her lands in exchange for an annuity seem a more likely explanation. It was not uncommon for noble ladies to retire comfortably to nunneries for their last years. The Minories in London was a popular choice, but Elizabeth went instead to the monks' guest suite at Bermondsey, where Henry V's widow, Catherine of Valois, had spent her last months. The abbot, John de Marlow, had been one of those who had officiated at Edward IV's funeral. The Clare family had been the abbey's chief benefactors and Edward was the last male representative of the family. Elizabeth, as his widow, therefore had a particular claim on the abbey's hospitality, little though the monks may have relished the idea of a queen-dowager and her household in residence.[12]

Anne Nevill, queen of Richard III, is an altogether more shadowy figure. Her husband, in the view of a major recent biographer, was a 'genuinely pious and religious man'.[13] His interest in and support of scholars was more in the tradition of the Lancastrian kings than that of his brother, Edward IV. He was a noted patron of Cambridge both before and after he became king. The chief beneficiaries were King's and Queens' Colleges, and much granted to the latter was in the name of his queen, but there seems little doubt that the motivation was Richard's and not Anne's. He made his grants provisional upon the college recognising Queen Anne as a founder, a condition not unnaturally accepted. Anne, who was queen for little more than eighteen months before her death, seems not to have initiated any benefactions herself, but she was associated with most of her husband's, and it seems likely that she was as devout as he. The book of hours associated with Richard was made for the Beauchamp family and was almost certainly a gift from his wife, or more likely hers until her death. It was a much-used volume, clearly more valued for its content than its binding.[14]

Only when we come to Elizabeth of York, eldest daughter of Edward IV and Elizabeth Woodville and queen of Henry VII, do we find a consort whose piety and charity were truly queenly. Bernard André, her husband's official biographer, described her in the following terms: 'She exhibited from

[11] *CPL 1471–84*, 90–91, 563, 582–3.
[12] S. Chrimes, *Henry VII*, 1972, 76; A. Strickland, *Lives of the Queens of England*, 1857, ii, 368–9.
[13] Charles Ross, *Richard III*, 1981, 128ff.
[14] P. Tudor-Craig, *Catalogue of the Richard III Exhibition*, National Portrait Gallery 1973, 26–7.

her very cradle towards God an admirable fear and service; towards her parents a wonderful obedience; towards her brothers and sisters an almost incredible love; towards the poor, and the ministers of Christ a reverend and singular affection.'[15] Although this portrait might be dismissed as a mere panegyric, it can be substantially supported by evidence from the queen's own surviving privy purse expenses. These cover the last year of her life, from 25 March 1502 until her death in child-bed on her thirty-eighth birthday, 11 February 1503, and illustrate, as far as such payments can, her personal life.

Elizabeth performed her major duty as queen very promptly, and in gratitude for her safe delivery of Prince Arthur at Winchester founded a chapel there dedicated to Our Lady. Neither her mother nor Queen Margaret, who both had to wait far longer to give their husbands sons were moved to give thanks in this way. The queen also had the habit of sending priests on pilgrimages on her behalf. Sir William Barton undertook a month-long one travelling from Windsor to East Anglia, visiting, among other places, Hailes Abbey, Worcester, Walsingham and Stoke by Clare. His offerings at the shrines for the queen amounted to 48s 4d, and she allowed him 10d per day for expenses.[16] Elizabeth's Maunday money in 1502, 3s 1d paid to each of thirty-seven poor women, came out of her privy purse, as did the cost of three yards of cloth given to each of the women.[17] Various religious guilds like the fraternity of St George at Southwark, the Brotherhood of Jesus at Grantham or the Brotherhood of St Ursula in London were recipients of her charity, usually for sums in the region of 3s 4d or 5s. The sum of five shillings was her customary offering at a major feast, such as Ascension Day or the feast of the Holy Trinity, though at one which was especially significant to the queen personally, she might offer as much as twenty-five shillings, and on both Good Friday and Easter Sunday 1502 she offered 66s 8d. The abbess of the fashionable London convent, the Minories, was a regular recipient of the queen's alms, and so were two of her nuns, Dame Katherine and Dame Elizabeth, together with a third, the daughter of William Crowther, one of the queen's gentlemen ushers. On 4 August 1502, Elizabeth bore the cost of making 'little Anne Loveday' a nun at Elstowe, a sum totalling £6 13s 4d.[18]

The queen's almoner, Richard Payne, was the household officer responsible for the main distribution of her charity, particularly on her journeys from one royal residence to another, but Dr Underwood, her confessor, was sometimes asked to give alms to a recipient the queen specially noted. On one occasion Master Harding, the clerk of her closet, was refunded for 'money by him given in alms at divers times by the Queen's commandment'.[19] The queen's

[15] N. H. Nicolas, *Privy Purse Expenses of Elizabeth of York*, 1830, xcv.
[16] Nicolas, 3.
[17] Nicolas, 1, 74.
[18] Nicolas, 7, 51, 77; 10, 13, 65, 96; 8, 37.
[19] Nicolas, 59, 50.

charity extended from impulse payments to those in need encountered by chance, such as the friar of St John's for burying the men hanged at Wapping or the man of Pontefract who had lodged Earl Rivers (the queen's maternal uncle executed by her paternal uncle, Richard III) just before his death, to the financial support given to her sisters.[20] These younger daughters of Edward IV were married by Henry VII to English noblemen, but without marriage portions. Family pride and Elizabeth's generous nature made her pay annuities of up to £50 each to Cecily, Anne and Katherine, and £120 p.a. to their husbands for their support so that they might not be totally dependent. When Katherine's husband, William Courtenay, later earl of Devon, had his lands seized by the crown, the queen brought Katherine into her household and undertook the complete support of their children. Her youngest sister, Bridget, became a nun at Dartford Abbey and Elizabeth made regular payments to the abbess for her expenses.[21] Unlike her mother, her aunt Queen Anne, or Queen Margaret, Elizabeth of York was no public benefactor of education, her charity was small-scale but universal. Yet it was clearly recognised by her husband's subjects, for it was she and not one of her immediate predecessors who was known as 'the good'.[22]

The queens of the late fifteenth century, it would seem, were not generally noted for their piety or charity. The love given by the people to Elizabeth of York demonstrates that goodness and charity in a queen were recognised and prized. There had been pious queens before, Eleanor of Provence as the widow of Henry III took the veil at Amesbury, but she was not known for her charity, indeed rather the reverse, and was highly unpopular. Piety alone was not enough. Only when it was part of a generous, charitable and loving nature did it ensure that the queen was held in widespread affection. In the centuries since the Conquest, only Matilda of Scotland, wife of Henry I, and Philippa of Hainault, wife of Edward III, had won the epithet 'good' before Elizabeth of York. There were, however, two royal ladies of the period whose piety was legendary and who cannot be excluded from this study. They were the kings' mothers, Cecily Nevill, duchess of York, mother of Edward IV and Richard III, and Margaret Beaufort, countess of Richmond and Derby, mother of Henry VII.

Cecily's piety has been analysed in great scholarly detail by C. A. J. Armstrong, who describes it as 'true humility accompanied by dignity, a responsibility towards others felt not only as a duty of high rank but as the product of intimate devoutness'.[23] She was deeply attracted to the mystical form of contemplative piety dominated by the two saints, St Catherine of Siena and St Bridget of Sweden. The cult of St Bridget was particularly

[20] Nicolas, 14, 78.
[21] Nicolas, xciv.
[22] Strickland, 457.
[23] C. A. J. Armstrong, 'The Piety of Cecily, Duchess of York', in his *England, France and Burgundy in the Fifteenth Century*, 1983, 138.

strong in England and it centred on the great double abbey at Syon on the Thames, a few miles from London. Although founded by Henry V, it was the York family that was particularly devoted to the Order and Cecily who was the driving force. Edward IV was regarded by Syon as its second founder and his youngest daughter, to whom her grandmother stood sponsor, was given the name of Bridget, hitherto virtually unknown in England. The life led by Cecily in her later years at her principal residences of Berkhamsted and Baynard's Castle in London was monastic in almost everything save vows. A record of her daily round has survived in a household ordinance of post-1485 when she was seventy.[24] It consisted of private and public devotions broken only by public business, and relaxation allowed only after supper. Her chapel was sumptuously furnished with valuable plate, vestments, jewels and books and her will contains many of these as bequests. She also possessed a large number of rosaries and *Agnus Dei*, and her most precious reliquary was 'a crosse silver and guilte and berall, and in the same a pece of the holy crosse'.[25] Whether or not her granddaughter Bridget, Edward IV's seventh daughter, was always intended by Cecily for the church, or whether it was the girl's own inclination or reversal of fortune that led her to become a nun, she took her vows at Dartford, a strict Dominican house, which like Syon was a centre of mysticism. However, another granddaughter, Anne de la Pole, entered Syon and became its abbess. To Bridget and Anne Cecily bequeathed her books on mysticism.[26] The piety of Richard III can probably be traced to his mother's influence and certainly Queen Elizabeth's spiritual life owed far more to her grandmother than her parents, but Cecily's devoutness was inherited most strongly by her youngest daughter, Margaret of York, who became duchess of Burgundy. Margaret is recorded as performing corporal acts of mercy herself rather than delegating them, a humility rare in the wives of reigning princes. She was a patron of the Observant Franciscans, an order much admired on the continent, and is credited with persuading her brother, Edward IV, to invite them to England and offer them a site for a house close to his palace at Greenwich.[27] Only a fraction of Margaret's will now survives, but in it she bequeathed thirty *livres* p.a. to keep a student of theology at the universities of Louvain and Lille.[28]

Lady Margaret Beaufort adds a new dimension to this group of devout English ladies of the royal family. First cousin of Cecily Nevill, Lady Margaret's piety was of the active rather than contemplative kind. Although she wore hair shirts or girdles on certain days every week, spent hours every day at her devotions, and received the permission of her third husband, Thomas Stanley, earl of Derby, to live chastely, her life was far from the

[24] Armstrong, 140ff.
[25] *Wills from Doctors' Commons*, ed. J. G. Nichols and J. Bruce (Camden Society lxxxiii), 1863, 5.
[26] *Wills from Doctors' Commons*, 2–3.
[27] Ross, *Edward IV*, 273–4.
[28] Armstrong, 152n.

simple round of masses, offices and devotional reading favoured by Cecily in her old age. Margaret was a great landowner in her own right, mother of the reigning king, over whom she possessed considerable influence, and a woman of notable intellect. Her religious and charitable benefactions were legion and she retained a personal interest in many of them. For instance, she kept twelve poor people at Hatfield, providing them with lodging, food and clothing, which was easy enough for a wealthy woman to do, but she also nursed them herself when they were ill and sat with them when they were dying.[29] Among her benefactions to the church were a chantry at Wimbourne, co. Dorset, where her parents were buried, three chantry priests at Westminster Abbey, for whose altars she gave books, vestments and plate, and apparently the delightful gift of her manor house at Torrington, co. Devon, to the village priest because she was distressed by the long walk he had from his house to the church.[30]

It is, however, with education that Lady Margaret's name is most closely linked. In about 1502 she appointed as her chaplain a Cambridge scholar named Dr John Fisher, his predecessor, Dr Robert Fitzjames, having moved on to become, successively, bishop of Rochester, Chichester and London. Fisher was already renowned for his extraordinary devotion and thereafter exerted a considerable influence on her. His opinion of Lady Margaret was equally high, for he described her as having 'in maner all that is praysable in a woman eyther in soule or in body', and being 'of singuler wysedome ferre passynge the comyn rate of women'.[31] She owned a great number of books and translated some devotions from the French so that they could be printed in English. She was also not above commanding Caxton and his fellow printers to print devotional works she particularly favoured.[32] According to Fisher she often complained that she had never been taught Latin properly when she was young, though she knew enough to understand the services. It is generally accepted that it was Fisher's influence which led her to patronise his university to the degree she did. Before he entered her household her patronage had been more equably distributed. In late 1496 and early 1497 she had been granted licences by her son the king to found two perpetual readerships in theology, one each at Oxford and Cambridge, with grants of land not exceeding the value of £20 p.a. to pay for the readers.[33] Dr John Roper at Oxford and Dr John Fisher himself at Cambridge were then appointed to read approved works of divinity to the students for an hour each day. In 1505 she moved on to a much greater task: the refounding of God's House, Cambridge, where Fisher had begun his career, as Christ's College.

---

[29] 'The Month's Mind of the Lady Margaret', in *The English Works of John Fisher*, ed. J. E. B. Mayor (EETS xxvii), 1876, 297.
[30] C. H. Cooper, *The Lady Margaret*, 1874, 42, 59, 105.
[31] *English Works of Fisher*, 291.
[32] Cooper, 45, 54, 87, 108.
[33] *CPR 1497–1509*, 79.

Margaret framed the statutes in 1506 for an establishment consisting of a master, twelve fellows and forty-seven scholars, half of whom were to come from nine northern counties. She took considerable personal interest in the college, far more, certainly than the queens could, or chose to, show in Queens' College. She visited the half-finished building and reserved rooms for herself in the college which in her absence were to be used by Fisher, whom she appointed visitor for life. She endowed it with seven advowsons, five manors and various lands, including those of Creke Abbey, co. Norfolk, which had escheated to the Crown and been granted to her by her son with licence to assign to Christ's College.[34]

In about 1508, obviously pleased with her achievements in Cambridge, Margaret turned her attention to the ancient Augustinian hospital of St John, which she decided to refound as an academic college for a master and fifty scholars. Nothing was formally done in her lifetime, nor in her will, but a codicil stated her intentions and left it to her executors to fulfil them. This they did, not without difficulty and largely owing to the vigour and determination of Fisher. Other provisions in her will increased endowments to Christ's College and the chantry and free school at Wimbourne and also provided for her manor of Walton to be repaired and put at the disposal of the students during any period of contagious sickness in Cambridge.[35]

In some ways Margaret's will, made in 1508, exemplifies many of the late fifteenth-century attitudes to religion.[36] It instructs her executors in minute detail about the services to be held at her death, in her own chapel, the parish church of the place where she died and in the churches of the fifteen adjoining parishes, those parishes through which her cortège passed and those where it halted overnight on its way to her final resting place in her son's chapel in Westminster Abbey. She dealt generously with her household servants and dependants and appointed her executors, chief of whom were Bishops Richard Fox of Winchester and John Fisher of Rochester, and then in a great schedule she detailed her specific legacies and benefactions, some of which have already been mentioned. The heir to those of her lands not already set aside for charitable purposes was, of course, the king, by this date her grandson, Henry VIII. Many of her household possessions were bequeathed to her family and friends, but all the furnishings of her chapel, plate, jewels, vestments, books and altarcloths, she asked to be divided equally between her two Cambridge colleges.[37] In her preoccupation with masses and her considerable founding of chantries, Margaret was illustrating the overwhelming belief of her time, that the souls of the donors and their families would benefit in direct proportion to the number of masses said for

---

[34] *CPR 1497–1509*, 415, 519, 543; Cooper, 100, 103–4.
[35] Cooper, 110, 121.
[36] *Test. Vet.*, i, 517–21.
[37] Cooper, 121.

them. That the masses should be supplemented by pious and charitable acts was a further belief exemplified by Margaret in her lifetime. The fact that much of her charity was educational made her exceptional in the fifteenth century. It was not until the Reformation had loosened church control over education and chantries no longer absorbed such a substantial proportion of charitable giving that Englishmen began to follow her example in large numbers.[38]

In contrast, Margaret's cousin, Cecily Nevill, was the inheritor of a much earlier attitude to religion, that of the supremacy of the monastic life. If she had not been a duchess, surely she would have joyfully taken the veil. As it was, she lived as closely by the rule as her position allowed and encouraged two of her granddaughters to do what she could not. Queen Elizabeth of York lived far less austerely than her grandmother or her mother-in-law, enjoying the pleasures of the court she led. She watched players and dancers, listened to musicians, hunted and kept greyhounds, and even gambled at cards and dice, yet she paid the strictest attention to her religious duties and her charities were legion. While the lives and wills of the Nevill-Beaufort ladies show what importance they, like most of their contemporaries, placed on the external trappings of fifteenth-century religion, the masses for the dead, the rosaries, the indulgences, the rich furnishings of chapels, yet these could not mask the intense devotion of three generations of royal ladies. They set an example of piety and good works that no post-Reformation queens could hope to emulate and few medieval ones had equalled.

Bristol Record Office

---

[38] See J. A. F. Thomson, 'Piety and Charity in late medieval London', *JEH* xvi, 1965, 194–5.

The Last Days of Cleeve Abbey

Robert W. Dunning

In 1542, when John Leland was making his way through West Somerset, he spent some time at the house at Orchard near Williton which John Wyndham had recently acquired by his marriage to one of the Sydenham heiresses. From there he rode westwards, through a village called Washford, where he crossed a brook flowing from the Brendons down a narrow, fertile valley. On his right he noted a stone bridge; on his left, hardly a quarter of a mile away, was Cleeve Abbey. For Leland the abbey buildings were simply a landmark, a passing point of reference on the way to something more unusual than an abandoned monastery. He was making for the chapel of Our Lady of Cleeve, a mile or so away nearer the sea. The chapel, like the monastery, had seen better days: the visitors no longer came, for offerings to the famous statue of the Virgin were now frowned upon, and the 'ynne', the hostel specially built to shelter the pilgrims, was no longer in business.[1] Still, Leland could describe the 'ynne' as 'goodly' and the chapel as 'well-builded'. But their glory, like the glory of Cleeve Abbey nearby, had departed. The abbey of Vallis Florida in its delectable site beside the Washford River, and the chapel of Our Lady of Cleeve, a last flowering of devotion and spiritual enterprise, were both dismissed, the one a landmark for travellers, the other a recent curiosity.

Another traveller, with a different purpose, had taken the same road only six years before. Sir Thomas Arundell, one of the king's surveyors, rode past Cleeve towards Cornwall armed with 'letters of dissolution' for the lesser houses in Somerset 'and heard such lamentations' for the dissolution of

---

[1] *Leland's Itinerary in England and Wales*, ed. L. Toulmin Smith, 1906–8, i, 164–5. For a brief history and description of the abbey, see *VCH Somerset* ii,115–18, and R. Gilyard-Beer, *Cleeve Abbey: official guide*, HMSO, 1959.

Cleeve that he wrote with some concern to Cromwell. There was, Arundell reported, a local rumour that the king had exempted the abbey from suppression under the Act of 1536 which dissolved houses whose yearly value was less than £200.[2]

Arundell had already written in his doubt to the Chancellor of the Court of Augmentations, asking whether he should proceed at Cleeve or not, for the house apparently did not appear among his papers. Was this, he now enquired of Cromwell, administrative oversight in an office which had, at the time, 'many other great matters' to attend to? Should he proceed on his return from Cornwall to dissolve the house, or might the king, indeed, spare it, for 'all the honest gentlemen in that quarter' were prepared to support a petition on behalf of the seventeen priest-monks there 'of very honest life and conversation' who had a reputation for keeping 'great hospitality to the relief of the country'.

There was another doubt in Arundell's mind concerning his own earlier dealings with Cleeve. He had been one of the surveyors who had produced the valuation on which the fate of the house now depended. He and his colleagues, rating it at £155 9s 5¼d, had thus brought it well below the £200 limit of the 1536 Act of Suppression.[3] Yet the abbot had recently admitted to the collector of a subsidy that he ought justly to pay more than the survey valuation; he was, in fact, prepared to find 1,000 marks to save his house. Had the surveyors somehow made a miscalculation; could the house still be saved?

Arundell's letter to Cromwell, written from St. Columb in Cornwall, is undated. James Gairdner assigned it to 1537, and it has consequently been assumed that Arundell's plea was at least temporarily successful, and that the house did not fall until that year.[4] But there is no other evidence to date Arundell's letter to 1537, and the surviving accounts reveal quite clearly that the house surrendered in 1536: two accounts for the period 4 February (the date of the Act of Suppression) to Michaelmas 1536 indicate by their very existence that the property had by the end of that period come into the king's hands, and one contains more precise information – that the abbot was responsible for the income of the house until 6 September 1536.[5]

But were Arundell's suspicions about the income of the monastery justified? Was Cleeve under-rated or was it, in common with many others, struggling against inflation or the effects of over spending? Had there been a profligate building programme, were the demands of neighbours becoming sinister, or, surely not, were there rather more religious than the house could support?

[2] W. A. J. Archbold, *The Somerset Religious Houses*, 1892, 84–6, from BL MS Cotton Cleop. E.iv, 257; calendared in *LP* xii (i), 2.
[3] *VE* i, 218.
[4] *LP* xii (i), 2; *VCH Somerset* ii, 117; *MRH*, 112, 117.
[5] PRO, SC6/Henry VIII/3127, 7298.

chapter house at Cleeve in October 1525 and signed by Abbot William Dovell and nine members of his community.[24] The second is the list of monks, beginning with the pensioned former abbot and prior and followed by the names of thirteen monks each given 26s 8d as a 'regard' when their house was closed.[25] The third is the statement of Sir Thomas Arundell that there were seventeen priests there.[26] A gloss on these figures is provided by the record of ordinations of Cleeve monks. Here there are serious short-comings in the sources. No ordination register survives for Bath and Wells diocese after 1526, but from 1509 onwards for a few years Cleeve monks regularly travelled to Exeter or elsewhere in Devon for orders, usually at the hands of the same bishop, the Cluniac suffragan Thomas Chard.[27] Exeter ordination registers survive until after the Dissolution, but no Cleeve monks appear in Exeter registers after 1518.[28]

From these sources it is possible to recover the names of 21 monks and to make some tentative statements about recruitment. The dates of ordination range between 1489 and 1525 and from 1500 onwards for two decades confirm an even flow of new blood, five in the first ten years, six in the next. Three more entered the house up to 1525, but thereafter the ordination lists fail. Yet in the last ten years of the life of Cleeve five more names were added to its family, five men who came at a time when its financial state was at its most precarious.

The ordination registers reveal a significant pattern, for if the monks are listed in order of seniority of ordination they fall into three quite distinct groups. First there are seven, ordained between 1489 and 1509 and still there in 1536, some of them old men, for whom the prospect of life outside the cloister might well have been difficult to face. Abbot Dovell, assigned a pension of £26 13s 4d, was well enough endowed to establish himself in decent state, and was still alive and receiving his pension in 1553.[29] Three others clung to the monastic life after 1536 and entered the sister house of Dunkeswell, not many miles away over the Devon border – only to find themselves turned out again three years later. One of them was John Webb, who had been at Cleeve since at least 1489.[30] He left Cleeve as prior of the house with a cash payment of £6 3s 11d, and received a pension of £6 when he left Dunkeswell.[31] John Gaye and John Bennett joined him at Dunkeswell, Gaye leaving in 1539 with the choice of the curacy of Sheldon and £6 13s 4d or, if he was too ill (he was ordained in 1500), a pension of £5 6s 8d.[32]

[24] Exeter, D & C MS 800.
[25] PRO, SC6/Henry VIII/7298.
[26] BL MS Cotton Cleop. E.iv, 257.
[27] D. M. Smith, *Guide to Bishops' Registers of England and Wales*, 1981, 35; *HBC*, 268.
[28] Devon RO, Reg. Oldham, fo. 130v is the last reference to a Cleeve monk.
[29] PRO, SC6/Henry VIII/7298; Archbold, 151.
[30] SRO, Reg. Stillington, fo. 233.
[31] PRO, SC6/Henry VIII/7298; *Monasticon* v, 679.
[32] SRO, Reg. King, fo. 122; *Monasticon* v, 679.

Bennett, somewhat younger, was awarded a pension of £4 13s 4d.[33] Of the remainder of that group there is no trace. They, too, may have sought refuge in a sister house like Forde or Buckland, for which no pension lists have been found; they may simply have not survived the trauma of removal.

The next group of Cleeve monks presents a more speculative problem. There are five men, ordained between 1511 and 1517, only one of whom signed the agreement of 1525.[34] If they were still in the house at that date they were certainly not in receipt of the 'regard' paid in 1536. Had they died meanwhile, perhaps in the plague which may have hit the house in the 1520s or 1530s?[35]

The third group, nine in all, were by 1536 men of forty years old or less; the oldest was ordained in 1518, and three more were in the house by 1525.[36] All were still there in 1536, and perhaps the most senior was that John Baker who received a pension of £5 when he was driven out of the Cistercian house at Newenham in Devon in 1539.[37] The fate of only one other of those younger monks is known: he was John Hooper, later to be the reforming bishop of Gloucester and Marian martyr.[38] The remainder cannot be traced; they do not seem to have found a calling at least among the parish clergy of Bath and Wells diocese.

None of this argument is to make out a case for the spiritual state of the house at Cleeve, but it is of some importance that five men should have sought a vocation when the prospect of a comfortable lifestyle was at least problematical. And did these new recruits possibly add to the pressures on the financial stability of the house? In the country at large there were forty-six Cistercian houses larger than Cleeve in terms of income. Fountains was by far the richest, worth £1,115 and having thirty-two monks at the suppression.[39] In the West Country, Forde was valued at £347 and supported fourteen monks; near neighbour Dunkeswell, with an income of £295, had eight pensioned monks (including three from Cleeve); Buckland's thirteen monks were supported by an income of £241; and Newenham's ten (one from Cleeve) enjoyed £227.[40] These figures as they stand certainly suggest that the size of the community at Cleeve was a significant factor in its financial instability.

When the abbey estate was surrendered to the Crown in September 1536 much was already in lay occupation including four of its five granges. The

[33] Ordained priest 1510: Devon RO, Reg. Oldham, fo. 103v; *Monasticon* v, 679.
[34] Exeter, D & C MS 800.
[35] PRO, E134/31 Elizabeth, Easter 23.
[36] Thomas (*recte* John) Baker, ordained 1518: Devon RO, Reg. Oldham, fo. 130v; Exeter, D & C MS 800.
[37] *Monasticon* v, 694.
[38] Strype, *Ecclesiastical Memorials*, 1721, iii, pt. ii, 80.
[39] *MRH*, 113, 119.
[40] *MRH*, 112–13, 116, 118–19.

and drinke' at the abbot's table and the same for his servant, 'daily and nightly livery' of bread and ale or beer at his 'pleasure and demand', seven loads of wood each year and food for two horses. Should Walker fall ill or 'if it shall please the said Edward for his own singular mind and pleasure', he might have his meals delivered to his rooms.[55]

Walker was not the only personal drain on the abbey's resources. John Mychell and Widow Margaret Jobson each received bread and ale, fish or meat, and fuel, and John was assigned a chamber, a pension of 53s 4d and a suit of clothes in the abbot's livery each year.[56] Margaret had a small pension and candles. Between them they cost the abbey 16s 2d in cash for the part year February to September 1536.[57]

Is there any evidence at Cleeve of a profligate building programme so commonly found in the last phase of English monastic life? The great building work at Cleeve, undertaken in the mid-fifteenth century by Abbot David Juyner, is still to be seen in the magnificent frater range, and Abbot Dovell is credited only with minor repairs and additions to the gatehouse and with work on the west cloister, unfinished at the suppression but supported just two years earlier by a legacy of £60 from the vicar of the neighbouring parish of Stogumber.[58]

One other project of Abbot Juyner may be seen as a last spiritual as well as architectural flowering at Cleeve. Under the cliffs at the southern edge of the abbey's estate stood a small chapel, known from its position as the chapel of St Mary by the Sea. In 1452 it was virtually destroyed by a landslip, only the figure of the Virgin miraculously escaping damage. Within three years a new building arose further inland, and in 1455 it was consecrated.[59] In 1466 the abbey was licensed to hold a weekly market and two fairs to raise money to repair or extend the chapel, which soon became for the people of West Somerset a place for public ceremony, probate business and solemn oath taking, but principally a place of pilgrimage.[60] An 'ynne' was built beside the chapel to give shelter to visitors, and a small settlement seems to have grown up there, including butchers' shambles.[61] Only the name of the hamlet, Chapel Cleeve, and a fragment of the 'ynne' in the mansion called Chapel Cleeve Manor, survives from this spiritual enterprise, which clearly had an economic value: offerings before the statue of the Virgin in 1536 totalled £20 and rents there were worth a further £9 3s 4d.[62] But the chapel's four bells

[55] PRO, E315/91, fo. 35.
[56] PRO, E315/91, fos. 54v–55v.
[57] PRO, SC6/Henry VIII/7298.
[58] Wells Wills, ed. F. W. Weaver, 1901, 153; Gilyard-Beer, 8.
[59] Reg. Bekynton, 178–9, 251–2.
[60] CPR 1461–7, 527; VCH Somerset v, 52 and references there given; Som. Med. Wills, 1531–58, 14.
[61] Leland, i, 165; PRO, SC6/Henry VIII/3127.
[62] PRO, SC11/567.

were soon silent, the chapel itself let.[63] Within a year or two the chapel and the 'ynne' were simply matters of antiquarian curiosity.

Three centuries and more of religious observance were brought to an abrupt end in September 1536. If there were regrets on spiritual grounds, they were not voiced in public. There is no reason to doubt the genuineness of the 'lamentations' in the countryside at the end to the abbey's hospitality, nor yet any reason to question Arundell's judgement on the 'honesty' of the monks.[64] But a community so heavily in debt to secular neighbours and an abbot showing obvious favour to members of his own family, were no longer the spiritual force they could have been. Perhaps the religious had all become too familiar, with names like Washford, Clyve and London too closely associated with the parish outside. People in later years remembered the abbey as just another tithe owner and collector of rents; remembered Abbot Dovell for coming to take part in a disputed claim to some common land; or for sheltering at Leigh grange when plague visited the villages in the valley; remembered how the monks 'came into a broomey close . . . having each of them a newe paire of gloves upon their hands and there did pull upp the young broomes ther growen until their newe gloves were well worne and their hands sore with drawing of broomes'.[65] As for their calling, people remembered their white cowls, but a witness in 1589 did not know 'what the monks of the abbey were, but he heard say they were white-monks' and recalled that his father had seen one of them buried in a white garment 'such as they were supposed to wear'.[66] By then the seven bells which used to ring across the Flowery Valley had long been forgotten, the vestments of purple velvet and white damask long since sent away for the king's use.[67] The Daily Office, continued for a while by Cleeve monks at Dunkeswell and Newenham, may well have been maintained in private wherever former brethren found a home. But in a remote part of Cleeve's former estate, at the old grange at Leigh, the Old Faith was revived by a secular priest in a gentleman's household and then maintained by a succession of Benedictines who regarded Leigh as the centre of a mission in West Somerset.[68] What still survives at Cleeve are buildings substantial enough to bring to the imagination of even the most casual visitor a real insight into the monastic life of England in the years before it was so swiftly brought to an end.

Victoria County History, Somerset

---

[63] PRO, SC6/Henry VIII/7298.
[64] Archbold, 84–6.
[65] PRO, E134/31 Elizabeth, Easter 23; SRO, DD/WY 46/2/25a; *Somerset and Dorset Notes and Queries*, xxx, 1979, 404.
[66] PRO, E134/31 Elizabeth, Easter 23.
[67] PRO, SC6/Henry VIII/7298.
[68] *VCH Somerset* v, 52.

University of London, work which has shed light on the Church of the fifteenth century in its theological reality, its polity and government, and its social and economic rooting in the land. Readers may find in it also, incidentally, material relevant to some of the ecclesiological tasks of our own day.

University of Exeter

Propositio Facta Coram Anglicis

A Theme Expounded before the English

Most reverend and renowned fathers, men famed for your learning and wisdom, brothers most dear to us in the love of Christ, the University of Paris salutes with joy your devotion, your burning zeal, your mission so arduous yet so demanding of praise! With joy, I say, this University, which loves, admires and fosters all that is good, welcomes you. Here there is no envy, nor rejoicing in iniquity, but only rejoicing in the truth.[1] Why should we not, therefore, rejoice in the truth which you embrace, as ever, and hold fast in your bosom, and which now, with tenacity and zeal, you strive with every nerve to bring to good effect?

Now the particular theme of our address in your honour is aptly expressed in the words of Hosea the prophet, Hosea 1: *'And the children of Israel and the children of Judah shall be gathered together'*.[2] So we may gladly exclaim, 'Behold, how good and joyful a thing it is, brethren, to dwell together in unity';[3] that is, to come together and gather together in one council; for in the council of the upright and in the congregation[4] are seen the mighty works of God. And such is the sacred and venerable council to which your mission is directed, to be celebrated, with God its author and guide, at Pisa – and fruitful may be your coming there, such is all our wish and our hope! Indeed, the Truth himself says that every kingdom divided within itself shall be brought to desolation,[5] but every kingdom united in itself stands. And Sallust says the same: with concord small things grow, with discord the greatest fall apart.[6] Why, then, should hope not run high, while the Church is gathered, while a solemn assembly is called and the elders come together?[7] Look well on this word, especially since we hold fast the most sure promise of Christ when he

---

[1] I Cor. 13: 4, 6.
[2] Hos. 1: 11.
[3] Ps. 132 (133): 1.
[4] Ps. 110 (111): 1.

[5] Mt. 12: 25 (Vulg. *contra se*. Mk. 3: 23, *in se dividatur*).
[6] *De Coniuratione Catalinae*, VI.
[7] Joel 2: 15f.

said 'Where two or three, etc.'[8] We have heard, furthermore, with joy and gladness that *they shall be gathered* etc.

However, lest my discourse should weary or burden you by ranging too widely or wandering too far, let us compress, if we may, all that is to be said, and all that may be drawn from my text, into four sentences taken from the text, from words immediately adjoining it; and let us see what God says in them, for he speaks peace to his people.[9] For after God has said through Hosea '*And the children of Israel and the children of Judah shall be gathered together*' — that is the first sentence — at once he adds, '*and they shall appoint themselves one head*' for the second; then, '*they shall go up from the land*' for the third; and '*great shall be the day of Israel*'[10] for the fourth.

Let us begin, therefore; and we shall pursue and find, I venture, four sufficient causes[11] whereby the children of Israel and Judah shall be gathered together; for they who are the one people of God are now by abominable division — unspeakably wicked — rent asunder, as once befell Rehoboam and Jeroboam in a type or figure, as Scripture records, III Kings xvii (*sic*);[12] and these two elements blended together amount to a material reason[13] for holding this council. We shall find, moreover, the final cause lucidly expressed in the second sentence, 'And they shall appoint themselves one head'. Then the dispositive and, so to say, efficient cause for holding the council is touched upon when it is said in the next sentence, 'and they shall go up from the land'; and what is this land, in mystical interpretation, but earthly affection? What, therefore, is 'to go up from the land' but to arouse oneself powerfully from the earthly affections, by which many have been and are still held down, to spiritual and divine affections, and, being so roused, to rise in full vigour, as any of us may hear God calling him from on high? 'Arise, thou that sleepest';[14] and again, 'Arise, out of your rest'.[15]

We have next what I may call the formal cause, the one which quickens this embryonic council into life. This, the form or shaping principle,[16] is the living and effectual seed of God, the seed of the Holy Ghost which possesses in itself the power to form and to re-form the unity of the whole, the whole body of the Church, in one faith, and hope, and charity,[17] under one God and Lord, through every joint, as the Apostle draws it out in Ephesians iv.[18] This is indicated in this word 'Israel', which by interpretation means 'God's seed', or 'God has sown'. And of what sort is this seed? Plainly, that of which the prophet says elsewhere, 'unless the Lord of hosts had left to us his seed, we should have been as Sodom, we should have been like unto Gomorrah',

---

[8] Mt. 18: 20.
[9] Ps. 84 (85): 9.
[10] Vulg. *Jezrahel*.
[11] Accessible notes on how the Scholastics, following Aristotle, used *causa* may be found in the glossaries of the Blackfriars edn of St Thomas Aquinas, *S.T.*, vols. 2 (1963) and 9 (1967).

[12] I Kg. 11: 26ff.
[13] *ratio*: as in n. 11, vols. 9, 11 (1970) and 14 (1974).
[14] Eph. 5: 14.
[15] Ps. 126 (127): 2.
[16] *forma*: as in n. 11, vol. 9.
[17] I Cor. 13: 13.
[18] Eph. 4: 16.

principal head of the Church, unchangeable and abiding, as the Apostle testifies: 'the head of the Church', he says, 'is Christ'.[35] And 'Christ abides for ever', as he says again, 'having an everlasting priesthood'[36] and papal dignity. It is therefore for our salvation, O Christ, that thou art our head; from thee flow all senses and all life-giving movements in the Church, spiritual and of pure grace – and therefore thy Church can never be acephalous, without a head, nor widowed from thee her spouse. None the less, before thine ascension to the Father, thou didst leave behind a vicar for thyself on earth as a sort of secondary head, one following another as tide follows tide, in place of thine unchanging essential priesthood and papacy, indefectible and abiding to the end of time, when thou wilt put down all rule and all authority and power, and deliver up the kingdom to God the Father.[37]

But now, alas! fathers and brethren, two contestants[38] defame this supreme head, in that they both insist on representing him at once, a thing abominable to God, or on being his vice-gerent, or on succeeding to his place. So far are we fallen into this impious abuse that they have made themselves enemies of the Church in its very head. It is in fact proper to the unity of the papal priesthood that only one priest and sure vicar of Christ on earth should be set in succession to Peter, and not that it should be said, in Pharisaic strife as the Apostle once complained, 'I am of Gregory, I of Benedict'.[39] It were more in accord with holiness, and more befitting filial love towards a mother, to relinquish the papal dignity and the see of Peter to a third, who would possess it in peace, under whom the children of Israel and Judah would be gathered together, one people of God, than that obedience should be divided by sedition most foul, and the flock scattered as though there were not one fold and one shepherd;[40] as though again it were unseemly that the children of Israel and the children of Judah should be gathered together.

For some time I pondered these things in the hidden council of my heart[41] before they were openly explored, whilst, as you know, the sensual man does not mind the things of God[42] but speaks of the things of earth – he is indeed numbered among the sons of Hagar of whom Scripture says that they sought the wisdom that is of the earth;[43] he is wedded indeed to that same earthly wisdom, sensual and devilish,[44] not to that which is from above; and therefore his understanding is darkened.[45] This sensual man, I say, impatient, brutish, headstrong, asks why it is necessary for the children of Israel and Judah to be gathered together: is the right of the parties so uncertain? is it, moreover, either lawful or expedient that a general council be called now? It

---

[35] Eph. 5: 23.
[36] Hebr. 7: 25. *et papatum* is not in the Vulgate text.
[37] I Cor. 15: 24.
[38] Gregory XII and Benedict XIII.
[39] I Cor. 1: 12.
[40] Jn. 10. 16.
[41] Ps. 43 (44): 22.
[42] I Cor. 2: 14.
[43] Baruch 3: 23. Vulg. *prudentiam*.
[44] James 3: 15.
[45] Eph. 4: 18.

is not lawful, he goes on, because a general council cannot be held without a pope, or unless there has been restored to him, first of all, that obedience of which he has been deprived. How can it be right, furthermore, that things which have been established in custom and use over the longest periods of time should be brought into question again as though they were in doubt? or that the true and just party should expose himself to the risk of condemnation – for the result of judicial proceedings is uncertain, they are led into error and they err. Finally, of what use is it to strive against God's will and providence, who in his righteous judgement permits heresies to arise[46] and says that it is necessary that offences should come;[47] who also said, 'Think not that I came to send peace on earth, but a sword';[48] who, finally, once forbade the children of Israel and Judah to be gathered together, in that he declared that he had himself brought about their division.[49] Many and mighty were the sounds which the sensual man was preparing to bark dog-like against the holding of the council, declaring it to be neither lawful, nor proper, nor expedient, so much so that I tremble, I confess. Nevertheless, I say to him: Be silent, troublesome and foolish man, or wait until all the considerations which I have begun are finished. You will hear unmistakably things which can reduce your objections to silence. I have stayed on this and spun it out, rather against my will, in order to fill out my third and fourth considerations more freely.

The third consideration: the gathering together of the children of Israel and Judah must be brought about as if by a dispositive cause, one which sets aside the obstacle, at the point where 'they go up from the earth'; that is, following the moral interpretation, where they rise from earthly affections to heavenly and become spiritual rather than sensual; and where renouncing the letter which kills they embrace the spirit which gives life;[50] with care being taken, however, against anything excessive, lest excessive claims for the spirit should cause the flesh to be overwhelmed with the spirit.[51] So I ask, fathers and brethren, can there be any reason why the gathering of this general council has been so long delayed other than that for so long the spiritual men, who, if the Apostle is to be believed, shall judge everything,[52] have not been listened to? And lo! how the renowned University of Oxford determined long ago to work for a Council – for which it cannot be too highly praised – and communicated that decision to France I know, for I was there when this conclusion of the Compendium was expounded from the text of Joel, 'Call a solemn assembly, gather the elders'.[53]

But long before that, when the schism was first beginning to shew itself, the University of Paris determined formally in a unanimous judgement that

---

[46] I Cor. 11: 19.
[47] Matt. 18: 7.
[48] Matt. 10: 34.
[49] I Kg. 10: 31 etc.
[50] 2 Cor. 3: 6.

[51] Gerson's characteristic caution against a too liberal use of *epikeia*.
[52] I Cor. 14: 24.
[53] Joel 1: 14.

lowest administrative grade, whatever that may be; for this is supernaturally ordained, arising only out of the good pleasure of its bountiful founder. And I do not think that master Henry of Hassia would ever have wished to maintain the contrary when he posited that the Church could set up for itself a supreme pontiff had he not been directly set up by Christ; for he adds that the Church could have done this as taught and authorised by the Holy Ghost; and this is a probable opinion.

Fifthly: the Church the mystical body constituted in one head, Christ, will always have at every juncture[61] those degrees of dignities and ministrations of which we have spoken. This is plain from the text 'Until we all come etc.' [into the unity of the faith].[62] For this reason the Church is said to be espoused to Christ eternally, Hosea i.[63] It is said further that it has in itself the seed for its own propagation and preservation to the end of time.

Sixthly: the Church constituted in one head, Christ, while the law is as it is, will not be left to continue embodied in one solitary woman, nor indeed in lay persons alone;[64] on the contrary, there will be bishops and other faithful priests until the end of time.

Seventhly: the Church may be said to have a two-fold element, bringing it into one; one is of things transitory, the other of things permanent and, we may say, essential. Of the first sort are mortal persons in their several degrees; of the second sort are those degrees themselves, whether of dignities or of ministrations. So we have popes and the papacy, bishops and the office of bishop, and so on. Popes come and go; the papacy abides.

The eighth point: the Church is constituted, in its transitory and, in a sense, material elements, in the ministry of men according to the law given at the first and implanted in the body of the Church itself; and as it has in itself that same living seed, efficacious for the propagation and preservation of itself in a succession specific to that seed, as much in its transitory parts, and in their material succession, as in the essential parts. The truth of this is clear from the word of the Apostle: 'no man taketh this honour to himself' etc.;[65] and also from his saying about the preachers, 'how shall they preach if they be not sent' etc.[66] And this truth could be turned with similar effect to the deposition, degradation and cutting away of parties causing scandal; but that is left aside for the moment.

The ninth point: the Church has the keys of order and jurisdiction in one form in itself and in another form in its transitory parts; so that, for example, the keys were given to Peter as his authority and for him to exercise, but to the Church universally and for its support; or given to the Church in the first place and to Peter[67] in the second.

---

[61] Eph. 4: 16.
[62] Eph. 4: 13.
[63] *sic. recte*, Hos. 2: 19.
[64] An opinion quoted by William of Occam, *Dialogus* I. V. 34.

[65] Hebr. 5: 4.
[66] Rom. 10: 15.
[67] Matt. 16: 19.

The tenth point: the Church is constituted like an army arrayed with banners,[68] or like a body utterly entire and perfect, so that it stands not within the power of the pope or of any other person whatever to disorder or mutilate it essentially in any of its parts. Hence not even the pope might bring it about that there were no more bishops, nor priests with cure of souls, nor cardinals, inasmuch as these are the successors of the Apostles in the holy Church of God. For all these degrees were sown by Christ like seed in the primitive Church, tiny as it was, in which the grades of the ecclesiastical hierarchy were not yet unfolded as we discern them now – as an ear of corn has all its future yield in one grain, and as the nut tree is virtually contained in the nut. Philosophers call this the inception of form in matter.

In the eleventh place: the Church, though it can neither institute the papacy nor dispense with it, can nevertheless, by itself or by a general council representing it, decree a method of choosing the pope other than that which obtains now, as appears elsewhere. It can also renounce a pope even though duly elected, and appoint another, if this seemed to be expedient for the edifying of the Church, as in a case of grave scandal, or in a case of doubt unresolvable otherwise than by the resignation or deposition of the pope; or in some other such case. For any shepherd is appointed for the good of the flock; but when his guardianship turns to its serious hurt, he is accounted a hireling, or rather a thief, or even worse a ravening wolf if he persists in lording it so destructively. And on this is founded the possibility of undertaking the way of cession, at least so far as concerns its effect – though this the rivals deny and are unwilling to undertake. Here is established also, in a matter of truth like this, how a church urging the pope to resign or deposing him if, swayed by an all-consuming lust for power, he refuses to do so, is not to be adjudged as persecuting him but rather as fulfilling its duty in every possible way – to him, to God and to the Church as a whole.

The twelfth point: the Church may lawfully and with good reason call itself together in a particular event without the pope and without his authority. Accordingly, since an assembly may be convened in two ways, the one by agreement or assent or in charity, the other by authority, it is beyond dispute that the first manner of assembling can be without the pope, for it so happened often enough, both in the time of the apostles and in the time of the holy Emperors, and among Catholics who often came together in one before they were convened or authorised by the pope. This is clear in the first four councils mentioned in the Acts of the Apostles:[69] from the very first, when Peter had not yet become pope, when they were all gathered together to make proof of the testimonies fulfilled in the resurrection. It follows that every free assembly, not subject to tyranny, has this power of bringing itself into being. It is clearly seen in confraternities and in many charitable associations.

---

[68] Cant. 6: 3.

[69] Acts 2: 14; 6: 2; 15: 4; 21: 17.

The Monks as Landlords: The Leasing of the Monastic Demesnes in Southern England*

J. N. Hare

Twenty years ago, Professor Du Boulay commented on the neglect of the history of the substantial landowners after the early fifteenth century and on the tone of gloom that was generally adopted when considering the leasing of the manorial demesnes: a tone 'more suited to a tale of decline than of new beginnings'.[1] Since he wrote this, a series of important studies have taught us much about the policies of late medieval landowners. Yet the fifteenth century still seems to be a period of relative neglect, and nowhere has this been more obvious than on the monastic estates that have played such an essential role in our understanding of developments in earlier centuries. It is as a contribution to this neglected topic as well as an examination of one point of contact between church and laity that this study is gratefully offered.

The approach adopted has been to trace the leasing of the demesnes and the subsequent development of estate policy by a group of southern monasteries from c. 1400 to c. 1530. The latter date has been chosen in order to exclude any changes that may have resulted from fears of impending dissolution. This study has evolved from an earlier examination of agrarian conditions on lay and ecclesiastical estates in Wiltshire during a similar period,[2] and its origin is reflected in the choice of the monastic estates now

* This article was one of the projects begun during my tenure of a schoolteacher fellowship at Liverpool University in the spring term of 1984. I am very grateful to the University and to Hampshire County Council for providing me with this opportunity, and to the School of History for its hospitality. The manorial accounts, which almost always ran from Michaelmas to Michaelmas, have been referred to by the year in which the account closed.

[1] F. R. H. Du Boulay, 'A Rentier Economy in the later Middle Ages: the Archbishopric of Canterbury', *EcHR*, 2nd ser. xvi, 1964, 427.
[2] J. N. Hare, 'Lord and Tenant in Wiltshire, c.1380–c.1520, with particular reference to regional and seigneurial variations' (London Ph.D., 1976).

examined. All possessed properties included in the earlier study. Any selection of a small group of monasteries cannot hope to be fully representative. This one is, dominated by wealthy and long-established houses, the pre-conquest foundations of St Swithun's Cathedral Priory and St Mary's nunnery, both at Winchester, and by William the Conqueror's great foundation at Battle. But younger monasteries are also represented by the Cistercian abbey of Netley and by the limited surviving documentation from the lesser Wiltshire houses. Geographically, the study concentrates on the counties of Wiltshire, Hampshire and Sussex. Most of the manors were to be found on the chalk downlands of Wessex, but others were situated in very different environments: the claylands of north-west Wiltshire, the clays and gravels of the Hampshire basin, and the Weald of south-east England. Our manors thus represent something of the rich geographical, historical and agrarian diversity of the monastic lands of southern England.

This diversity was reflected in monastic estate policies, and was already apparent by 1400. This may be seen by examining developments on two great estates: those of St Swithun's Priory, Winchester, most of whose lands consisted of large chalkland manors in Hampshire and Wiltshire, and of Battle Abbey, whose lands centred on Kent and Sussex. On the former estate, direct cultivation was still very much the norm as it had been throughout the later fourteenth century.[3] Some leasing had occurred, but this was on smaller and sometimes peripheral estates, thus the small isolated manor of Westwood had been leased by 1364, Wroughton between 1373 and 1387, Hannington from 1380–86, in 1389 and from 1394, while Stockton and Silkstead were leased from 1396.[4] But these were exceptions and the priory estate remained characterised by a continuation of large-scale demesne agriculture. In this, it typified the monastic lands that lay nearby, as on the estates of Romsey Abbey or St Mary's Abbey, Winchester.[5] Here in the chalklands of Wessex, monastic demesne agriculture continued largely unchanged into the following century, although the practice of leasing the demesne arable had already begun to spread on some of the larger lay estates.[6]

Such continuity of estate policy was not, however, reflected in developments

---

[3] J. S. Drew, 'Manorial Accounts of St Swithun's Priory, Winchester', in *Essays in Economic History*, ii, ed. E. M. Carus-Wilson, 1962, 25–6; Winchester Cathedral Library (hereafter WCL) Stockbook (of livestock on priory manors, 1390–92); J. Greatrex, 'The Administration of Winchester Cathedral Priory in the time of Cardinal Beaufort' (Ottawa Ph.D., 1972), appendices B–D.

[4] WCL Box 39/1; Box 52, court rolls; Greatrex, 'Administration', appx A, ii; BL MS Add. Roll 24352 and 53.

[5] PRO SC6/1052/2, H. G. D. Liveing, *Records of Romsey Abbey*, Winchester 1912, 194–5; WRO, 192/20 (court rolls) and 192/28.

[6] Hare, 'Lord and Tenant', 102–10. For general accounts of Wiltshire agriculture in this period see R. Scott, 'Medieval Agriculture' in *VCH Wilts.* iv, and J. N. Hare, 'Change and Continuity in Wiltshire agriculture in the later Middle Ages' in *Agricultural Improvement: Medieval and Modern* (Exeter Papers in Economic History), ed. W. Minchinton, 1981, 1–18.

between 1471 and 1483. By 1484, the priory had ceased to run its own flocks except at the home manor of Barton.[23] Nor was such continued activity in pastoral farming at all atypical of the monastic estates of the area. St Mary's Abbey at Winchester maintained large flocks of over 1,000 sheep at Urchfont until between 1471 and 1477, and of over 600 sheep at All Cannings until between 1478 and 1481, long after it had leased the demesne arable.[24] Meanwhile, Netley Abbey kept flocks on its chalkland manors of Kingston Deverill and Waddon (Dorset) until the 1490s even though the former's arable had been leased a century before.[25] Wilton Abbey, most of whose estates lay in the chalklands, maintained a flock at nearby Brudcombe until at least 1486, although the arable had already been leased, and it was still engaged in large-scale wool supply in the early sixteenth century. Thus in 1521 it was alleged in court that the abbess had failed to fulfil an agreement to provide £180 worth of wool from the abbey wool house. She argued that the wool had been provided, and although not all of it need have come from her estates, the case still suggests the continuation of large scale monastic flocks.[26] Lacock Abbey still had a large flock at Chitterne in 1476, although it seems to have ceased cultivating the arable there.[27] This continued maintenance of a large sheep flock, long after the arable had been leased, was typical of the chalklands. It was paralleled on the Duchy of Lancaster estates where large-scale sheep flocks were kept at Collingbourne, Everleigh and Aldbourne for at least half a century after the leasing of the arable. These sheep flocks were eventually sold in 1453.[28] Such continued extensive sheep farming represented an awareness not merely of the value of the wool and of the meat, but also of the manure of a large flock enclosed within a fenced area.[29] Yet it was a development that was not found outside the chalklands in our area. At Bromham, Battle's sheep flocks ceased with the lease of 1425–31, although arable cultivation was resumed from 1431 to 1443.[30] Nor was it to be found on any of the other leased manors of Battle Abbey or on those manors of Netley Abbey that lay outside the chalklands.[31]

Apart from these chalkland sheep-farming activities, our monasteries had leased most of their lands by 1450 or shortly afterwards. But most of them continued to cultivate some land, albeit a diminishing amount. At St Swithun's Priory, the monks continued to cultivate at Barton, the great manor that encircled much of the city of Winchester. Here the arable demesne was temporarily leased in 1465, but cultivation was restored by

[23] J. S. Drew, *Compton near Winchester*, Winchester 1939, 60; WCL, Boxes 29–30 and 46.
[24] E.g. WRO, 283/18 and 24/2; WRO, 192/28.
[25] WRO, 192/32.
[26] WRO, 492/8; *VCH Wilts.* iii, 237.
[27] PRO, Wards 2/94c/9.
[28] Hare, 'Lord and Tenant', 67–72, 114–5.
[29] Hare, 'Change and Continuity', 7–8.
[30] Hare, 'Lord and Tenant', appx.
[31] Based on examination of PRO account rolls (SC6).

1479 and continued until the manor was leased in 1538.[32] Battle Abbey continued to cultivate a small group of large food-producing manors: Alciston, Lullington, Barnhorne and Wye.[33] Netley Abbey cultivated at least three manors in *c.* 1460: Roydon had been leased from at least 1436 until 1459 and was then cultivated in 1461, 1462 and 1463, while Townhill and Waddon were cultivated in 1459 and 1461 respectively. For neither of the two latter places do we possess any earlier account rolls, so that it is not clear whether the abbot was continuing to cultivate these demesnes or whether seigneurial cultivation had been resumed.[34] At Lacock Abbey, a *valor* of 1476 covering the whole estate describes only three manors as being leased, but the list of livestock with it suggests that on only one manor did the abbey continue with both arable and pastoral farming, while on another a large sheep flock was all that was maintained. At Lacock itself the abbey kept a mixed home farm until the Dissolution, while at Chitterne sheep are the only livestock mentioned and the reference to sales of grain may refer to a cash valuation of a rent in kind.[35] Other monasteries also maintained home farms. Thus Monkton Farleigh still kept such a farm in 1526, although it had also continued to cultivate the demesne at Chippenham until at least 1461.[36]

Such home farms might continue in operation until the Dissolution of the monasteries, but several of these were leased in the 1490s and it is perhaps to this decade that we should look for the final transformation of the monks to their role as rentiers. Such seems to have been the case at Battle. Here, the demesne at Lullington had been leased from 1466, but that at Barnhorne was leased after 1494 and that at Alciston in 1496.[37] This late leasing parallels developments further west, where in the 1490s Glastonbury Abbey leased its remaining demesnes and where Tavistock Abbey was in the course of so doing.[38] In other ways too, the last decade of the fifteenth century marked a distinct stage in the leasing of the demesnes. On the estate of St Swithun's Priory, leases were now frequently enrolled in the Chapter Register. This increased concern with the registration of the leases may be seen elsewhere at this time on the estates of Westminster Abbey and of the archbishops of Canterbury.[39] These enrolled leases of St Swithun's also seem to be for substantially longer terms than previously, now frequently being for forty

[32] WCL, Box 9/36, 38, 41; F. R. Goodman, *Valley and Downland*, Winchester 1934, 47.
[33] Brandon, 'Cereal Yields', 412; for Wye see above, n. 12.
[34] PRO, SC6/980/2, 18, 24–7; SC6/983/10, 833/20.
[35] PRO, Wards 2/94c/9.
[36] WRO, 192/29.
[37] Brandon, 'Cereal Yields', 412; J. A Brent, 'Alciston', 97, 101.
[38] I. J. E. Keil, 'The Estates of Glastonbury Abbey in the later Middle Ages' (Bristol Ph.D., 1974), 108; H. P. R. Finberg, *Tavistock Abbey*, Cambridge 1951, 256–7.
[39] B. Harvey, *Westminster Abbey and its Estates in the Middle Ages*, Oxford 1977, 153; F. R. H. Du Boulay, 'Calendar of the Demesne Leases made by Archbishop Warham' in his *Documents Illustrative of Medieval Kentish Society* (Kent Records xviii), Ashford 1964, 266; *The Register of the Common Seal of the Priory of St. Swithun, Winchester*, ed. J. Greatrex, Winchester 1978, *passim*; WCL, Register of the Common Seal, vol. II.

estate, seigneurial agriculture continued on the fertile manors in western Sussex, long after its nearer Wealden properties, such as the home manor of Marley, had been leased.[50] Here as we shall see, estate policy reflected the great regional variety of agricultural development.

Nor did the leasing of the demesnes mean that the monastic landlords retreated into an entirely passive role. They could, and did, show a readiness to spend and to innovate. In the chalklands, the leasing of the demesne arable had been accompanied by the continuation of large-scale sheep rearing and grazing by flocks whose dung helped to maintain the fertility of the soil, and thus also the yields of the lessees and the rents of the landlord. Although the folding of large sheep flocks may not yet have been as systematic as it was later to become,[51] landlords, both lay and ecclesiastical, were already aware of the value of the flocks in manuring the arable.[52] Thus in 1436 and in 1448, Netley Abbey received about half as much from renting out its flock at Kingston Deverill for manure, as it received from the total wool sales.[53] Although the size of the seigneurial sheep flocks tended to be smaller than in the later fourteenth century, heavy investment was still needed. The picture was not one of consistent decline, and lords might spend to halt and reverse this, as at Stockton where St Swithun's Priory was building up its flock in the later 1440s and 1450s. Moreover, on some manors the lord gave up his breeding flock and depended on purchase for the renewal of large flocks. This was the practice on the manors of Urchfont and All Cannings, belonging to St Mary's Nunnery at Winchester, and it has also been found on the lay manor of Aldbourne.[54]

Further east, Battle Abbey provided a noteworthy example of 'high farming' on those manors where it still maintained direct cultivation. Here, on these Sussex manors, it showed high seeding rates, high productivity, convertible husbandry, continuous cropping of a third to a half of the arable using a legume crop, and heavy manuring.[55] It showed flexibility in cropping and stocking. Thus at Barnhorne, the run-down of the sheep flock was accompanied by a strengthening of the cattle stock with a notable expansion in the early 1420s, while at Alciston the sheep flock was rebuilt in the early 1440s.[56] The productivity of their Sussex manors has led to the suggestion

[50] Searle, *Battle*, 324–37.
[51] T. Davis, *General View of the Agriculture of the County of Wiltshire*, 1794, 20–21; E. Kerridge, 'Agriculture 1500–1793' in *VCH Wilts*. iv, 54–5.
[52] Hare, 'Continuity and Change', 7–9.
[53] WRO, 192/32.
[54] WRO, 192/28, John Ryland's Library, Manchester, Rylands Charter 170. A ewe flock had survived at Urchfont until at least 1414 (Hampshire Record Office, Winchester City Records, Shelf 13, Box 6).
[55] Brandon, 'Cereal Yields'; *idem*, 'Demesne Arable Farming in Coastal Sussex during the Later Middle Ages', *AgHR* xix, 1971, 126–34.
[56] P. F. Brandon, 'Agriculture and the Effects of Floods and Weather at Barnhorne, Sussex, during the late Middle Ages', *SAC*, cix, 1971, 84; Brent, 'Alciston', 97; PRO, SC6/742/31 and 35.

that we should see the monks of Battle as, 'amongst the foremost farmers of their day, obtaining heavier harvests on model farms than lesser lordships . . .' and its rural economy as 'unsurpassed in productivity in Sussex'.[57]

Even when the demesne lands had been leased, the monks could show a readiness to resume cultivation, so that the process of leasing was less the inevitable development that, in retrospect, it now appears. We have already seen several examples of such resumption in the early stages of leasing and how Netley Abbey may have returned to direct cultivation in the 1460s. A later example is provided by the Cistercian abbey of Stanley whose lands were concentrated around the claylands of north-west Wiltshire. Its account roll for 1528 shows that all its demesnes had been leased, but that now part of the rent from the lease of Stanley itself and of four other properties was not received because the abbot had occupied them for his greater profit.[58] A monastic superior might even undertake the role of lessee, as did the prior of Ivychurch, who leased nearby land from the bishop of Winchester.[59] Nor did the final leasing of the demesnes remove for ever the demands on monastic finances. Although the demesne lessee was expected to finance the maintenance of the manorial buildings, the lord was expected to pay for any substantial building programme,[60] such as the reroofing of the great barn at All Cannings in 1471.[61]

The contrasting leasing policies pursued within the confines of a single estate mean that we cannot simply explain the diversity of leasing in terms of more conservative or more advanced monastic landlords. Rather, the monastic estates seem to reflect the regional patterns that applied to both lay and ecclesiastical estates. This was certainly the case in Wiltshire although developments did not occur at the same speed on the two types of estate. But in both cases, leasing seems to have occurred earlier in the north and west of the county and only later on the chalklands, while seigneurial sheep farming frequently continued long after the arable land had been leased. Thus the continuation of the great monastic sheep flocks, paralleled the situation on the estates of the Duchy of Lancaster, the Lords Hungerford and the bishops of Winchester and of Salisbury.[62] Here too, there seems to be no noticeable difference between monastic and non-monastic estates in rent movements or in the lord's ability to collect the anticipated revenue. Together they show some of the same regional and chronological variations.[63] The same was also true of the demesne lessees of both types of manors: in the chalklands the

---

[57] Brandon, 'Cereal Yields', 420.
[58] PRO, SC6/Hen. VIII/3958.
[59] *Register of the Common Seal*, 193.
[60] Hare, 'Lord and Tenant', 121–3 and 126–7.
[61] WRO, 192/28 (1471).
[62] Hare, 'Lord and Tenant', 54–74.
[63] Hare, 'Lord and Tenant', chapter III. See also my 'The Wiltshire Risings of 1450: political and economic discontent in mid-fifteenth century England', in *Southern History*, iv, 1982, 18–19.

demesne was leased wholesale and to one man, while elsewhere it was often leased piecemeal or to a group of tenants.[64]

The scattered estate of Battle Abbey shows the regional influences in a different way. Its Wealden lands often lay close to the abbey, but with soils that were poorly suited to arable farming. Here even the 'home farm' of Marley was leased at an early date. In general, the eastern lands of the abbey followed an early, hesitant and sometimes reversible path to leasing, similar to that pursued by the cathedral priory at Canterbury. By complete contrast, its Wiltshire manor of Bromham might be expected to have been leased early, as it was peripheral to the main estate and had always served as a supplier to the abbey of cash and not of food. Instead it reflected the practices of its ecclesiastical neighbours and was not finally leased until 1443.

A monastic manor might thus have more in common with its lay neighbours, than with other manors on its own estate. This should not be surprising for the former would share common geographical environments and influences. The monks were, moreover, closely, and perhaps increasingly, integrated into the lay world. Estate administration was merely part of the relationship. Monastic, episcopal and lay estates all shared the same officials, while the latter could themselves be lay landlords. John Whittocksmede served as steward on the Wiltshire manors of Battle and Hyde Abbeys, was active in the administration of other lay and ecclesiastical estates, and was a leading participant in local government.[65] Bartholomew Bolney was the steward of Battle Abbey from the 1420s to 1477, and also served Archbishop Stafford, as well as being a prominent figure in local government and the possessor of a carefully accumulated estate.[66] At Battle, Professor Searle has drawn attention to the close integration of the lay and monastic world. The abbey had once created the town, but by the middle of the fifteenth century, the abbot's council had come to be dominated by the urban oligarchy, who in turn provided several of the monks and abbots.[67] The close relationship between monk and layman was perhaps reflected, in physical form, in the attention given here and elsewhere to the rebuilding of the abbot's hall, the main meeting place between their two worlds. Both at Battle and at St Swithun's Priory, our period was to see the erection of such a new and much grander hall;[68] similar rebuilding was also undertaken just outside our area, at Forde, Muchelney and Milton Abbeys.[69]

---

[64] J. N. Hare, 'The Demesne Lessees of Fifteenth-Century Wiltshire', *AgHR* xxix, 1981, 1–15.

[65] J. Wedgwood, *A History of Parliament*, vol. I. *Biographies of members of the commons house 1439–1509*, 945; *VCH Wilts.*, v, 33; Hare, 'Lord and Tenant', 319.

[66] Searle, *Battle*, 422; *The Book of Bartholomew Bolney*, ed. M. Clough (Sussex Record Society lxiii), 1964.

[67] Searle, *Battle*, 432–5.

[68] H. Brakspear, 'The Abbot's House at Battle', *Archaeologia* lxxxiii, 1933, 158–60; VCH *Hampshire*, v, 59.

[69] N. Pevsner, *The Buildings of England: South and West Somerset*, 1958, 249; Royal Commission on Historic Monuments, *West Dorset*, 1952, 244, and *Central Dorset*, ii, 1970, 193–5.

As the monks leased the demesnes, so their dependence on the laity increased. The monks now rarely visited their manors and increasingly relied on the lay stewards. This tendency may be observed at St Swithun's Priory. Here the monks themselves had previously been active in visiting their estates, but by the end of the fourteenth century they had come to depend for supervision on a small group of secular officials. John Mounter in the 1380s and 1390s, Robert Hayhod, from 1390 to 1422, and John Grenefeld, from 1411 to the 1440s, made frequent appearances on the account rolls as they visited and supervised various manors.[70] The first two men were described as the lord's clerks and Grenefeld was given a corrody in 1427 for his past and future services to the priory.[71] It is unusual during this period for there to be any indication of a monk visiting the Wiltshire manors, but this occasionally happened, and seems to have become temporarily more frequent in the 1430s, 1440s and 1450s. Thereafter, the leasing of the demesne flocks removed the need for frequent visits of supervision, and henceforth the monks came to rely on the lay stewards and auditors who held the manorial courts and audited the accounts. Other smaller monasteries may possibly have been more dependent on their own monks or abbot, as is suggested by the scanty documentation from Netley Abbey. But here too, the religious relied heavily on non-monastic officials like John Langport, who was receiver of the estate in 1442, and was found supervising at Kingston Deverill and Raydon from 1459 to 1462.[72]

The evidence of our monastic estates reminds us of the considerable regional variations within the medieval economy. By 1420, the leasing of the demesnes had become the norm in so many parts of England, as on the estates of Canterbury, Coventry or Durham Cathedral Priories and of Westminster Abbey.[73] Yet it had only just begun to make inroads into the monastic estates of the chalklands of Wessex. But the developments in our area were also reflected elsewhere. The continued active investment in sheep farming, long after the demesne arable had been leased, was paralleled on the Cotswold manors of Winchcombe and Westminster Abbeys or on the estates of Coventry Cathedral Priory.[74] Such continued involvement was also apparent in the expensive land reclamation carried out by Canterbury Cathedral Priory even after it had already leased its demesnes.[75] By 1500, the

[70] Based on the Wiltshire account rolls and on Greatrex, 'Administration', 239–40, 283.
[71] Register of the Common Seal, 46.
[72] WRO, 192/32; PRO, SC6/980/24–7.
[73] R. A. L. Smith, Canterbury Cathedral Priory, Cambridge 1943, 192; R. A. Lomas, 'The Priory of Durham and its Demesnes in the Fourteenth and Fifteenth Centuries', EcHR, 2nd ser. xxxi, 1978, 345; Harvey, Westminster Abbey, 150–1; C. Dyer, Warwickshire Farming, 1349–c.1520, Preparations for Agricultural Revolution (Dugdale Society Occasional Papers), Oxford 1981, 4.
[74] R. H. Hilton, 'Winchcombe Abbey and the Manor of Sherborne', in Gloucestershire Studies, ed. H. P. R. Finberg, Leicester 1957, 111; Harvey, Westminster Abbey, 150–1; Dyer, Warwickshire Farming, 16.
[75] Smith, Canterbury Cathedral Priory, 203–4.

monasteries of southern England had returned to the role of rentier, but this was a process that was only just complete. Even then, as the case of Stanley Abbey suggests, the story was not yet finished, and this apparently unusual example of the renewal of direct farming can be paralleled on individual estates elsewhere.[76] But in general, the southern monasteries conform to the pattern that is familiar in other parts of England: the monks were to remain as rentiers, attentive to the value of their rents but not involved in direct cultivation.

The evidence from our southern monasteries suggests that the century before the reformation was neither a 'landlord's purgatory', nor one of rapid retreat into inertia. The monks, like their lay neighbours, had responded with flexibility to the influences of geography and of a changing world. The management of many of the monastic estates reveals initiative and invest-ment. The farming of the later Middle Ages has elsewhere been described as one of 'preparations for agricultural revolution'.[77] Here too, the changes were to provide an essential basis for future developments. In Wiltshire, there was a growing contrast between the chalklands and the 'cheese country' such as was to characterise the farming of succeeding generations. The characteristic and vital large-scale character of subsequent chalkland farming and flocks would depend on the survival of the demesne and its lease wholesale to a single tenant, such as had now occurred.[78] In addition, in the east of our area, many of the methods associated with later agricultural developments were already to be seen on the monastic estates. With few exceptions, the monks do not seem to have been particular pioneers in these changes, their work being paralleled by that of their lay neighbours. They were part of wider changes that were to outlive the monasteries themselves. The century before the Reformation had seen the monks acquiring a new role, but it was a change that may more appropriately be seen in terms of evolution rather than of doom, and of new beginnings rather than of decline.

Peter Symonds' College, Winchester

---

[76] J. Youings, 'The Church', in *The Agrarian History of England and Wales, iv, 1500–1640*, ed. J. Thirsk, Cambridge 1967, 312–15.
[77] Dyer, *Warwickshire Farming*.
[78] Hare, 'Change and Continuity', 1–19.

The Labourer is Worthy of His Hire? – Complaints About Diet in Late Medieval English Monasteries*

CHRISTOPHER HARPER-BILL

In 1492 the bishop of Norwich, in the course of a visitation of his own cathedral priory, ordered that 'since the labourer is worthy of his hire, there should be served to the brethren in refectory, in hall and elsewhere the same number of dishes and the same quality of food and drink as in former times was the custom'.[1] Complaints about conventual diet were among the most common grievances voiced at visitations in the century before the Reformation, and frequently visitors, who in this matter had greater opportunity than in some others to test for themselves the truth of allegations, issued injunctions relating to the satisfactory provision of victuals and beverages. The extant visitation records, although only a fraction of those compiled, include successive enquiries in the large dioceses of Lincoln, Norwich and Coventry and Lichfield, and are sufficiently extensive to serve as a barometer of conditions in the non-exempt houses of late medieval England.[2]

It should not be difficult for anyone who has spent any part of his life in an institutional environment – boarding school, residential college or the armed services – to appreciate the central importance which food and drink assume in the communal consciousness. Apart from overt cruelty or depravity, few things so alienate a community from its leader or officials as the provision of meagre or unwholesome diet. St Benedict himself had recognised this, for it was in relation to food and drink that he delivered his most urgent strictures against murmuring, which he so abhorred.[3] Later medieval visitors were well

* I am grateful to Professor Rosalind Hill for suggesting this topic to me, and for her comments.

[1] *Norwich Vis.*, 5–6.
[2] *Linc. Vis. 1420–49*; *Linc. Vis. 1517–31*; *Blythe's Vis.*; *Norwich Vis.*
[3] *RSB*, cap. 34, 40.

95

aware of the danger of dissension if the religious did not feel that they were receiving their due. In 1478, for example, Bishop Redman ordered the abbot of Dale to provide suitable bread and drink, lest for the failure of decent victuals murmuring should arise.[4]

The dietary expectations of English religious in the fifteenth century were, however, very different from those of the earliest followers of St Benedict. It is incontestable that there had been in the later middle ages a general relaxation of the primitive regulations.[5] Constant attempts were made to mitigate the long period of fast from September to Ash Wednesday, when only one meal a day was allowed, except on Sundays; this was, in fact, a stipulation ill-suited to cold northern winters. Despite the prohibition in the Rule of the flesh of four-footed animals, meat was increasingly eaten outside the refectory, and this was sanctioned by Pope Benedict XII in 1336.[6] The toleration of the *peculium*, the small personal allowance of money, and the provision of an increasing number of private apartments within the monastery, also gave opportunity for unsanctioned indulgence in private eating and drinking. By the fifteenth century, moreover, standards of living had improved outside the cloister, and it is not surprising, although a matter of lament for contemporary critics and later historians, that the religious should share the higher expectations of their secular kinsfolk.[7]

The relaxation of the Rule was accepted, with regret, as inevitable even by as ardent a reformer as King Henry V. Although the 'King's Articles' of May 1421 inveighed against the 'infirmity' of contemporary monks, it was acknowledged that long and established custom had reduced the dietary regulations of the Rule of St Benedict to a mere form of words. It was demanded merely, in accordance with the bull *Summi Magistri* of 1336, that on all meat days throughout the year half the convent should take *prandium* in the refectory, being content with milk foods, fish and meat products, such as tripe and sausages, and eating no meat elsewhere during the rest of the day. It was stipulated that for this purpose officials actually present in the house on that day should be included in the total number. Similarly, the winter fast of one meal a day should be maintained by all except the weak and infirm,

---

[4] *CAP* ii, no. 358.
[5] Knowles, *RO* i, 280–85; ii, 240–47. See also E. Bishop, 'The Method and Degree of Fasting and Abstinence of the Black Monks in England before the Reformation', *Downside Review* xlvi (1925), 184–237. The regime sanctioned by Pope Benedict XII for the Augustinian canons was, in accordance with the customs of the Order, slightly less austere than that of the Benedictines; see *Chapters of the Augustinian Canons*, ed. H. E. Salter (CYS xxix), 1922, 258–60.
[6] In some houses the refectory fell into disuse. At Humberstone in 1440 it was stated that the monks had not eaten in the *frater* for twenty years, except on Good Friday, and at Redlingfield in 1514 the nuns had not eaten there for five years, and it was used for other purposes (*Linc. Vis. 1420–49* ii, 141; *Norwich Vis.*, 139).
[7] F. R. H. Du Boulay, *An Age of Ambition*, 1970, 35–6; C. Dyer, 'English Diet in the Later Middle Ages', in *Social Relations and Ideas: Essays in Honour of R. H. Hilton*, ed. T. H. Aston *et. al.*, Cambridge 1983, 191–216, especially 216, where he refers to the 'dietary optimum' in the fifteenth century.

the aged and those below twenty years, but the customary list of exceptions – principal and double feasts, feasts of twelve lessons, and the season from Christmas to the octave of Epiphany – was condoned.[8]

The legitimisation of relaxation by the highest authority is well illustrated by two indults granted to major English houses in the fifteenth century. In 1417 Pope Martin V validated an indult granted by John XXIII to the abbot and convent of Westminster that, notwithstanding the prohibition by the statutes of the Order of the eating of meat from Septuagesima to Quinquagesima Sunday, they might according to the custom of their house eat dishes flavoured and cooked with gravy, except on canonical fast days.[9] In 1454 the prior and convent of Durham informed the pope that from Septuagesima to Quinquagesima Sunday the monks ate pancakes and sausages made for the most part from flesh, and since they had little space for taking exercise, because of this unwholesome food they were often afflicted by various illnesses, so that they could not attend divine service. Also, they received many noble guests, particularly on Christmas Eve, and when this fell on a Sunday, it was most inconvenient and expensive that the guests ate meat, while the monks were bound to eat fish. The pope responded to their complaints with an indult that, provided there was no canonical impediment and that they did so outside the refectory, they might eat flesh or any other dish enjoyed by their guests on Sundays, Mondays, Tuesdays and Thursdays from Septuagesima to Quinquagesima, and also on Christmas Eve when it was a Sunday.[10]

Thoroughly respectable communities, therefore, sought to legitimise their lapses from primitive and austere dietary custom. Yet within the parameters of generally accepted contemporary practice, there does not seem to have been a general decline into luxurious living, gluttony or insobriety. It is hardly surprising that in the course of many visitations an individual religious was censured for his lack of moderation in food, or more commonly in drink. This is no more symptomatic of general decline than the isolated instances of sexual misconduct, and it was rare for a visitor to detect such faults in an entire community. Where this did happen, it was normally merely one aspect of a total breakdown of religious discipline, as in 1442 at Newnham, a thoroughly disordered house, where the canons apparently neglected their liturgical obligations every morning as they gorged themselves and each chose his individual dishes for the rest of the day, or at Bardney in 1437, a community rent by faction, where the religious used separate forms of diet in the refectory as they each chose.[11]

Such particularism in diet was obviously disruptive of community spirit,

---

[8] *Benedictine Chapters* ii, 112–13.
[9] *CPL 1417–31*, 48.
[10] *CPL 1455–64*, 5–6.
[11] *Linc. Vis. 1420–49* ii, 15; iii, 236.

but it was not a common phenomenon, and far more often the religious were near unanimous in complaints of the paucity or poor quality of the food and drink served to the convent. In some monasteries, conditions sound to have been truly appalling. At Butley in 1532 the visitor heard that the refectory, exposed to the harsh wind of the Suffolk coast, was always cold, and unbearably so in winter, so that the canons regularly contracted chilblains and other ailments. Despite their proximity to the sea, there was a shortage of fish, both fresh and salted, while they had little meat, and that mostly infected beef. The vegetables were no better, to which the best testimony was the serving lad who had finished them up and was now suffering from an undiagnosed illness. The wine was very bitter, and during Lent coarse bread was served to the canons. They got a brew fit only for labourers, while the prior and his servants, who constantly insulted the brethren, enjoyed much better. That these complaints were justified is indicated by the injunctions issued by the visitors.[12] Such stark conditions were surely made more intolerable by the fact that the house was far from impoverished, and that in this period lavish hospitality was displayed to visiting nobility.[13]

Resentment was often caused by the maintenance by the superior, even in the smallest houses, of a separate establishment. At Peterborough in 1437 it was alleged that the abbot's household was consuming a vast quantity of wine, to the detriment of the convent. At Thornholm in 1440 one canon complained that they were served with stale bread, and the prior with a better sort.[14] At Nunappleton in 1534 the prioress was enjoined by the visitor that there should be no difference between her food and that of the convent.[15] At St James Northampton in 1442 the abbot was accused of partiality in invitations to his chamber or hall, where now by convention meat might be eaten; some he invited twice or three times, others never.[16] In 1494 at St Benet of Holme it was complained that some had not been called to eat in the hall for seven or eight weeks.[17]

The prioress of Campsey Ash on the eve of the Dissolution, however, made no distinction between herself and her nuns. In 1532 the episcopal visitor was informed that she did not provide enough food for the convent, and that what they did have was unwholesome, like the skinny ox which had recently been slaughtered to prevent its death from natural causes, and the roast lamb which habitually came to the table burnt. The only thing which could be said in favour of the prioress was that she was every bit as mean at her own table,

---

[12] *Norwich Vis.*, 285–9.
[13] *The Register or Chronicle of Butley Priory, Suffolk, 1510–1535*, ed. A. G. Dickens, Winchester 1951, especially 50–52.
[14] *Linc. Vis. 1420–49* iii, 276, 365.
[15] 'Visitations in the Diocese of York holden by Archbishop Edward Lee, A.D. 1534–5' (unsigned), *YAJ* xvi, 1902, 443–4.
[16] *Linc. Vis. 1420–49* iii, 245.
[17] *Norwich Vis.*, 61.

but, of course, the house was discredited when noble guests complained of her parsimony.[18]

Certainly the malicious head of a small community could cause great hardship to his brethren. The canons of Marton in 1531 unanimously accused their prior of the most uncharitable behaviour. He had diminished greatly the quantity of meat and drink, and what they did get was more likely to poison than to nourish them, for the wine was sour, and they were served with stinking beef crawling with maggots. When they remonstrated with him, he told them to be content, or they would get worse in the future. He slaughtered many fewer beasts than his predecessors, and the rare guests who came rose from the table as hungry as when they sat down. Most of these evils arose because he had conferred upon his secular kinsmen the offices normally occupied by the brethren, and one of these, the kitchener, was so negligent that he regularly lost four or five oxen at a time, which had to be cast to the dogs.[19]

In many small houses, poor diet was obviously the result of poverty. In 1440 the prioress of Legbourne, a house whose income was only £38 a year, was enjoined to provide sufficient food and clothes, so that the nuns did not need to resort to their friends for the necessities of life. At Ankerwyke, with eight religious and an annual income of only £32, one nun asked for sufficient food to allow her to maintain religious observances. At Fineshade in 1434, the visitor ordered the prior to provide out of the annual income of £56 sufficient service in food and clothing, and prohibited the admission of any new brethren, so that the present community should not be utterly destitute.[20] During the visitation of the diocese of Norwich in 1514, complaints about the quantity of food served to the religious were made at Broomhill, Thetford, Wymondham, Walsingham and Flixton.[21]

At more prosperous monasteries, complaints were more often directed against the quality of the diet. In 1427 an heartfelt petition was delivered to the pope by the abbot and monks of Reading. In the preparation of conventual food, as well as for the diluting of their drink, they used water from a stream called 'Carenterbrook'. Recently, some sons of iniquity had begun, out of malice, to foul this water, and the religious often became so ill that they could not celebrate divine office. The prior of Wallingford was ordered by the pope to prohibit this pollution, by threat of excommunication if necessary.[22] More often, however, the blame for unwholesome food lay within the monastery itself, and the quality of the bread and meat attracted the most complaints. At Bruton in 1452 Bishop Beckington ordered that the bread should be made of pure wheat only, and that the quality should be in

[18] Norwich Vis., 290–92.

[19] J. S. Purvis, 'Notes from the Diocesan Registry at York', YAJ xxxv, 1943, 397–9.

[20] Linc. Vis. 1420–49 i, 64; ii, 5, 186.

[21] Norwich Vis., 86–8, 96–7, 114, 142–3.

[22] CPL 1417–31, 515.

accordance with custom and the practice of other religious houses. At Muchelney he instructed that only good and unspoiled grain should be used.[23] At Broomhill in 1514 it was complained that the bread was bad because the grain was not winnowed before milling, and at Wellow in 1525 the unwholesome loaves were made of barley.[24] At Halesowen in 1478 a complaint was made to Bishop Redman that the canons received insufficient bread, made not of wheat but of other grains, which was unsuitable and dishonourable to the ministers of Christ's altar. The bishop ordered that the bread should henceforth be made of wheat and suitable for priests.[25]

Red meat was, of course, prohibited by the Rule of St Benedict, although universally accepted in practice by the fifteenth century.[26] Much of the meat served, however, even in the greater houses, sounds to have been distinctly unappetising. At Winchester in 1492 the subprior complained of the poor quality of the beef and mutton, and at Peterborough in 1518 it was alleged that the abbot slaughtered skinny sheep, tainted oxen and sick pigs for the conventual meals.[27] In 1442 it was claimed that the kitchener of the abbey of St James patronised a Northampton butcher who was his kinsman, and that he provided meat that was invariably unsavoury and sometimes stinking and unhealthy.[28] At St Frideswide's in 1520 the prior apparently provided for the convent the worst cuts of meat, calves' shoulders and sheep's necks, and the visitor ordered that he should henceforth provide wholesome food, and enough of it.[29] A canon of Worspring complained in 1526 that the only meat they had was salted.[30] There was less genuine cause for grievance among the nuns at Studley, whose main complaint in 1530 was that often on Thursday and Sunday evenings they were served only with beef, and were not given the choice of mutton.[30] St Benedict had indeed stipulated that two cooked dishes should be set before the religious, but he had not envisaged that either should be meat.

In 1421 King Henry V's commissioners had acknowledged that it was difficult to provide for convents far from the sea or well-stocked rivers a sufficient supply of foods other than meat.[31] There are, indeed, a surprising number of recorded complaints of the scarcity of fish, even from a house as close to the Norfolk coast as Walsingham, while at Flixton in the early sixteenth century, on the three fast days of the week the nuns ate only butter and cheese, and occasionally milk.[32] Sometimes, however, the shortage was

---

[23] *Reg. Bekynton*, 182.
[24] *Norwich Vis.*, 86–7; *Linc. Vis. 1517–31* iii, 120.
[25] *CAP* ii, no. 432.
[26] *RSB*, cap. 39.
[27] Register of Archbishop John Morton, Lambeth Palace Library, i, fo. 89v; *Linc. Vis. 1517–31* iii, 81.
[28] *Linc. Vis. 1420–49* iii, 245.
[29] *Linc. Vis. 1517–31* iii, 48.
[30] *Linc. Vis. 1517–31* iii, 110.
[31] *Benedictine Chapters* ii, 112.
[32] *Norwich Vis.*, 115, 142–3.

due to maladministration, as at Bardney in 1437, where almost four hundred pike in the stewponds had been squandered by the sub-cellarer, who gave them away to his friends in the town two or three at a time.[33] Yet the hardship here was only relative, for it was complained that whereas the convent used to be served with three or four kinds of fish, now only two were provided. At Thornholm in 1440 there was a shortage because the convent's fishermen never bothered to repair their nets.[34]

It is hardly surprising, in an age when beer was the normal beverage consumed by the religious, with wine as the only alternative, that the quality of ale provided for the convent should be a frequent cause of complaint. It was even alleged at the visitation of Peterborough in 1518 that there was a certain papal bull by force of which the abbot, if he did not provide a decent brew, was *ipso facto* excommunicate.[35] The most common grievance was that the conventual ale was thin or weak, but occasionally the complaint was more specific. At Stone priory in 1518 the subprior stated that the beer was often murky and clouded with dregs, at Bruton in 1526 it was said that the brew was watery because oatmeal was mixed with the barley, and at Holy Trinity Ipswich it was served to the convent before it had time to mature.[36] Often the religious petitioned the visitor for the removal of the brewer, as at Repton in 1518, where the subprior declared him to be unfit for his office, and at Burton in 1524, where the office was said to be conducted to the scandal of the house.[37]

The poor quality of beer served in so many houses had unfortunate consequences for the regularity of religious observance. Within many monastic precincts there were established beer cells, where the inmates might buy drink. At Maxstoke in 1518, where the refectorer stated that the conventual beer was unwholesome, the prior said that such a beer cell had been established out of necessity. Between 1518 and 1524 at Darley, where again the brew provided for the canons was unsatisfactory, the father of one of them sold beer in a cell in the first gate.[38] Such outlets existed also in nunneries. At St James Canterbury in 1511 a married laywoman sold beer within the precincts, and at Esholt in 1534 an injunction was issued against such an establishment.[39] At Spalding in 1438 one monk prayed that the sale of wine within the cloister buildings be prohibited, and at St Mary's York in 1534 it was ordered that the wine shop should be closed.[40] At Ixworth in 1514

[33] *Linc. Vis. 1420–49* ii, 19.
[34] *Linc. Vis. 1420–49* iii, 364.
[35] *Linc. Vis. 1517–31* iii, 81.
[36] *Blythe's Vis.*, 39; 'Visitation of Religious Houses and Hospitals, 1526', ed. H. C. Maxwell-Lyte, *Collectanea* i (SRS xxxix), 1929, 218; *Norwich Vis.*, 293–4.
[37] *Blythe's Vis.*, 8–10, 12, 147.
[38] *Blythe's Vis.*, 21–2, 62, 151–3.
[39] M. Bateson, 'Archbishop Warham's Visitation of Monasteries, 1511', *EHR* vi, 1891, 22; *YAJ* xvi, 452.
[40] *Linc. Vis. 1420–49* iii, 30; *YAJ* xvi, 447.

one canon, far from attempting to conceal the sale of drink within the monastery, complained angrily that the door of the ale house was in the wrong place, so that the brethren had to stand in the rain as they queued to purchase their beverages.[41]

One of the most common complaints lodged by superiors against their brethren in late medieval visitations was that they wandered off to a neighbouring town to frequent taverns. Visitors, however, often recognised that it was the poor brew provided within the monastery that provoked this ill-disciplined behaviour. At Muchelney in 1455 an injunction was issued that the abbot should cause better and stronger beer to be brewed, so that neither he nor the convent should be driven to seek ale in nearby towns.[42] At Ely cathedral priory in 1515 Archbishop Warham's commissary, accepting the fact that the ale supplied by the *granator* was not fit for pigs, and that he had withdrawn the drink which the monks used to have in the cloister after dinner, ordered that a wholesome brew should be supplied within the house, rather than that they should be sent into the town to drink.[43] At Repton in 1518 it was ordered that a new brewer should be appointed, and in the meantime decent beer should be provided, so that the canons did not need to go out to ale houses, to the detriment of divine service.[44]

Often the quality of monastic diet was ruined by the carelessness, or even malice, of the conventual servants. There were frequent complaints of insolence. At Walsingham in 1494 it was alleged that the servants abused the brethren and called them *fatuos* when they asked for food and drink for visiting relatives.[45] At Ramsey in 1518 a servant in the refectory was said to be encouraged in his rudeness by the prior.[46] It was said at Gracedieu in 1440 that the secular serving folk held the nuns in contempt, and that they sat around in small groups eating to the point of gluttony, while at Walsingham in 1514 the prior's servants filched the food from the canons' plates.[47]

Even more serious was an unsatisfactory butler or steward. The overbearing insolence of these officials was a matter of complaint at Missenden in 1518, Ixworth in 1526, and Westacre in 1532.[48] Jud the butler of Canons Ashby was in 1530 noted as a sower of discord, who made free with the conventual food and drink and sometimes put salt in the canons' beer, and at Elstow in the same year the steward was accused of failing lamentably to

---

[41] *Norwich Vis.*, 84.

[42] *Reg. Bekynton*, 254.

[43] 'Ely Chapter Ordinances and Visitation Records, 1241–1515', ed. S. J. A. Evans (*Camden Miscellany xvii*, Camden Society 3rd series lxiv, 1940), 66.

[44] *Blythe's Vis.*, 8–10.

[45] *Norwich Vis.*, 59.

[46] *Linc. Vis. 1517–31* iii, 84.

[47] *Linc. Vis. 1420–49* ii, 120–23; *Norwich Vis.*, 114. There were also complaints of insolent servants at St Benet of Holme in 1494, Holy Trinity Ipswich in 1514 and Buckenham in 1526 (*Norwich Vis.*, 61, 136, 247).

[48] *Norwich Vis.*, 240, 309–10; *Linc. Vis. 1517–31* iii, 17.

provide cattle and sheep at the right time.[49] These officials, if unchecked by the superior, had great opportunities for corruption. At Humberstone in 1440 the butler, who was said to be not merely the second but the chief abbot, was accused of sending out into the town as much food as the community consumed.[50] At the small nunneries of Stixwould in 1525 and Little Marlow in 1530 the steward was said to be making great profit from his office.[51]

It is perhaps only to be expected that monastic cooks attracted even greater opprobrium if satisfactory service was not provided. Many of them apparently took little trouble to serve up food in an attractive way. At Thornton in 1440 the food was served unsalted and not fully cooked,[52] and at Westacre in 1520 it was complained that different foods were served piled up on the same dish.[53] At Lilleshall in 1520 it was considered that the quality of the food might be improved if they had one of their own brethren as *coquinarius*.[54] In some cases the behaviour of the cook was considered to be not unconnected with the poor service provided. At Dunstable in 1442–43 the cook was surly and puffed up with pride, and discriminated between the canons in the dishes he set before them, while it was probably no accident that the female cook of Gresley, who in 1524 had been spotted wrestling with the prior in his chamber, had little skill in the kitchen.[55] Cooks, too, had ample opportunity for peculation. The cellarer of Markby complained in 1438 that William the cook, although he had a corrody for himself and his household, diverted to his house in town much of the conventual food.[56] The cook of Holy Trinity Ipswich in the early sixteenth century was alleged to have acquired a luxurious house in town from the profits of the kitchen.[57] At Hickling in 1526 it was stated to the visitor that the cook, who was a kinsman of the prior, had the running of the whole house; when he had arrived he was poverty-stricken, now he was rich at the expense of the community. He insulted and belittled the brethren, provided no suitable food for the sick, and his wife, the conventual washerwoman, only bothered to do the job once a week.[58]

The feeding of the poor was traditionally a responsibility of the religious. In their reception special attention should be shown, because in them is

---

[49] *Linc. Vis. 1517–31* ii, 100–101, 126. The butler or steward was also stated to be incompetent at Horsham St Faith in 1492, St Frideswide's in 1520 and Westacre in 1532 (*Norwich Vis.*, 19, 309–10; *Linc. Vis. 1517–31* iii, 48–9).

[50] *Linc. Vis. 1420–49* ii, 141–2.

[51] *Linc. Vis. 1517–31* iii, 8, 104.

[52] *Linc. Vis. 1420–49* iii, 372

[53] *Norwich Vis.*, 166.

[54] *Blythe's Vis.*, 58–9.

[55] *Linc. Vis. 1420–49* ii, 85; *Blythe's Vis.*, 148–9.

[56] *Linc. Vis. 1420–49* iii, 221.

[57] *Norwich Vis.*, 136.

[58] *Norwich Vis.*, 212–13.

Christ more truly welcomed.[59] Capitular legislation reiterated the obligation to distribute in entirety the remains of conventual meals in alms, and those who infringed this ruling were to fast for three days on bread and water. The doors of the cloister were to be closed against undeserving seculars to prevent them getting their hands on the remains of *prandium* and *cena*, and obedientiaries were forbidden to feed their servants from this source.[60] Whatever the proportion of monastic revenues devoted to alms on the eve of the Dissolution, it is clear from visitation records that in the century before the Reformation many communities felt scant obligation to support the local poor from their own tables.[61] Waste and the diversion of alms in food was one of the complaints most regularly laid by conscientious individuals. In the diocese of Lincoln between 1432 and 1447 such waste of food was detected at thirteen monasteries, ranging from the tiny Cistercian nunnery of Nun Cotham to the rich communities of Peterborough and Ramsey, and in several cases reiteration at successive visitations reveals the inefficacy of episcopal injunctions in this, as in other matters.[62]

Such diminution of alms might, of course, be the result of poverty and the resultant inability to provide an adequate diet for the religious themselves, but there are many indications that this was not always the case. At Peterborough in 1432 the alms from table were sent to a third eating place, 'ly Chymney', access to which was now prohibited by the visitor, where they were shared out among the brethren.[63] At Ely in 1403 surplus food was apparently used by individual monks as payment in kind to seculars, and at Thornton in 1440 the alms had been converted into corrodies which were sold.[64] It was alleged that the master of the works at Darley in 1518 diverted surplus food to the beer cell within the precincts run by his own father.[65] At Newnham in 1442, Darley in 1521, St Benet of Holme in 1526 and Norwich in 1532 the excessive number of hounds was blamed for the lack of fragments for distribution.[66] Sometimes the remains were given to the servants of the house, in direct contravention of the statutes, and elsewhere it was found that the superior, cellarer, or the convent as a whole gave the food to their kinsfolk or friends.[67] At Ramsey in 1432 it was enjoined that the alms of the house

---

[59] *RSB*, cap. 53.

[60] *Benedictine Chapters* i, 36–7.

[61] For discussion of the level of almsgiving, see Knowles, *RO* iii, 264–6.

[62] Waste was reported or censured at Bardley, Croyland, Daventry, Kyme, Laund, Markby, Newnham, Nun Cotham, Nutley, Peterborough, Ramsey, Spalding and Thornton (*Linc. Vis. 1420–49* i, 2, 37, 89, 102, 105; ii, 14, 20–21, 39, 179; iii, 223, 234, 249, 255, 309, 311, 313, 372–5).

[63] *Linc. Vis. 1420–49* i, 102.

[64] 'Ely Chapter Ordinances', 55; *Linc. Vis. 1420–49* iii, 372.

[65] *Blythe's Vis.*, 21–2.

[66] *Blythe's Vis.*, 62; *Linc. Vis. 1420–49* iii, 234; *Norwich Vis.*, 215.

[67] Given to servants at Bardney, 1437 (*Linc. Vis. 1420–49* iii, 14), Shrewsbury, 1524 (*Blythe's Vis.*, 132–4), Westacre, 1526 (*Norwich Vis.*, 249–50). Given to friends and family at Folkestone, 1511 (*EHR* vi, 28), Peterborough, 1518 (*Linc. Vis. 1517–31* iii, 81), Maxstoke, 1518 and Burton, 1524 (*Blythe's Vis.*, 13, 146–7).

should be distributed by the clerks of the almonry to the poor at the gate, and that no monk was to grant such alms to any person, of whatever kinship, without special licence.[68] Yet at Keynsham in 1451, where Bishop Beckington found it necessary to order every canon eating in the refectory to put aside a portion of his meals for the common alms on pain of half rations at the next meal, they were allowed to send helpings to parents and relations without seeking the prior's permission.[69]

A similar disregard was often shown for the dietary requirements of ailing brethren. St Benedict had laid the greatest stress on the obligation of the superior: 'Before all things, and above all things care must be taken of the sick, so that they may be served in very deed as Christ himself.'[70] The York provincial chapter of 1221 had stipulated that the cellarer should every day visit the sick monks, enquiring into their needs and providing the diet best suited to their illness. If he failed in this, after the third admonition he was to be deprived of office. In 1343 the obligation to visit daily the infirmary was placed upon the prior or subprior, in company with the kitchener.[71] The care given to the sick was a matter of routine enquiry at visitations, and complaints were made with distressing regularity. Between 1518 and 1530, lack of suitable food for ailing religious was reported to the episcopal visitors in thirteen houses in the diocese of Lincoln, and in most cases an injunction was issued.[72] In Norwich diocese between 1492 and 1532, eight communities were found to be failing in their obligations to their sick members, and the fact that complaints were made at Westacre priory four times in this period reveals once more that episcopal injunctions had at best very short-term effect.[73]

This neglect of the sick was not confined to small and impoverished houses. At Ramsey in 1439 it was complained that the infirm monks received no delicacies, but only coarse food like beef and bacon.[74] Only a penny a day was allowed for the food of a sick brother at Peterborough in the early sixteenth century.[75] Allegations of insufficient provision for the sick were made at the cathedral priories of Winchester in 1492 and Norwich in 1492 and 1526, while at Worcester in 1525 Cardinal Wolsey's commissary issued an injunction for the daily visiting of the sick and the preparation by the

---

[68] *Linc. Vis. 1420–49* i, 105.
[69] *Reg. Bekynton,* 260–62.
[70] *RSB,* cap. 36.
[71] *Benedictine Chapters* i, 239; ii, 48.
[72] At Ashridge, Bourne, Chacombe, Daventry, Eynsham, Goring, Legbourne, Markby, Missenden, Peterborough, Stansfield, Stixwould, Studley (*Linc. Vis. 1517–31* ii, 76, 82, 106, 113, 143, 156–7, 181; iii, 13, 17, 80–81, 99, 102, 109–10).
[73] At Butley, Carrow, Coxford, Hickling, Norwich, St Benet's, Walsingham, Westacre (*Norwich Vis.,* 5–6, 51, 102, 112, 114, 204, 218, 275, 277, 279–81).
[74] *Linc. Vis. 1420–49* iii, 306.
[75] *Linc. Vis. 1517–31* iii, 80.

kitchener of such food as their ailments required in a cleaner fashion than had been customary, on pain of claustration for one week.[76]

Complaints about the quality, quantity and distribution of food and drink were, therefore, among the most common grievances expressed at visitations during the last century of English medieval monasticism. To some historians, this preoccupation with diet in communities dedicated to the service of God and to individual poverty will be distressing, further evidence of the decline from primitive ideals, and symptomatic of the transformation of the monasteries into little more than collegiate chapters. Others, in this secular age, may derive wry but not unsympathetic amusement from the timelessness of dietary preoccupations within any residential community, whatever its *raison d'être*. From the accumulation of complaints and injunctions, however, some general points do emerge. Amongst the religious of the more prosperous houses, the isolated complaints of those who wished for stricter dietary observance were far outweighed by the plethora of demands for receipt in full of everything to which the community believed itself entitled according to those modifications and relaxations of the Rule which had taken place in the later middle ages. Yet there is much evidence that far from all monasteries were havens of luxury whose inmates enjoyed a very high standard of living. Even in the best endowed houses mismanagement, corruption or malice might have disastrous effects upon the dietary régime of the community, while the reiterated complaints from smaller convents of short rations, consisting mainly of the cheapest and least wholesome provisions, are an indication of great economic stringency. The frequency with which visitation injunctions responded to the complaints of the religious indicates that responsible secular clergy often found the monastic diet to be deficient either in quality or quantity.

In many houses, the management of the internal economy had been taken over by a lay administrator, often a kinsman of the superior, who managed the domestic budget to his own advantage and to the detriment of the conventual table, while some communities had to contend, even while they ate, with insolence and hostility from the servants of the refectory, who evidently had little respect for their monastic masters. There were, of course, instances of abuse by the religious themselves, such as the drinking parties and gluttonous feasts denounced by Bishop Beckington at Bruton and Muchelney.[77] Yet it is instructive that the frequenting of taverns and ale-houses, so often cited as an example of monastic dissoluteness and indiscipline, was frequently attributed by visitors to the negligent failure of superior or officials to provide decent beverages within the precincts. Perhaps the

[76] Reg. Morton i, fo. 89v; *Norwich Vis.*, 5–6, 204; 'The Visitations and Injunctions of Cardinal Wolsey and Archbishop Cranmer', ed. J. M. Wilson, *Associated Architectural and Archaeological Reports* xxxvi (2), 1922, 362.

[77] *Reg. Bekynton*, 181–2, 253.

most serious and distressing indictment of the religious that emerges from this survey of visitation material is lack of charity, manifested not only in the frequent diminution or withdrawal of alms in food from the monastic table, but also in that individualism in the cloister which so often led to a lack of communal concern for the dietary welfare of ailing brethren.

St Mary's College, Strawberry Hill

John Whethamstede, The Pope and the General Council

Margaret Harvey

If one asks how, about 1440, English ecclesiastics judged recent developments in the church (especially the general councils) an answer is difficult to find. Thanks to Professor Crowder and Dr Schofield a great deal can be discovered about the attitude of the English Crown to the pope and council, and such was the nature of fifteenth-century English church government that a picture of unanimity was presented to the outside world.[1] Dr Schofield has convinced us that the English Crown gave no support to the conciliarists who opposed Eugenius IV, but we know very little about the debate (if any) behind the seeming unity and equally little about the views of individuals.[2] Yet Piero da Monte in 1438 and 1439 wished his readers to understand that loyalty to the pope might be precarious and, though he wrote to show what a good job he had done, there may have been some truth in the point.[3]

To survey the whole field would be beyond my competence, so I wish in this article to examine only the views of one man, John Whethamstede, abbot of St Albans. He has attracted a great deal of attention from historians but more for his humanism (or lack of it) than for his theological views.[4]

---

[1] C. M. D. Crowder, 'Henry V, Sigismund and the Council of Constance, a re-examination', *Historical Studies* iv, 1963, 93–110; A. N. E. D. Schofield, 'England and the Council of Basel', *Annuarium Historiae Conciliorum* v, 1973, 1–117. I must thank Dr Schofield for his help.

[2] Schofield, 4.

[3] J. Haller, *Piero da Monte (Bibliothek des Deutschen Historischen Instituts in Rom* xix), Rome 1941, 41 no. 52; 62–8 no. 69.

[4] The most detailed recent work on Whethamstede is D. R. Howlett, 'Studies in the works of John Whethamstede' (unpublished D.Phil., Oxford 1975). I must thank Dr Howlett for a great deal of help and for allowing me to use and quote from his thesis. See also E. Hodge, 'The Abbey of St Albans under John Whethamstede' (unpublished Ph.D., Manchester 1934), where much of W's work was identified and a list of sources given, though many were not identified; E. F. Jacob, 'Verborum Florida Venustas', in *Essays in the Conciliar Epoch*, Manchester 1953, 185–206, esp. 187–96; W. F. Schirmer, *Der Englische Frühhumanismus*, 2nd edn, Tübingen 1963, 73–89, 136–8; R. Weiss, *Humanism*, 25–7, 30–38; D. Knowles, *RO* ii, 193–7, 267–8; A. Grandsen, *Historical Writing in England* ii, 1982, 371–86.

Professor Knowles pointed out that he seemed to be a conciliarist but otherwise his theological position has remained unexamined.[5] Yet he had a considerable amount to say on recent church history, most of it very enlightening. He was in an exceptionally good position both to know about recent events and to read recent and older literature of the controversies about papal power. He had been *prior studentium* of Gloucester College, Oxford and maintained his scholarly interest afterwards. He was abbot of St Albans twice: from 1420 to 1440 and again from 1452 to 1465. During the first period he attended the council of Pavia-Siena, leaving some account of his journey and his impressions.[6] He was selected by his fellow Benedictines to attend Basel, and though he did not go, there is evidence in his writings that he was interested in its activities.[7] St Albans was an important house, constantly being visited by great men. In addition Whethamstede belonged to the circle of Humfrey, Duke of Gloucester, and thus not only knew exceedingly well-informed men, like Humfrey himself or Bekynton the royal secretary, but also had access to an excellent library to supplement an already good collection in St Albans.

Whethamstede was a prolific writer but from my point of view his most interesting work is his *Granarium* part I. This is an historical dictionary or encyclopedia, dealing with a variety of topics and persons, ranging from *Anglia* to *Johannes XXII, papa*. The section A–L exists in full, though not in its final form, and there are a few items left from the lost M–Z section.[8] The date of this work is a matter of dispute but Whethamstede seems to have worked on it over a number of years, from at least 1438. Duke Humfrey presented a copy to Oxford in 1444, and Dr Howlett must be correct to think that the major part of the work dates to Whethamstede's period of retirement after his first resignation as abbot in 1440.[9]

---

[5] Knowles, *RO* ii, 268.

[6] W. Brandmüller, *Das Konzil von Pavia-Siena 1423–24 (Vorreformationsgeschichtliche Forschungen* xvi), Münster 1968, i, 27, 31, 37–8, 93, 100, 103; ii, 6, 9.

[7] *Benedictine Chapters* iii, 105 no. 261; *Historiae Dunelmensis Scriptores Tres (Surtees Society* ix), 1839, appx ccxxvii.

[8] A–L is BL MS Cotton Nero C VI (hereafter Nero). This is Whethamstede's own working copy (Howlett, 174–5; Hodge, 170–77). For its incompleteness see below n. 9. I have used BL MS Arundel 11 (hereafter Arundel) for both sections of *Granarium* and Cambridge, Gonville and Caius College, MS Gonville 230 (hereafter Gonville). The last is W's own commonplace book (Howlett, 152, 173).

[9] Howlett, 246. For the date 1444, Weiss, *Humanism*, 34 n. 1; *Ep. Ac. Ox.* i, 235; A. Sammut, *Unfredo Duca di Gloucester e gli Umanisti Italiani (Medioevo e Umanismo* xli), Padova 1980, 78. Hodge wished to date it 1438 but Howlett has pointed out that Nero fo. 90v has a copy of the decree of union with the Greek church, dated 6 July 1439, under the heading *Eugenius IV*. Copies were being circulated in England by Piero da Monte from 26 August (Haller, *Piero da Monte*, 111) and he sent one to Whethamstede (*ibid.* 120–21). Also a marginal note in Nero fo. 90v refers to the union with the Armenians. Their decree was dated 22 November 1439 (Cambridge, Emmanuel College MS 142 (hereafter Emmanuel) fo. 164r for letter of Eugenius IV sending news of it to England on 23 November, with copy *ibid.* fos. 162r–163r). The government acknowledged receipt on 8 February 1440 (*Official Correspondence of T. Bekynton*, ed. G. Williams (*RS*, lvi), 1872, ii, 51).

First of all let us examine what Whethamstede has to say about the councils held in his own lifetime: Pisa, Constance, Pavia, Basel and Florence.

On Pisa he had little to say. He used it as an example of a council justifiably called without papal consent, noted that it elected Alexander V and that it first used organisation into nations, which, he maintained, was the method of organisation approved by the council of Constance and used until, under pressure of French hatred of England, it was abandoned by Basel.[10] Evidently Whethamstede had no *Acta* of Pisa: his sources for his information on Alexander V were: *sparsim in gestis Romanorum pontificum et in cronica Martini ac in continuacione*.[11] *Acta* of Pisa were probably scarce in England. I know of only one contemporary reference to ownership; the *Acta* of Pisa, Constance and Basel in three paper volumes, given by Thomas Burton to Durham College, Oxford and used by Thomas Gascoigne.[12] But, though Burton, who had been at Basel, became rector of Whethamstede in 1440, there is no evidence in Whethamstede's existing work that he had access to these books.[13]

On Constance, by contrast, the information is full and detailed. There is an account of the schism to 1415, a detailed account of the relations of John XXIII with the council, including many documents and summaries of proceedings.[14] He tells of Benedict XIII's recalcitrance and gives the decree deposing him, describes Gregory XII's refusal to accept Pisa but his final acceptance of Constance, with his resignation via his proctor Carlo Malatesta and the honourable provision for him by the council.[15] Jerome of Prague's recantation is given.[16] There is an account of Hus, stating that he was a follower of Wycliffe who refused to be silent when his bishop ordered it and so he was cited to Constance. The document of his reply to his interrogation was given, with the decree condemning him and a list of six condemned articles.[17] Under *Concilium* and *Papa* Whethamstede quoted *Haec Sancta* verbatim, referring to *Frequens* and to the question of tyrannicide.[18]

There is no doubt about the source of all this abundance: he refers to it himself many times: *autor recollectionis actorum concilii Constanciensis*.[19]

---

[10] Lack of papal consent: under *Concilium*, Nero fo. 46v; Alexander V, Nero fo. 4v; under *Ecclesia*, Nero fo. 71r and more generally under *Nacio*, Gonville, 128 and 270–84 (slightly fuller in Arundel fos. 113r–117v) for organisation. *Concilium* in Nero fos. 46v–50v contains much the same points on organisation (slightly fuller in Arundel fos. 34r–40v).

[11] See previous note.

[12] T. Gascoigne, *Loci e Libro Veritatum*, ed. J. E. Thorold Rogers, Oxford 1881, 116, 121, 157, 164, 165.

[13] *BRUO* i, 319–20; J. E. Cussans, *History of Hertfordshire* iii, *Hundred of Dacorum*, 1879, 346.

[14] Nero fos. 157r–163r.

[15] Deposition: Nero fos. 28r–28v; fate of Gregory: *ibid.* fos. 116r–118r.

[16] Nero fos. 144r–145r.

[17] Nero fos. 165r–167r.

[18] *Concilium*: Nero fo. 50r; *Papa*: Gonville 251–70; *Frequens* and tyrannicide: Nero fo. 50v.

[19] Nero fo. 118r.

He certainly had an *Acta* of Constance and from it he either cited whole documents or paraphrased and summarised the notary's connecting narratives. The most likely source, as Dr Hodge pointed out, is the *Acta* now in the British Library as Cotton Nero E V, which came into Duke Humfrey's Library by purchase from the executors of Thomas Polton, who died in 1433.[20] Whethamstede had certainly read his documents very carefully and he gave a faithful account of what he had before him.[21]

On Pavia-Siena of course Whethamstede has his own letters and recollections from which it is clear that he was critical of the pope and hoped for more than was achieved.[22] All he says in *Granarium* is that the sentence against Wycliffe was made more severe and was to be proclaimed on major feasts.[23] That was the only substantial legislation produced by the council.[24]

On Basel the information was not abundant, considering how long the council had continued and the variety of matters discussed. He knew that the method of organisation had changed from that of Constance and that the assembly was grouped according to its aims into *domus fidei*, *domus pacis* and *domus reformationis*.[25] He gave a summary account of the quarrel between Eugenius IV and the council but the only document is the council's bull of 25 June 1438 deposing the pope.[26] He referred to the Hussites (under *Heresis: De Pragensibus*) and summarised the four articles which he says they presented to the council, though without telling us more, and refers us to the (now lost) section *Praga* for further information.[27] This is not very much, though it is worth remembering that the article on Eugenius IV is unfinished in the existing manuscript (which seems to be Whethamstede's working copy) and that the article *Concilium* in that version does not include Basel in its list of councils (though there is another version of the item which does).[28] This suggests very strongly that these sections were actually being written in 1439.

What were his sources? First and foremost we would expect him to have consulted and corresponded with some of the English delegates themselves. Correspondence was brisk and Bekynton's letter book was full of it.[29] We

---

[20] Hodge, 216; Sammut, 108.

[21] Compare official *Acta* with his account of John XXIII's promise to resign: Nero fos. 158r–159v, and BL MS Nero E V fo. 7v *et seq.*

[22] *Annales Monasterii S. Albani a J. Amundesham*, ed. H. T. Riley (*RS* xxviiia), 1870, i, 118–86 and esp. 179–81, with n. 6 above.

[23] Under *Concilium*, Nero fo. 50v.

[24] J. D. Mansi, *Sacrorum Conciliorum Nova et Amplissima Collectio*, Venice 1757–98, xxviii, cols. 1060–63; Brandmüller, i, 145; ii, 20–28.

[25] Under *Ecclesia*, Nero fo. 71v and in general under *Nacio* see n. 10. Arundel fo. 117v has: *hec omnia colligi possunt ex his que scripta sunt in libris conciliorum sed precipue et magis summatim ex his que scripta sunt de rebus, actis et gestis in sacrosancto concilio apud Constanciam.* This does not occur in Gonville.

[26] Nero fos. 89r–90v.

[27] Nero fo. 136v.

[28] Nero fo. 50r ends with Pavia-Siena as council 43 and gives no sources. Arundel fo. 40v adds 44: *erat concilium celebratum sub Eugenio quarto apud Basiliam in partibus Germanorum.*

[29] Schofield, *passim*, for the many letters which remain.

know that Whethamstede was in correspondence with the abbot of York but others whom he knew were certainly writing to one another with news.[30] Furthermore, by the time he was writing about Basel the bulk of the English at the council had returned home and thus could be consulted personally.[31] There seems however to be evidence that he used *Acta* of Basel. In talking about the Hussites he refers to the evidence that he has used and although it is difficult to disentangle some of the reference from the general sources for heresy, two are clear: *Acta* of the council of Basel and (presumably mentioned separately because not part of the *Acta*) a certain letter sent by the leaders of the kingdom of Bohemia to the Princes of the Empire.[32] So straightforward a reference to *Acta* seems to suggest a volume like Nero E V, and Dr Hodge even suggested that he might have used Emmanuel College Cambridge 142, which belonged to Norwich Cathedral Priory and contains *Acta* of general sessions 1–16, that is till February 5, 1434, along with miscellaneous papers, including Hussite material. These may have been simply a collection of papers later bound into this volume, but all seem to have a Norwich connection.[33] But the *Acta* here, and also at least one other English example, Oxford, New College MS 138, would have told him little beyond that Basel welcomed the Hussites, and certainly did not give their four articles.[34] Whethamstede probably owed his knowledge of these to his mysterious letter from the citizens of Prague. If he had been using documents from Basel one would have expected him to cite the articles in the form and order agreed for debate in 1433 between the council delegates and the Hussites.[35] Emmanuel 142 in its appended papers, not its *Acta*, has a copy of that agreement, where the order is communion, public sin, preaching and endowment, whereas Whethamstede has communion, preaching, endowment and public sin.[36] Furthermore his version seems to talk overtly about disendowment, which not all versions of the articles did and which suggests a

---

[30] *Memorials of St Edmunds Abbey*, ed. T. Arnold (*RS* xcvi) iii, 1896, 252–4.

[31] Schofield, 81.

[32] Nero fo. 137r.

[33] Hodge, 218–19. The *Acta* of general sessions are fos. 14r–61r. Session 16 is in a different hand. For Norwich Cathedral MSS see N. R. Ker, 'Medieval Manuscripts from Norwich Cathedral Priory', *Transactions of the Cambridge Bibliographical Society* i, 1949, 1–28 and esp. 3 and 22. William Worsted, prior of Norwich, was at Basel from 2 March 1433 till late in 1434 (Schofield, 28, 49, 62, 63–4; *BRUO* iii, 2089–90).

[34] Mansi xxix, col. 27–31 has the welcoming letter of Basel to the Hussites from *Acta* of the type of Emmanuel. The other English example, Oxford New College MS 138 has *Acta* from sessions 1–19 (fo. 276r *et seq.*) i.e. to 7 September 1434 but omits the welcome to the Hussites. On the manuscript see R. W. Hunt, 'The Medieval Library', in *New College, Oxford 1379–1979*, ed. J. Buxton and P. Williams, Oxford 1979, 328.

[35] On the question as a whole see F. G. Heyman, *John Zizka and the Hussite Revolution*, Princeton 1955, chapter 10. The articles for debate at Basel are in *Monumenta Conciliorum Generalium Saeculi XV. Concilium Basiliense*, Vienna 1857–96, i, 444–5 no. 184.

[36] Above n. 27; Emmanuel fo. 169r.

document like that known to the papal legate to Bohemia in July 1420.[37] Whethamstede's letter looks like a copy of a Czech manifesto, perhaps that of July 1420. Where would he have got it? A possible source would be Cardinal Beaufort himself or more probably Beaufort's chancellor Nicholas Bildeston, whom Whethamstede would have known from their time at Pavia-Siena and with whom he shared humanist interests (and some of the same friends).[38] Bildeston had been with Beaufort on his 1427 crusade and Beaufort visited St Albans on his return from Bohemia in 1427.[39] Beaufort seems to have taken the trouble to study the views of his opponents so he must have known some version of the four articles.[40]

It therefore seems more probable that for information on the Hussites Whethamstede was relying not on *Acta* of Basel but on information on the Hussites from other sources.

Acta is in any case an ambiguous term. There certainly were official, notarised copies of the decrees of general sessions of the council and of synodal letters, though the existing copies of these in England came in the seventeenth or eighteenth century.[41] The contemporary English manuscripts are incomplete and seem to cover only the period when the English were officially present at Basel.[42] Once the bulk of the delegates had departed (by the end of 1434) it seems that information depended on the sending of copies of individual *Acta*, such as Piero da Monte was certainly receiving.[43] Thus when Whethamstede refers to *Acta* he might mean individual copies of decrees rather than a whole volume such as we know he must have had for Constance. Existing English *Acta* do not include the bull deposing Eugenius IV, for example, but we know that da Monte received copies from Basel by 24 July 1439 and sent one at once to the royal confessor.[44] Likewise Whethamstede mentions the union with both the Greeks and the Armenians at Ferrara-Florence.[45] We know that da Monte had sent him a copy of the

---

[37] H. Kaminsky, *A History of the Hussite Revolution*, Berkeley and Los Angeles 1967, 369, 373 n. 32. For versions see F. M. Bartoš, 'Manifesty města Prahy z Doby Husitské', in an offprint from *Zborniku* vii, Prague 1932, 253–309, appx, 275–309. The version nearest to Whethamstede's, though less extreme on endowment, is 278–82. The version known to the legate in F. Palacky, *Urkundliche Beiträge zur Geschichte des Hussiten Krieges*, Prague 1872, i, 34–5.

[38] *BRUO* i, 187–8; Weiss, *Humanism*, 19, 25–7.

[39] G. A. Holmes, 'Cardinal Beaufort and the Crusade against the Hussites', *EHR* lxxxviii, 1973, 721–50, esp. 724, 726, 735; *Amundesham* i, 28.

[40] Bartoš, 'An English Cardinal and the Hussite Revolution', *Communio Viatorum* vi, 1963, 47–54.

[41] J. Haller, *Concilium Basiliense*, Basel 1896, i, 1–12 for the variety of sources; BL MS Harley 3972 (for which see C. E. Wright, *Fontes Harleiana*, 1972, 438, 168–9, 367–9) signed by the council notary Michael Galteri fo. 92v with corrections by him fos. 2v, 3v, 9v, 10r, 25v. Bodleian Library MS Roe 20 (SC 266), synodal letters, given in March 1630 by the proconsul of Gdansk to Roe and thence to Oxford University. Signed by Galteri fo. 69r. For Galteri see J. Dephoff, *Zum Urkunden und Kanzleiwesen des Konzils von Basel*, Hildesheim 1930, 65.

[42] Above n. 33 and 34.

[43] Below n. 46.

[44] Haller, *Piero da Monte*, 97 no. 95. By 31 July he assumed that Beaufort would know of it (105 no. 99).

[45] Above n. 9.

bull of union with the Greeks, and we may suppose that he knew of the similar Armenian document from the official copy sent by the pope.[46] The English were very sparsely represented at Florence, though Andrew Holes, king's proctor and another of the Duke Humfrey circle, was present unofficially, but official documents were certainly being sent to this country and information was certainly available.[47]

Whethamstede is thus well informed about the councils held in his own life-time and seems to have been interested particularly in the council of Constance. What did he think of the conciliar movement and its theory? The best approach to this question is to ask what he thought constituted a general council. His definition *iuxta quosdam* is as follows:

> A universal council of the church is a gathering made by lawful authority, to any place, from every grade of the hierarchy of the catholic church, excluding no faithful person who ought to be heard, to deal. . . . with what is necessary for the rule of the church.[48]

Lawful authority is the pope, except in three cases:

  i. If the pope is absent by death, natural or civil, and it is necessary to call the council.
  ii. If, sufficiently required, he contumaciously refuses to call a council to the detriment of the church.
  iii. If, contrary to the statutes of general councils, he extends the dates for celebrating councils.

In these cases (*iuxta varios*) power to call a council rests with the church, as happened, says Whethamstede, at Pisa in our own day, for the removal of schism.[49]

The definition is thoroughly conciliar. It accepts the definition of itself given by the council of Pisa and it certainly accepts as binding the decree *Frequens* of the council of Constance. It is followed by a rather startling list of forty-three (or forty-four if Basel is included) councils to 1438, for which Whethamstede may have been copying some document (though, if so, it was not an *Acta* of Basel) but which has marked peculiarities.[50] For instance there are thirty-eight councils up to Lateran IV but including none of the twelfth-century Lateran councils, and of the later councils it includes Lateran IV, Lyons 1274, Vienne, Constance and Pavia-Sienna, thus omitting Pisa. The later part of this list resembles lists made by many of Whethamstede's

---

[46] Above n. 9; J. Gill, *The Council of Florence*, Cambridge 1959, 308; *Bekynton* ii, 51–3.

[47] J. G. Greatrex, 'Thomas Rudbourne, monk of Winchester and the council of Florence', *SCH* ix, 1972, 173–4. For Holes *BRUO* ii, 949–50.

[48] Nero fo. 46v.

[49] Nero fo. 46v: *quemadmodum nostris practizatum fuerat temporibus in concilio celebrato apud Pisas in quo papa nullus personaliter aut procuratorie comparuit sed tantummodo cardinales aliiique viri ecclesiastici ad tollendum horrendum scisma quo tunc diutius Christi ecclesia fuerat scandalizata. . . .*

[50] As Howlett, 246. Was it perhaps *autor conciliorum*, Nero fo. 47r under *Nicea* in the list of councils?

contemporaries, but at most these included thirteen general councils.[51] Perhaps, of course, Whethamstede did not intend his list to be only of general councils, but, if not, it is strange that he omits the twelfth-century councils and Pisa, the latter certainly approved by him as a general council. The list does not help very much in understanding Whethamstede's views.

His attitude to recent events is more illuminating. He accepted the council of Constance's own view of its friends and enemies: disapproving of John XXIII, approving of Gregory XII in so far as he resigned and accepting as normative organisation by nations and *Frequens*.[52] He by no means wholly supported Eugenius IV but totally disapproved of Basel's action in deposing him, which is dismissed as uncanonical.[53]

That this is more than the dutiful attitude of a loyal English churchman who supported his own government is suggested by abundant evidence that Whethamstede was very well read in controversial literature on the power of the pope and that he inclined to a conciliar view. The evidence comes chiefly from the article *Papa*, now preserved only in Whethamstede's own notebook in Gonville MS 230.[54] This is a discussion of six views of papal power, with a list of the main writers who had held each view. Frequently one finds that there are verbatim quotations from the authority being cited, as is often the case elsewhere in *Granarium*.

The article begins with a definition of the word *Papa*, rejecting the views of those (anonymous here) extreme papalists like Alvarus Pelayo in *De Planctu Ecclesie* or Alexander de Sancto Elpidio who maintained that *papa* meant *pater patrum* and indicated how much the pope was to be honoured, in favour of those *quibus major adhibenda est fides* who gave an historical account.[55] By gradual usage a title which had originally applied to major bishops in Africa was used by them when writing to the bishop of Rome and so came to be his title. Whethamstede took this explanation from *Dialogus inter orthodoxum et catechuminum* (of which more later) which he much admired and which presented a very Greek view of the church, with the pope *primus inter pares* and the local bishop enjoying much power.[56]

The first of the six opinions about the pope follows: those who contend that

[51] R. Baümer, 'Die Zahl des Allgemeinen Konzilien in der Sicht von Theologen des 15. und 16. Jahrhunderts', *Annuarium Historiae Conciliorum* i, 1969, 288–313, esp. 291–2, 297.

[52] For nations, Gonville, 127. It was: *expresse contra decretum concilii Constanciensis* to change the organisation of councils. Gregory XII is called *maturus vir* for his action (Nero fo. 116r).

[53] Nero fos. 89r–89v. Of the cardinals who supported the deposition of Eugenius by Basel he writes: *ibique unum habentes in corde aliud vero in ore quasi filii degeneres in patris depositionem non minus callide quam calumniose laborabant*. Of the deposition he says: *demum in eum licet canonice multum prepeditum talis* (89v) *qualis invalidaque satis sententia deprivationis lata erat*.

[54] Pp. 251–70. Howlett, 152, 173.

[55] Alvarus in J. T. Rocaberti, *Bibliotheca Maxima Pontificia*, Rome 1698, iii, 137 (Chapter 54) and see below n. 80. Alexander, Rocaberti ii, 11 (Chapter 10) and n. 57 below; for quotation Gonville 251.

[56] Dialogus, Book II, cap. 3 (see below n. 91 and 92). The writer rejects *pater patrum* or *admirabilis* as explanations of *papa*.

all authority both secular and spiritual derives from the pope and who prove this by arguing that the pope's role is that which most resembles God's in the celestial hierarchy. Secular authority is merely accessory to spiritual exercised by the pope. The writers who are said to hold these views are Alexander de Elpidio and Augustinus (Triumphus) of Ancona.

The Alexander de Elpidio reference is no doubt to *De Ecclesiastica Potestate*, written by the Augustinian Hermit in 1324.[57] Whethamstede quotes from it elsewhere and had clearly read it, though there now seems to be no English manuscript.[58] The Augustinus Triumphus reference was no doubt to his *Summa de Potestate Ecclesiastica*, completed in 1326, of which Whethamstede had had a copy made for St Albans for which he made a *tabula* of contents.[59]

At the other extreme from these very papalist ideas were those of the Waldensians and their followers. They so restricted papal power as to allow the pope no temporal rule nor any temporal possessions. Whethamstede listed the passages of scripture adduced in support of these views and said that they believed that no pope since Sylvester I had been a true successor of St Peter.

Here the sources are more difficult to determine. When discussing heresy elsewhere in *Granarium* Whethamstede seems to imply that he got his information on Waldensians from a work called *Opus vite*, attributed by Bale to Cardinal Adam Easton, at least one of whose other works Whethamstede certainly knew, doubtless from the library of Norwich Cathedral where they had been deposited in 1407.[60] If *Opus Vite* was the source it is now lost.

A third body of opinion was represented by Petrus de Palude and James of Viterbo, who gave such wide powers to the pope that in temporal and spiritual matters he could do anything and be questioned and judged by no-one. The pope could do no wrong and even if he were a manifest heretic he deposed himself, with the deposition merely declared by men. The pope could be resisted for disgraceful behaviour but not deposed.

The work of James of Viterbo mentioned is no doubt *De Regimine Christiano*, written in 1302, but this does not seem to be one of the books which

---

[57] Rocaberti ii, section 7, 23–264. I know of no English MS, though M. Krammer in his edition of *Determinatio Compendiosa* (*Fontes Iuris Germanici Antiqui*), Hannover and Leipzig 1909, xxii, Rocaberti, 23 and Hodge, 241 thought a copy existed in Cambridge, Emmanuel College MS 9 fos. 109v–122v, but this is only *Determinatio*, attributed to Alexander. On him see M. Wilks, *The Problem of Sovereignty in the Later Middle Ages*, Cambridge 1963, *passim*; R. Scholz, *Unbekannte Kirchenpolitische Streit-Schriften aus der Zeit Ludwigs des Bayern (1327–54)* (*Bibliothek des Kgl. Preuss. Hist. Inst. in Rom*, ix), Rome 1911, 232–4.

[58] Nero fo. 35v, under *Cardinalatus*.

[59] *Amundesham* ii, 269; T. Tanner, *Bibliotheca Britannico-Hibernica*, 1748, 441.

[60] Nero fo. 137r: *in illo egregio opusculo quod intitulatur Opus vite*, but I have found no reference to Easton as the author. For Norwich and Easton see H. C. Beeching and M. R. James, 'The Library of the Cathedral Church at Norwich', *Norfolk Archaeology* xix, 1917, 67–116, esp. 72; Ker (as n. 33), 11n. and 21. For the Bale reference, *Index Britanniae Scriptorum*, ed. R. L. Poole and M. Bateson (*Anecdota Oxoniensia*, ix), Oxford 1902, 5 (*ex actis eiusdem Joannis* [Whethamstede]); Hodge, 215–16.

Whethamstede either owned or could borrow: indeed, I know of no English manuscript.[61] Furthermore, whereas one can usually be fairly sure that Whethamstede had actually read what he cites because he gives either precise references or obvious quotations (this is the case with Alexander de Elpidio), no such thing is the case with James. Possibly therefore he only knew of this authority at second hand and the source could be the work of Adam Easton, in whose *Defensorium* James is used.[62]

In the case of Petrus de Palude the problem is different. Whethamstede had made a *tabula* of what is called his *De Ecclesiastica Potestate* and elsewhere there is a verifiable reference to Petrus's *De Potestate Pape* . . . or is it?[63] The problem is that two books passed for the work of Petrus in the fifteenth century, one, certainly his, being *De Potestate Pape*.[64] The other, much more common, is *De Causa Immediata Ecclesiastice Potestatis*, which is in fact by Guillaume de Pierre Godin.[65] Besides the attribution of this to Petrus in many manuscripts, the latter borrowed extensively from him, thus making identification more difficult. There is no English manuscript of the work by Petrus but there is one of the *De Causa*, which belonged to Philip Polton, nephew of Bishop Polton who owned the Constance *Acta* later used by Whethamstede, and attributing the work to Petrus de Palude.[66] Whethamstede was certainly quoting one or other work, and the balance is slightly in favour of *De Causa*, with the identification made more likely by the fact that *De Causa* was much the more common and by the title of the work indexed by Whethamsted.[67]

Whethamstede's fourth chosen viewpoint allowed the pope to hold possessions and indeed maintained that he had been given the whole of Western Europe by Constantine. This was evidently a moderate view of papal power,

---

[61] H.-X. Arquilliere, ed., *Le plus ancien traité de l'église, Jacques de Viterbe, De Regimine Christiano*, Paris 1926.

[62] For instance MS Vat. Lat. 4116 fo. 293r refers to James' opinion on the derivation of powers and fo. 297r on the origin of royal power.

[63] The *tabula*, Tanner 441, is said to be of *De Ecclesiastica Potestate*. Nero fo. 48r under *Chalcedon* has: *veluti testatur expresse Petrus de Palude Leoni pontifici Romane urbis acclamatum erat a clero his verbis: Leo sanctissimus apostolicus vivat per annos multos patriarcha universalis*. For this see Stella (as next note), 136, lines 25–7; McCready (as n. 65), 208, lines 610–12.

[64] Ed. P. T. Stella, Zurich, 1966.

[65] Ed. W. D. McCready, *The Theory of Papal Monarchy in the Fourteenth Century (Pontifical Institute of Medieval Studies, Studies and Texts* lvi), Toronto 1982.

[66] All Souls College, Oxford, MS 47 fos. 1r–75r. Polton died in 1461, McCready, 43–4. The whole is a composite manuscript. J. W. Eadie, *The Brevarium of Festus*, 1967, 29, suggested that it was a Duke Humfrey MS, but the Festus which Duke Humfrey was seeking from Pier Candido Decembrio was *De vocabulis* not *Brevarium*, cf. M. Borsa, 'The correspondence of Humphrey, Duke of Gloucester with Pier Candido Decembrio', *EHR* xix, 1904, 524; Sammut, 196.

[67] Use of the phrase (Gonville 256): *qui solutus est humanis legibus non tenetur in suo regimine obedire illis* suggests *De Causa*. Elsewhere W. quotes extensively from the section where this occurs (cf. v, lines 434–640 with Petrus 267) but although the whole section in *De Causa* is word for word in *De Potestate*, the borrowing by Godin stops short of the passage with this phrase, which thus seems unique to *De Causa*, v, line 663. I would like to thank Professor McCready for help.

giving pope and king separate spheres and not deriving the one from the other. The chief holders of these more moderate views were given as Dante, *De Monarchia*, Thomas, *De Potestate Papali*, Alvarus, *De Planctu Ecclesie* and Marsilius, *De Ecclesiastica Potestate*.

Not all of these references are as straightforward as they seem. Dante of course did write *De Monarchia* (*c.* 1313) but it is by no means certain that Whethamstede had read it.[68] The views of church property for example are not Dante's: at most he would allow the pope to receive property as a guardian and does not approve wholeheartedly of property-holding by the church.[69] Almost the only point on which Whethamstede's account and Dante agree is the derivation of the powers.[70] Knowledge of *De Monarchia* was very rare in fifteenth-century England and indeed the reference here has been taken as the very first mention.[71] Whethamstede certainly knew and read (in Latin) the *Commedia* and would know about Dante from Serravalle's commentary from Duke Humfrey's library, which he had certainly read.[72] But there is no evidence that either St Albans or Duke Humfrey's library included *De Monarchia*.[73] In fact a more likely source for a knowledge which was only superficial would again be Adam Easton's *Defensorium*, which Whethamstede had copied and for which he made a *tabula*.[74] In the extant portion of this enormous work Easton refers frequently to *De Monarchia*, in particular to those parts of Book 3 where the scriptural authorities which were used to support arguments that the church had both spiritual and temporal authority are refuted.[75]

A work by Thomas called *De Potestate Papali* ought to be by Aquinas, but he wrote no book on the papacy. A clue to the real identity of the work may

[68] Ed. P. G. Ricci, Verona 1965.

[69] *De Monarchia* III, x; Ricci, 256–61, esp. 259–60.

[70] *De Monarchia*, III, xiii–xvi; Ricci, 268–75.

[71] Weiss, 'Per la conoscenza di Dante in Inghilterra nel quattrocento', *Giornale Storico della Letteratura Italiana* cviii, 1936, 357–9, esp. 359.

[72] Weiss, 'Per la conoscenza', 359 and n. 6, with reference BL MS Add. 26764 fo. 79v (Howlett, 21, this is *Palarium*): *Vero quare omnes Romani pro maiori parte sunt binomii vide in Commento Johannis Ariminensis super Comediam Dantis capitulo sexto bene citra medium.* This is added as a footnote (Whethamstede's own). The reference is correct: see F. B. a Colle ed., *Fratris Johannis de Serravalle . . . translatio et commentum totius libri Dantis Aldhigheri*, Prato 1891, 886 (which is part III chapter 6). Similar correct ref. in footnote fo. 110v. For the commentary in Duke Humfrey's library see Sammut, 82–3.

[73] Sammut, 83 no. 259: Duke Humfrey owned a *librum Dantis, secundo folio a te*, which Paget Toynbee first (in a letter to the *Times Literary Supplement*, 15 March 1920, 187) identified with *De Monarchia* but finally (*ibid.*, 22 April, 256) with *Commedia* in Italian.

[74] For the work in St Albans *Amundesham* ii, 269; Howlett, 11; Tanner, 441. Under *Cardinalatus*, Nero fo. 35v he refers to *Cardinalis Norwycensium secunda parte sui defensorii capitulo decimo.* Only the prologue and Book I now remain (Vat. Lat. 4116, copied 1431–2). For references and extracts, Pantin, 'The *Defensorium* of Adam Easton', *EHR* li, 1936, 675–80.

[75] M. Grabmann, '*Das Defensorium ecclesiae* des Magister Adam, ein streitschrift gegen Marsilius von Padua und Wilhelm von Ockham', *Festschrift Albert Brackmann dargebracht*, ed. L. Santifaller, Weimer 1931, 569–81. Dante references: fo. 323r: *insuper Dans in libro suo de Monarchia Mundi libro tercio ostendit quod duo gladii, de quibus Lucas loquitur evangelista, non significant duplicem potestatem.* This is *Monarchia* III, ix, 1–8, Ricci, 251–3. Others: fos. 293r, 294r–95v, 299r, 325r.

come from a book with the title *De potestate papali* left to All Souls College Oxford by John Norfolk in 1467, which had as its *secundo folio: interdum contingit.*[76] This is the incipit of the *De Potestate Regia et Papali* by John of Paris, which is probably the notable tract *De Potestate papali et regali* which Whethamstede had had copied for St Albans.[77] This identification is made more likely when a comparison of John of Paris with Whethamstede's summary shows that Whethamstede seems to quote or paraphrase John. For instance he uses an example comparing the power of a *pater familias* with a *magister morum* and a *magister militum*. John uses the same illustration.[78] Likewise a reference to Pope Benedict IX and the way he was treated by the Emperor seems to come from John.[79]

Alvarus Pelayo, OFM, wrote *De Planctu* between 1330 and 1340.[80] Although there seem now to be no English manuscripts Whethamstede could have had access to this from the library of York, from which Piero da Monte was trying to borrow it in 1436.[81] Whethamstede was in touch with both da Monte and the abbot of York.[82] The summary of views certainly suggests that he had read it, though it is an oversimplification to suggest that it shared a viewpoint with the other works cited with it.[83] Whethamstede had certainly read and quotes accurately from Alvarus's *Collirium* which was one of his sources of information about the beliefs of the Greeks.[84]

Presumably Marsilius *De Ecclesiastica Potestate* is Marsilius of Padua's *Defensor Pacis*, written in 1324.[85] This seems to have become known in England only in the fifteenth century and the four extant English manuscripts are of that date, one owned by Thomas Gascoigne, Chancellor of Oxford, who died

[76] *BRUO* ii, 1363; N. Ker, *Records of All Souls College Library 1437–60* (*Oxford Bibliographical Society* n.s. ix), Oxford 1971, 18 no. 487 and Addenda 216.

[77] The John of Paris identification was first suggested to me by Professor J. A. Weisheipl, to whom I am most grateful. I have used J. Leclerq, *Jean de Paris et l'ecclésiologie du XIIIᵉ siècle*, Paris 1942, and F. Bleienstein, *Johannes Quidort uber königlich und papstliche Gewalt* (*Frankfurter Studien zur Wissenschaft von der Politik* iv), Stuttgart 1969. Extant MSS are listed by T. Kaeppelli, *Scriptores Ordinis Praedicatorum* ii, Rome 1975, 522. See Howlett, 180 no. 58.

[78] Gonville 260, from John, chapter 5: Leclerq, 184; Bleienstein, 88–9.

[79] Gonville 261, from John, chapter 22: Leclerq, 251; Bleienstein, 196.

[80] I have used Rocaberti, iii, 23–266 and checked with the ed. Lyons 1517. See N. Iung, *Un Franciscain theologien du pouvoir pontifical au XIVᵉ*, Alvaro Pelayo (*L'Eglise et L'Etat au moyen age* iii), Paris 1931, 46–52.

[81] Haller, *Piero da Monte*, 20 no. 30.

[82] Da Monte was in touch with W., e.g. Haller, 120–21 no. 108. As president of the English Black Monks W. was in touch with the abbot of York, *Benedictine Chapters* iii, 105 no. 262 and above n. 30.

[83] The second conclusion (that Christ acted sometimes as king, which shows that both roles derive immediately from him) suggests *De Planctu* caps. 51 and 56. On the other hand his statement that the Emperor holds the temporal sword immediately from Christ is not supported by the very confused exposition of Alvarus caps. 13, 37, 57. Iung quotes some of this, 142–3.

[84] Nero fo. 116v: *in Alvaro in suo Collirio parte sexta sparsim per totum*. The outline of part VI with a list of heresies is printed by Scholz, *Unbekannte* ii, 500–501. For the work see Iung, 59–63, with a list (not very reliable) of MSS, 62.

[85] Ed. R. Scholz (*Fontes Iuris Germanici Antiqui*) Hannover 1932. List of MSS, vii–xlv.

in 1458.[86] In many respects Marsilius's views did not agree with Whetham-stede's summary. For example Marsilius was very doubtful about the Donation of Constantine and at most conceded that it granted the pope certain provinces.[87] Marsilius certainly argued that the church ought to pay tribute to the Empire but did not conclude from this as Whethamstede did, that the church ought therefore to own its own property. He was in fact grudging about the church's right to property and argued against the legal distinction between use and ownership.[88] He would have allowed ecclesiastics what was necessary for their needs and to distribute alms but ownership of temporal goods remained vested in secular hands, with priests allowed a minimum. It is possible, therefore, that Marsilius is another writer whom Whethamstede did not know at first hand, and he could have been using the lost second part of Easton's *Defensorium*, which was devoted to a refutation of Marsilius.[89]

The fifth viewpoint is said to be supported by all the Greeks and by the author of *Dialogus inter Orthodoxum et Catechuminum*. The view summarised makes Peter *primus inter pares* and explains away all the texts used in the West to support Peter's primacy. Whethamstede seemed to be particularly impressed by historical evidence (from the Tripartite Chronicle) which showed that Peter did not preside at the first general council nor his successor at the next three: this he called a strong argument in favour of the view.[90] We have seen already how impressed he was by the historical explanation of the papal title.

The *Dialogus* was written in Siena, probably by the Dominican Bishop Michael Pelagallo, at a disputed date but probably 1388.[91] The writer was of the Roman obedience in the schism but markedly sympathetic to the Greek view of church government, with strong emphasis on the power of the local bishop and metropolitan as agents of reform. There are several references to the *Dialogus* elsewhere in the *Granarium* and the summary shows that Whethamstede had read it carefully.[92] Almost certainly he had had it copied, and it may have been among the volumes given by Duke Humfrey to Oxford in

---

[86] The Gascoigne MS is London, BL MS Royal 10 A XV, given by Gascoigne to Lincoln College, Oxford (Scholz, xxii).

[87] I xix 8, 131; II xxii 19, 437.

[88] II iv 9–10, 166–9; xiii *passim*, 275–300.

[89] Pantin, 'The Defensorium', 678.

[90] Gonville 262: *Tercia est talis et est fortis* . . . either the bishop of Alexandria or Antioch presided at Nicea, though proctors of the bishop of Rome were present, cf. Cassiodorus Epiphanius, *Historia Ecclesiastica Tripartita*, ed. W. Jacob and R. Hanslik (*Corpus Scriptorum Ecclesiasticorum Latinorum* lxxi), Vienna 1952, 82–3, 90.

[91] Kaeppelli, ii, 134–5; N. Valois, *La France et le Grand Schisme*, Paris 1896, i, 329, 398–9; Scholz, 'Eine Kirchenverfassung von Jahr 1406', in *Papsttum und Kaisertum. Forschungen . . . Paul Kehr zum 65. Geburtstag dargebracht*, ed. A. Brackmann, Munich 1926, 595–621. The dating argument based on Vatican Reg. Lat. 715 fo. 55r, which Scholz uses, is almost certainly wrong because this seems merely a note of when the MS was completed. When talking of why the French king took the side he did (Reg. Lat. fo. 41v; Emmanuel 9 fo. 202v) Book IV cap 15, the author refers to Charles VI as still under age, though he must have been writing in or before 1388.

[92] I have looked at Vatican Reg. Lat. 715; BL MS Harley 631 fos. 1r–40r (Scholz, *Defensor Pacis*, xxiii) and Emmanuel 9 fos. 176r–207v. The references elsewhere in W. are Nero fo. 33v, fo. 35v and Arundel fo. 125r. These are all correct.

1444.[93] It was probably not widely known in England (I know of only two English manuscripts) but it was diffused at the council of Basel and may have become more widely known because of that.[94]

Whethamstede was certainly interested in the Greeks. It is worth mentioning here that he frequently cites a work which he calls *De Erroribus Grecorum*, which appears to be the 1252 tract *Contra Grecos* of which he seems to have owned a copy: at least some of what he says seems to be direct quotation.[95] This work was one of the main sources of information about the Greeks at both Constance and Basel and several churchmen at those councils owned copies.[96] This is another example of how well read Whethamstede was in the literature of current controversy, though it is more unusual to find him sympathetic to the Greek view.

The final opinion is the Conciliar Theory, which, as Whethamstede says, is famous these days.[97] He summarises it by saying that it gives the pope plenitude of power on condition that he does not deviate from the faith nor pertinaciously scandalise the church with enormous crimes. In those two cases a general council is more powerful and can correct the pope or even, if necessary, depose him. Upholders of the view support themselves by quoting *Dist.* 93, *c.* 24 (Jerome's dictum that the world is greater than the city); from the argument that Christ's church must be a perfect society and could not be so if the pope could get away with criminal, incorrigible actions; and from the decree *Haec Sancta* passed by a general council which could not err. The decree is quoted verbatim.[98] The corollary of these views is that the council can correct and depose the pope, that if he resists the secular arm can be used against him and that if he refuses to call a council or dissolves it too quickly he can be corrected, suspended or even deposed.

---

[93] In the list of books copied for St Albans, given by Howlett from the badly burned BL MS Cotton Otto B IV, 180 no. 58 is *de deceptacione inter ortodoxum et orth (   )um*. Sammut, 73 no. 141 *ierarchiam subcelestiam* is probably this though I have not yet found the *incipit*.

[94] M. Steinmann, 'Altere theologische Literatur am Basler Konzil', in *Xenia Medii Aevi historiam illustrantia oblata T. Kaeppelli (Storia e Letteratura* cxlii), Rome 1978, 471–82, esp. 477.

[95] A poor version in *PG* cxl, cols. 487–574. On it see A. Dondaine, 'Contra Graecos, Premiers écrits polemiques des Dominicains d'Orient', *Archivum Fratrum Praedicatorum* xxi, 1951, 320–446. Refs. are Nero fo. 115v, 116v, 137r. Evidence of direct quotation e.g. On purgatory:

Nero fo. 115r	PG cxl col. 487
De tercio quo asserunt	
defunctorum animas nec	defunctorum animas nec
paradisi perfrui gaudiis	paridisi gaudiis perfrui
nec inferni seu purgatorii	nec infernorum supliciis
cruciari supliciis quousque	vel igne purgatorio citra
dominus ad adjudicandum	diem judicii aut ante latam
venerit et extremam tulerit	sententiam extremam
sententiam iuxta quod meritum	judiciis posse
uniuscuiusque aut demeritum	subjacere
exigit et requirit.	

[96] Dondaine, 425.

[97] Gonville 266: *quorum opinio famosior est hiis diebus.*

[98] Gonville 268.

Whethamstede's final comment was that these views are more acceptable and approved among catholics these days, which suggests that he too thought they were acceptable, though we know that he did not approve of the actions of Basel against Eugenius IV which were justified with his final argument.[99]

So Whethamstede was a conciliarist, if rather a confused one. He seems to have been convinced by the decrees of what he considered to be general councils and by arguments from history. What strikes one is how very well read he was, yet how very often he seems to have interpreted his sources to suit himself . . . and, of course, like many medieval writers he was not as well read as he seems. What is next needed is to discover how many English contemporaries were as well read, and, if any were, what they made of their reading.

Department of History, Durham University

---

[99] Gonville 270: *et est hec opinio acceptior probaciorque apud varios et precipue apud Catholicos hiis diebus;* and above n. 53.

Chantries, Obits and Almshouses:
The Hungerford Foundations 1325–1478[1]

MICHAEL HICKS

The new foundations of late medieval England are a neglected field of study. This is understandable, since the largest and best documented institutions were already ancient. The few later foundations of comparable size have not been overlooked. Large and imposing as university colleges and Henry V's abbeys were, however, they were not representative of late medieval benefactions, which were typified instead by almshouses, by schools and above all by chantries. Pioneering surveys of such categories have not been adequately followed up and the direction of much recent research has been away, towards specific status groups and classes of record. Both approaches are valuable and indeed complementary: without some understanding of the institutions themselves, breakdowns of benefactors and types of benefaction are little use. Nevertheless there are methodological drawbacks to each method: concentration on the fullest records or those most susceptible to quantitative analysis involves a loss of context and hence of relevant source material. The study of foundations in the round, using all the available evidence, offers a chance of fuller knowledge and understanding. This is the justification of the case study of restricted scope, which treats foundations within a natural geographical, institutional or intellectual framework – such as the city or county of York. Strangely there is still no case study of the most natural group of all – the foundations of a particular family – even though the family is accepted as an appropriate unit for economic, political and social history.

This paper fills the gap by studying the new foundations of the Hungerford family in the later middle ages. Emerging from obscurity only in the early

[1] Unless otherwise stated, all places are in Wiltshire and all documents cited are in the PRO.

fourteenth century, the Hungerfords reached the peerage in 1426 and weathered with difficulty the Wars of the Roses. Professor Rosenthal has identified them as notable benefactors of the Church and twelve chantries, seven obits, and two almshouses feature in this account.[2] The Hungerfords were lavish benefactors of the most conventional type.

TABLE I: The Hungerfords.

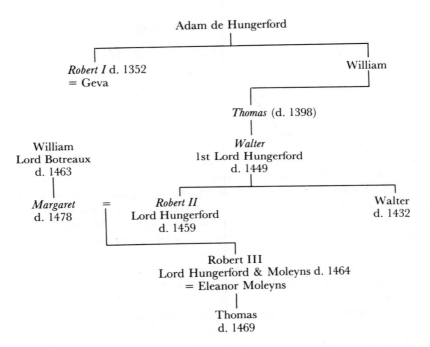

Dr Raban has shown that information on foundations derives mainly from two sources, the records of the crown and those of the Church.[3] This article has relied equally on the records of the patrons, comprising the Hungerford cartularies, estate accounts, deeds and wills. This third source not only yields more accurate evidence of particular foundations, but it facilitates interpretation by supplying the context specifically relevant in each case. A fresh approach can cast new light on familiar topics of broader significance, such as attitudes to inherited obligations, the financing of foundations, and alienation in mortmain. This study therefore amplifies and occasionally corrects the more wide-ranging surveys of other historians.

[2] J. T. Rosenthal, *Purchase of Paradise: Gift Giving and the Aristocracy*, 1972, 50–51.
[3] S. Raban, *Mortmain Legislation and the English Church 1279–1500*, Cambridge 1982, 10.

While ranging over the whole period, this study concentrates on the fifteenth-century foundations of Walter, Lord Hungerford (d. 1449) and his daughter-in-law Margaret (d. 1478). The first part is a chronological account of the individual foundations and contains the raw material for two substantial sections of conclusions.

TABLE II: Hungerford Foundations and Bequests.

		Robert d. 1352	Thomas d. 1398	Joan d. 1412	Walter d. 1449	Robert d. 1459	Margaret d. 1478
Religious houses:							
Benedictines	Bath (Soms.)				F		x
	Canterbury (Kent)				f		
Benedictine nuns	Amesbury (Wilts.)				x	x	
Cistercians	Stanley (Wilts.)	F					
Augustinian	Bruton (Soms.)				x		
	Edington (Wilts.)		F		x	x	x
	Ivychurch (Wilts.)	F					
	Launceston (Corn.)						x
	Lesnes (Kent)		F				
	Llanthony (Gloucs.)	f					
	Longleat (Wilts.)		F	x	x		
	Maiden Bradley (Wilts.)				x	x	x
Augustinian nuns	Lacock (Wilts.)				x		
Carthusians	Henton (Soms.)				x	x	
	Sheen (Surr.)				x		
	Witham (Soms.)					x	
Bridgettines	Syon (Middx.)						x
Trinitarians	Easton (Wilts.)	F					
	Hounslow (Middx.)						x
Dominicans	Bodmin (Corn.)				x		f
	Exeter (Devon)				x		
	Ilchester (Soms.)				x		x
	Salisbury (Wilts.)				x	x	x
Franciscans	Bridgwater (Soms.)				x		x
	Salisbury (Wilts.)					x	
Carmelites	Marlborough (Wilts.)				x		x
All friars	Bristol (Gloucs.)				x		
	Cambridge (Cam.)						x
	Exeter (Devon)				x		
	London				x		
	Oxford (Oxon.)				x		
Secular churches:							
Cathedrals	Salisbury (Wilts.)	F		x	f F	x	F
	Wells (Soms.)			x	x		
Colleges	Heytesbury (Wilts.)			x	x		
	Merton (Oxon.)				x		
	Salisbury, St Edmund (Wilts.)				x		
	Westminster (Middx.)				F		
Hospitals	Bedlam (Lond.)					x	
	Bradford (Soms.)					x	
	Calne (Wilts.)	F					
	Heytesbury (Wilts.)				F	x	x .

Parish churches							
Chippenham (Wilts.)					F	F	
Farleigh (Soms.)		x	x	2F	x		
Hungerford (Berks.)	F						
Salisbury (Wilts.):							
St Clement				x		x	
St Martin				x		x	
St Thomas			x		x	x	
Teffont Evias (Wilts.)			x	x			
Wellow (Soms.)				x	x	x	

Road: Standerwick causeway (Soms.).

Sources: foundations and wills.

Key: F = foundation; x denotes bequest; f = confraternity.

Walter (d. 1449) made bequests to a further 18 churches, Margaret to St Martin's Ludgate, the anchorite of London wall, and prisoners in two Salisbury gaols.

Sir Robert de Hungerford (Robert I, d. 1352) founded four chantries: at Holy Trinity chapel in Hungerford church (1326), where he was buried; at Salisbury cathedral (1334), where a capitular nominee celebrated for the souls of him and Archdeacon Walter de Hervy; at St Edmund's chapel in Calne church (1336), where the cantarist was nominated by (or perhaps was) the warden of the nearby hospital of St John and St Anthony; and at the Trinitarian friary at Easton, where Robert gave only £1 0s 4d income to endow an extra brother. Although a fifth chantry at the Augustinian priory of Ivychurch (1321) was stillborn, an obit was founded there in 1336 and the priory paid the pension that supported the cathedral cantarist. There was a second obit at the Cistercian abbey of Stanley.

A man of limited means, Robert put off alienating his endowments and some never reached the intended recipients. A royal licence to alienate a Salisbury messuage to Stanley Abbey was secured in 1331, but it had not been conveyed at Robert's death and could not then be completed, as no licence was forthcoming: this may indicate refusal by the immediate overlord, the bishop of Salisbury, or the expiry on Robert's death of the royal licence. Instead the property was sold and the abbey accepted the proceeds as endowment for the obit. In two cases, at Easton and Calne, the income was too small to support a priest and Easton in particular had a bad bargain, since it presumably paid Robert's £3 life annuity for sixteen years. The penalties imposed for non-performance were severe, in two cases tantamount to disendowment, which actually befell at Calne a century later.[4]

Robert's nephew Thomas bestowed his favours elsewhere. In 1365 he founded an obit for himself, his first wife, parents and uncle at the priory of Bonshommes at Edington. In 1377 a chantry at the Austin abbey of Lesnes (Kent) was his price for the quitclaim of the manor of Northwood in Lesnes. Thirdly, his will ordained a chantry at Longleat priory, near his residence at

---

[4] *VCH Wilts* iii, 291n, 325, 334; *CPR 1324–27*, 191; SRO, DD/SAS H348 (hereafter Hungerford cartulary), fos. 259v–60, 262.

Heytesbury.[5] He was actually buried at Farleigh Hungerford (Soms.) in the north chapel of St Anne, which he added in the 1380s to the parish church he had earlier rebuilt. His widow Joan provided in her will for the foundation of a chantry there for their souls and those of her ancestors.[6]

Thomas did not manage to complete his foundations in his own lifetime. It was to support two further canons that he had enfeoffed North Tidworth manor to the use of Longleat priory. By 1401 the priory had sold it for £106 13s 4d, which it lent to Walter for his pilgrimage to Jerusalem. In 1407 Walter was licensed to appropriate Rushall church to Longleat and in 1410 conveyed it the advowson and prescribed the ordinances of the chantry. Yet in spite of episcopal approval, no appropriation occurred. Walter later blamed his failure on an entail, not new but old and hence unbreakable, which certainly did exist.[7] His failure was surely fortunate for Longleat, since the endowment was inadequate for the commitments. Rushall church, taxed at only £10 before the establishment of a vicarage, was sufficient endowment only for one chaplain and North Tidworth was worth even less. Probably no chantry was established, since it passed unnoticed among Joan's bequests to Longleat in 1411 and £106 13s 4d remained due in 1449, when Walter ordered its repayment – without interest – subject to the return of the relevant deeds, the advice of Salisbury cathedral chapter, but apparently not to the establishment of his father's chantry.

In her will Joan required Walter to found a chantry at Farleigh with two hundred marks (£133 6s 8d) already in his hands. Although nothing permanent was done until 1426, Thomas's obit was scrupulously kept meanwhile.[8] By 1429 a daily mass was said by John the chaplain, perhaps John Gody, first perpetual chaplain, who was paid £2 salary and one shilling a week board, total £4 12s. Joan's scanty endowment and Walter's public commitments may have contributed to the delay, but another factor was probably the difficulty and/or cost of securing a royal licence to alienate in mortmain. Such licences almost dried up in Henry V's last years and Henry VI's minority council was anxious to keep the young king's rights

[5] J. S. Roskell, *Parliament and Politics in Late Medieval England*, 1981, ii, 37; Hungerford cartulary, fos. 261v–3; see below. Northwood had belonged to Thomas's parents, *HMCR* lxxviii, *Hastings* i, 215–16.

[6] R. Wilcox, 'Excavations at Farleigh Hungerford Castle, Somerset, 1973–6', *Somerset Archaeology and Natural History* cxxiv, 1981, 87–94; *Farleigh Hungerford Castle* (DOE Guide, 1979), 4; N. Pevsner, *North Somerset and Bristol*, Harmondsworth 1958, 191–2.

[7] Lambeth P(alace) L(ibrary), Reg. of Archbishop Stafford fo. 115; *CCR 1399–1402*, 325; *CPR 1405–8*, 384; *Reg. Hallum* nos. 1071–2; Salisbury C(athedral) M(uniments), Reg. Viringe p. 30; Devizes Museum (Canon Jackson's) Hungerford (Family) Collections, Places iii, fos. 57–8. For what follows, see K. L. Wood-Legh, *Perpetual Chantries in Britain*, Cambridge 1965, *passim*; J. I. Kermode, 'The Merchants of three northern towns', *Profession, Vocation and Culture in Later Medieval England*, ed. C. H. Clough, Liverpool 1982, 25.

[8] *Test. Vet.* i, 181; PRO, SC 6/970/29 m.3; /971/2 m.3d. In 1429 93 priests and 363 paupers attended and in 1430, 43 priests and 572 paupers (PRO SC 6/1119/9 m.2; Devizes Museum, Hungerford Colls., Personal i, 126). For what follows, see Hungerford Colls., Personal i, 133.

intact until he came of age, so the number of such licences dwindled.[9] Soon after becoming a councillor, Walter agreed to serve abroad at a council meeting on 18 February 1423, which was dominated by the concessions that he extracted for going. Among these the council agreed to his performance of a vow on his return.[10] While the vow is unspecified, surely only a licence to alienate would have required conciliar approval for its fulfilment? If so, it was not redeemed until 14 June 1426, when Walter had just become a baron and as treasurer of England was particularly influential.

By advice and assent of the great council the licence allowed alienation of £10 revenue for a chantry at the altar of St Mary, not St Anne, Farleigh Hungerford for the benefit of the souls of the king, Walter and his wife, his parents, their ancestors and all the faithful dead.[11] In 1431 the foundation deed ordained services for the souls of Walter, his wife, his parents, ancestors and all the faithful departed, but not for the king. The endowment comprised a house and £8 income, from which was to be paid the cantarist's salary, essential expenses and repairs, and the cost of Thomas's obit. Each 2 December the chaplain and seven other priests were to repeat matins and evensong of the dead and on 3 December, the anniversary proper, each was to say mass separately. For this the cantarist was to provide dinner and pay each priest 4d; thirteen paupers were to receive 1d each to pray for Thomas's soul and four others 1d each to remember him.

From 1428 the rector of Farleigh was also obliged to celebrate Thomas's obit at his own expense: he and seven other priests were to say the services of the dead the night before and a mass each on 3 December, each priest receiving dinner and 4d; another thirteen paupers were to receive 1d each; and two 1 lb tapers were supplied. This stemmed from the union of Farleigh with the adjoining parish of Rowley, across the boundary with Wiltshire and the diocese of Salisbury. Rowley was a deserted village with a rectory worth only 15s, too little for any rector to reside. Immediately after acquiring the advowson, Walter applied for the union of Rowley with Farleigh. The parishioners of Rowley agreed on conditions, which included the preservation of their church and the upkeep of the chancel by the rector of the combined living. As justification the bishop of Bath and Wells cited the pastoral needs of the people of Rowley and the poverty of the rector of Farleigh – a somewhat hollow claim in view of the extra burdens imposed. Over a third of the rector's extra income was appropriated to particular expenses and he and his successors were henceforth bound by oath on institution to observe the new arrangements on pain of a fine to the Wells cathedral fabric.[12] The real

[9] Griffiths, *Henry VI*, 88.
[10] Roskell ii, 113; *PPC* iii, 37–8.
[11] *CPR 1422–29*, 347. For what follows, see J. E. Jackson, *Guide to Farleigh Hungerford*, Chippenham 1879, 110–34.
[12] J. E. Jackson, 'Rowley *alias* Wittenham', *WAM* xiii (1872), 230–31, 235, 238–48; Salisbury CM, Reg. Harding fo. 92v.

beneficiary was Walter himself, who secured a splendid obit for his father at no cost to himself.

In 1426 Walter intended endowing his Farleigh chantry himself, but actually provided only a house, the balance being a pension of £8 from Bath cathedral priory, which also agreed to celebrate the obits of Walter, his wife and parents at an annual cost of £1.[13] This was not just another pension financed by alienations to a religious house, for it emanated from Olveston church (Gloucs.), part of the priory's preconquest estate. The exceptionally full documentation does not mention any consideration paid by Walter to justify acceptance by the monastery of perpetual commitments of £9 a year, a life pension of £32 above £20 stipend for the vicar, and the heavy cost of appropriation from a living worth only £21 4s 8d to it at the dissolution. It already enjoyed a pension of three and a half marks (£2 6s 8d) from the living and had fought off a challenge to its patronage in 1352.[14] Probably Bath priory already wished to appropriate the church, but could not because a royal licence was refused or was too expensive. Walter, however, already had a licence and as royal councillor and treasurer could have it adjusted to permit the appropriation. The council's warrant to the chancellor prescribed a reasonable fine, but in spite of the earlier licence, £40 was charged – four years' income: what would a wholly new licence have cost?[15] If this interpretation is correct, Walter paid for his chantry and obit by exercising his influence in council.[16]

At that same 1423 council meeting Salisbury cathedral chapter was licensed to acquire £50 income for the repair of the spire and for the increase of divine worship for the soul of the king and the donors of such new endowment. Walter was present and, as a member of the cathedral confraternity, presumably supported the application.[17] Perhaps he hoped to benefit from it and had already reached an understanding with the chapter. However that may be, it was under this blanket authority that in 1427 he was licensed to alienate to the cathedral land and the advowson of St Sampson's church, Cricklade and to appropriate the church. The gift was worth £16 13s 8d and the fine was £33 6s 8d, two years' purchase. In 1429 the property was conveyed, St Sampson's church was appropriated, and the chapter were bound to maintain a chantry of two priests, Walter's obit, and to mention him and his wife in their Sunday litanies. The chapter supplied a house in the close, subject to rent for earlier obits, and Walter erected a chantry chapel in the north nave arcade. Those commemorated were Henry V and Henry VI, Walter and his spouse, their heirs, his parents and grandparents, and his

---

[13] Jackson, *Farleigh Hungerford*, 112–17, 129–30, 133–4.
[14] Jackson, *Farleigh Hungerford*, 133–4; *VCH Somerset* ii, 78; *Monasticon* ii, 273; BL MS Egerton 3316 fos. 79v, 93v.
[15] PRO, C 81/690/2006–7; *CPR 1422–9*, 541–2.
[16] This point is expanded below, pp. 139–40.
[17] Salisbury CM, Reg. Pountney p. 1; *CPR 1422–9*, 70; *PPC* iii, 37–8.

great-uncle Robert I and great-aunt Geva. Of the actual income of £30 9s 2d, £16 was to be paid to the chaplains, £1 6s 8d was for essential expenses, £4 4s at least was for Walter's obit, and only £2 specifically for the spire. Should the endowment prove too little, it was the money for the belltower, doles and repairs that was to be withdrawn first.[18]

Heytesbury church housed an ancient secular college and lay within the peculiar of the dean of Salisbury, who was also dean of Heytesbury. There were two chantries dedicated to St Mary and St Katherine, of which the former was in Hungerford patronage by 1408. It was presumably with the dean's approval that Walter used an embassy to the Council of Constance to secure a bull transferring the chantry to his oratory at Heytesbury, which he proposed developing into a chantry college with more chaplains and clerks. This was justified, quite untruthfully, by poverty so grave 'that for a long time no priest has celebrated in it'. The prior of Bath, nominated to investigate, duly appeared at Heytesbury in 1415–16, but the scheme was stillborn.

In 1438 Walter proposed the union of the two Heytesbury chantries with another at Upton Scudamore, Robert I's at Calne, and the free chapel of Corston in Hillmarton, the latter three of Walter's patronage and all said to be too poor to support chaplains. Inquiries revealed all to be impoverished, with incomes ranging from 8s to £3 10s, but some did have incumbents. If amalgamated, they would provide a comfortable income of £8 1s 4d and a house for a single chaplain.

By contemporary standards the Hungerfords were a charitable family. Thomas supported ten paupers at Farleigh in 1377–78 and he, his wife and son all left money for their poor tenants. All Walter's foundations provided for charitable distributions and by 1428 he was pensioning thirteen paupers on his estates at 4d a week each, 17s 4d a year. It was logical to bring these pensioners together in a hospital, which he built at Heytesbury by 1442. Only on 19 July 1442 did Bishop Aiscough annex Corston chapel, Calne and Upton chantries to St Mary's chantry, Heytesbury, whose chaplain was henceforth to commemorate all the founders. Four days later Walter declared his trust, instructing his feoffees to hold two manors until they were licensed to amortise them to Heytesbury hospital. Meanwhile they were to pay £23 6s 8d annually to support twelve almsmen and two almswomen in his new hospital and to perform other almsdeeds on particular days for the soul of Walter and others specified. To this combined almshouse and chantry Walter had added a school by his death in 1449. One of a group of five such foundations established in 1422–42 by Walter and his associates in govern-

---

[18] *CPR 1422–9*, 390; H. de S. Shortt, *Hungerford and Beauchamp Chantry Chapels*, Salisbury 1970, 2–4; Salisbury CM, Reg. Harding fo. 43; Hungerford cartulary fos. 250–5v. For the next three paragraphs, see M. A. Hicks, 'St. Katherine's Hospital, Heytesbury: Prehistory, Foundation and Re-foundation 1408–72', *WAM* lxxviii (1984), 62–9.

ment, Heytesbury was undoubtedly influenced by Henry VI's college at Eton.

Heytesbury hospital was one of Walter's three later foundations. In 1441 a second chantry at St Mary's altar, Farleigh Hungerford was licensed to acquire £10 income. Those commemorated were King Henry V, King Henry VI, Walter and his first wife, his parents and ancestors. No fine was charged for the first licence, but fines were levied in ancillary licences and one alienation was rated higher than the inquisition valuation. Walter soon appreciated that his two chantry chaplains sufficed to staff the tiny church of Farleigh Hungerford if it was relieved of its parochial responsibilities. These were no doubt inconvenient, since it now lay within Walter's new outer ward of the castle. By 1443 he had rebuilt the parish church at a distance and had taken over the old church at his chapel. Apparently the second chaplain was transferred from St Mary's altar to the high or St Leonard's altar.[19]

St Mary's chantry in the south chapel of Chippenham church was founded jointly by Walter and his son Robert II. In 1442 they were licensed to alienate £10 income to a priest to sing for the souls of Henry V, Henry VI, Walter and his first wife Katherine, Robert II, Walter's other children and ancestors. Already complete in 1442, the chapel was endowed in 1447. £11 11s fine was charged.

Walter's standard endowment of a house and £8 stipend was unusually generous. His Salisbury chantry stands apart, since the chapter took on the selection and oversight of chaplains, which Walter therefore did not need to regulate. Two candidates were nominated by the chapter at each vacancy for Walter to select from. His other chantries were free-standing corporations, fully constituted benefices requiring episcopal institution, and were in his gift. In general his statutes made commonplace provision for visitations, preservation of property, and for the prevention of pluralism and exchanges. They were not particularly stringent, the chaplains being allowed to hold compatible offices of the Hungerford family and to have female visitors to stay. In Walter's lavish and wide-ranging will, his chantries took pride of place. He ordered his executors to remedy any deficiencies in statutes, endowments or equipment, and he assigned to his foundations first claim on his residuary estate.[20]

The principal obligation Walter left was the endowment of Heytesbury hospital, which eventually devolved on his daughter-in-law Margaret. The chantry, almshouse and school were united by 1454 in a single person, the *Magister Scolarum*, who maintained both paupers and chantry. Robert II had asked, so Margaret also claimed, that the endowment be completed and in

[19] *CPR 1441–6*, 94–5, 269, 327; *Reg. Bekynton* i, 3; *Survey and Rentals of Chantries, Colleges and Free Chapels*, ed. E. Green (SRS, ii), 1888, no. 119; *Reg. Stillington*, 2, 30, 33. For the next paragraph, see *CPR 1441–6*, 151; PRO, C 143/450/27.

[20] Jackson, *Farleigh Hungerford*, 118–27; *Reg. King*, 158; Hungerford cartulary, fos. 252–5v. For the next paragraph, see Hicks, *WAM* lxxviii, 64–6.

1469 she secured the consent of the Duke of Gloucester, holder of the reversion of her estates, who promised

> to be mediator and meanes to the kinges highnes and his effectual labour and diligence to get the kynges licence thereof in due fourme to be made within the space of xij monthes next folowyng or rather if he godely can or may at the costes of the said Margaret.

Edward IV signed the agreement, but it was not until 1472 that the licence was secured, endowment conveyed, and statutes compiled. The foundation now consisted of twelve poor men and only one woman, perhaps from economy, more probably because thirteen was the number commonly favoured in imitation of Christ and the Apostles.

Although not executrix to her father Lord Botreaux, Margaret inherited obligations on his death. In 1449 Lord Botreaux, his heirs and assigns were licensed to alienate 100 marks (£66 13s 4d) revenue to any religious house of his choice and in 1459 he initiated a series of inquisitions *ad quod dampnum* into his proposals to alienate lands in Somerset and Hampshire to Bath cathedral priory. In 1458–59 he ordained a chantry there and evidently also erected an almshouse for thirteen poor men.[21] Some properties may have been formerly alienated at his death, since they were held by the priory's feoffees in 1481, but others were recovered by his daughter and sold. It is not known what befell the chantry, but the almshouse was disendowed. Margaret had already decided not to complete it in 1469 and probably earlier, since the thirteen paupers of the first half of 1464–65 dwindled to twelve in the third quarter, eleven in the final quarter and, on average, only ten in 1468–69. In 1477 Margaret ordered

> þat my Fathers poremen at Bath be paide yerely every oon jd a day according to my saide lordes ordynaunce yerely duryng þe lyff of þe personys þat now remayneth þer and afterward to cesse.[22]

The almshouse does not recur.

By will of 1459 Robert II asked for burial before the altar of the newly canonised St Osmund in Salisbury cathedral. His wish was performed: in 1464–65 and 1468–69 a chaplain was celebrating there.[23] From 1469 on Margaret claimed that Robert had asked in his will for the foundation of a chantry of two priests there. No such provision appears in his will, otherwise lavish in pious bequests, and the proximity in date of his death renders such a change of plan unlikely. Certainly the form of the chantry was determined by Margaret. Dedicated to Jesus and the Virgin, it was housed in a new chapel abutting on the north side of the Lady Chapel in mirror image of the

---

[21] W. Dugdale, *Baronage of England*, 1675, i, 630; *CPR 1446–52*, 230; PRO, C 143/452/20, /30. For the next sentence, see *Anc. Deeds* iii, A5499; *CCR 1461–8*, 334–5.

[22] BL MS Cotton Julius BXII fo. 123; PRO, SC 6/1061/21 m.2; SC 6/1119/15 m.4; Devizes Museum, Hungerford Colls., Personal i, fo. 270v.

[23] *Som. Med. Wills, 1383–1500*, 186; PRO, SC 6/1119/14 m.4, /15 m.4.

Beauchamp Chapel of 1461 to the south. Chapel, altar and tomb were consecrated in 1471 by Bishop Beauchamp himself. Robert II's effigy was placed in an arch in the south wall overlooking both the new altar and, presumably, that of St Osmund. In 1472 Margaret was licensed to alienate forty marks (£26 13s 4d) revenue to Salisbury cathedral and conveyed to it the manors of Folke (Dors.), Imber and Winterbourne Homington and her two free chapels of Imber and Folke. She declared her statutes in the cathedral chapter house. Imber chapel was appropriated in 1474. Altogether the Hungerford chapel cost £823 to build and equip. The foundation deed named as beneficiaries Margaret and Robert II, their parents, John Cheyne and John Mervyn co-feoffees and co-founders, the king, Bishop Beauchamp and Dean Goldwell, but the prescribed prayers commemorated only Margaret and Robert II, their parents and children, and all those for whom they were bound to pray.[24]

Margaret's other benefaction was at Syon Abbey, where she was confined in 1470. She left her heart for burial there and paid £100 'et vltra' for the insertion in the Syon martyrology of herself, Robert II, Walter, Robert III and her grandson, all Lords Hungerford.[25]

The twenty-one statutes of Margaret's chantry at Salisbury are more detailed and exacting than those of Walter's comparable foundation and forty-eight provided for Heytesbury hospital. They share a common core of twelve. Margaret relied for continuity after death on Salisbury cathedral chapter rather than her heirs, who were not to be patrons. The chapter would collate to the chantry and the hospital was in the gift of the cathedral chancellor if resident, of the chapter if not. The chapter could remove cantarists and the hospital keeper not just for notorious crime, but for waste and immoral conduct. Supervision of the chantry was easy, but at Heytesbury Margaret offered financial inducements for annual visitations by the dean's official. Although a remarkably rigorous *code*, the individual regulations against waste and for management of the poor are commonplace.

Whereas the Salisbury cantarists had purely liturgical functions, the Heytesbury keeper was expected to say mass daily, to teach daily except on Sundays and feast days when he joined in matins, high mass and evensong in the church, and to manage the almshouse. Outside vacation, his freedom was extremely restricted. For these reasons the post was difficult to fill, even though the salary – £16 8s 8d with house and £1 for a servant – was double that of the Salisbury cantarists. Those commemorated were Robert II and Margaret, their parents, their ancestors, descendants and 'all the soulis thei

---

[24] C. Wordsworth, *Ceremonies and Processions of the Cathedral Church of Salisbury*, Cambridge 1901, 286; BL MS Cotton Julius BXII fo. 123; W(iltshire) RO, 490/1465d; WRO Registrum Rubrum, fos. 140–42; Hungerford cartulary, fos. 317v–27, 345–62; *CCR 1468–76*, no. 1122; see also R. C. Hoare, *History of Modern Wiltshire*, 6 vols. 1822–40, i (2), 128, 130.

[25] BL MS Add. 22285, fos. 49v, 71. The next three paragraphs are based on J. E. Jackson, 'Ancient Statutes of Heytesbury Almshouse', *WAM* xi, 1869, 289–308; Hungerford cartulary, fos. 322a–24; *VCH Wilts* iii, 337–8; Wordsworth, *Ceremonies*, 285–6.

be bounde to pray for', and Margaret's co-feoffees Cheyne and Mervyn.

Several statutes reflect Margaret's modification of Walter's intentions. Apart from Walter and his wife, those commemorated cannot be those whom Walter had in mind and the beneficiaries of the dissolved former chantries were omitted. Margaret's stress on the Virgin's chastity recurs in the statutes and her cult of Jesus no doubt explains her insistence on unmarried almsmen, on the restriction of numbers to thirteen, insisted on in her statutes, and in the emblazoning on their gowns of JHU.XRT. (Jesus Christ). St Katherine is not mentioned.[26]

This study illuminates the Hungerfords as religious patrons. They held many advowsons of parish churches, chantries and monasteries and acquired others deliberately, rather than as mere appendages to particular manors. Presentations advanced clients ranging from household chaplains to future bishops and a few were promoted from living to living. Naturally such dependants looked for patronage to the Hungerfords, who accepted their responsibilities and acted on them. Their arms on churches of their patronage, as at St Sampson, Cricklade, imply contributions to the fabric like those known elsewhere from their wills and accounts. They wholly rebuilt Farleigh church at least once and probably twice. Their bequests of vestments and ornaments, like Robert II's provision of a chalice for St Anne's, Teffont, often reveal first-hand knowledge of particular local needs. Over three generations they relieved their poorer tenants through bequests, through pensions and ultimately through collecting them in Heytesbury hospital. Only Margaret, however, seems to have patronised churches primarily because they were in her patronage and even her will benefited other institutions. The Hungerford arms feature on the Lacock Abbey cloisters, on the tower of St Andrew, Chippenham and at Mickle Hall, Oxford, none of which were of Hungerford foundation.[27] Some family livings were hardly patronised at all: in particular the chantries of their predecessors were generally neglected.

Neglect, however, was preferable to being sacrificed to higher priorities. Like other patrons, the Hungerfords often presented to their livings those who were certain to be absentees. They did not hesitate to employ parochial incumbents as household chaplains, receivers-general and in other posts necessitating non-residence.[28] Indeed many of their churches were scheduled

[26] Hicks, *WAM* lxxviii, 67–9. Unless otherwise stated, the rest of this article is based on the preceding sections and wills in Lambeth PL, Reg. Stafford fos. 115–16v; Reg. Arundel, ii, fo. 152; *Som. Med. Wills, 1383–1500*, 186–93; Hoare, *Wiltshire*, i (2), 95–100; Devizes Museum, Hungerford Colls., Personal i, fos. 271v–6; table II.

[27] J. E. Jackson, 'On the History of Chippenham', *WAM* iii, 1857, 43; J. M. Fletcher, 'The Tomb of Lord Walter Hungerford K.G. in Salisbury Cathedral', *WAM* xlvii, 1935–37, 448; Roskell, *Parliament and Politics* ii, 99.

[28] E.g. John Pratt, rector of Winterbourne Homington and household chaplain of Joan Hungerford, and John Carter, rector of Camerleton and receiver-general to Walter.

for appropriation, notably parish churches at Blunsdon St Andrew, Rushall, Cricklade and Rowley and free chapels at Corston in Hillmarton, Imber and Folke (Dors.), with potentially adverse effects on the ministry to the laity. They also suppressed chantries at Heytesbury, Upton Scudamore and Calne, diverting the endowments to other purposes. The standard justification for this, that the livings could not be filled and that divine service was thereby increased, is sometimes demonstrably untrue. The Hungerfords had to submit to local inquiries, where their arguments could be refuted and local opposition expressed. Where this happened, however, the bishops over-looked it in their eagerness to satisfy such great people, who as patrons were supposed to have the best interests of their foundations at heart. Bishops, of course, were quite accustomed to diverting parochial revenue into higher education and diocesan administration, to which they accorded a higher priority. Walter and Margaret thus acted within their rights and indeed in accordance with accepted contemporary standards, but they were not observing the spirit of the original founders' wishes.

Such transactions imperilled a founder's soul. Given the belief that every mass alleviated the founder's sufferings in purgatory, how could Walter justify stoking the flames by suppressing an existing chantry or by diluting its efficacy through annexation to another? In 1442, when refounding St Mary's chantry, Heytesbury, Bishop Aiscough had ordered commemoration of all the founders, which Margaret conveniently forgot. No doubt the claims of unknown and unrelated founders could be rejected painlessly, but how did Walter justify to himself the suppression of the Calne chantry of his great-uncle Robert I, whom he had himself commemorated elsewhere? It was accepted that references in another's masses were no substitute for masses of one's own, yet this fault was not uncommon.[29] Indeed it has often been observed that strange moral standards, even fraud, were perfectly compatible with genuine piety.

Each generation inherited obligations from its parents – wills to perform, foundations to complete, and vows to fulfil. Preoccupied with the future of his own soul and encouraged by the belief that the pains of purgatory could be alleviated after his death, the medieval testator devised a range of tasks, often numerous, strenuous, expensive and tedious, for his executors to perform. The burden (and indeed expense) often fell most heavily on the heirs. Walter's pious instincts were not those of his parents, yet he was absorbed by their foundations until 1429, when he was about fifty years of age. He himself left unfinished business that was not completed until twenty-three years after his death. As each defunct testator receded into the past and most bequests were executed, the living became increasingly concerned with their own interests. If Margaret can be believed, most of Robert II's legacies had been

---

[29] Wood-Legh, *Chantries*, 308; for what follows, see e.g. M. A. Hicks, 'The Neville earldom of Salisbury 1429–71', *WAM* lxxii/lxxiii, 1980, 145–7.

largely fulfilled by *c.* 1472, when she admitted to only £35 6*s* 8*d* still outstanding, which she enjoined her executors to carry out. She listed them again in 1476, again leaving them to her executors.[30] Whether her instructions were observed we cannot know, but Margaret's conscience was thereby salved. Likewise founders' heirs remembered the failed foundations at Longleat and Bath: Walter's qualms were assuaged by repayment of his debt and Margaret's by provision of life-pensions to the remaining almsfolk, not by execution of their fathers' wishes. These were conscience payments like the often derisory bequests for forgotten tithes. Heirs could close their eyes to sufferings in purgatory prolonged by their delay and neglect, yet – perhaps because of this – were only too aware that their wishes might be ignored and their foundations allowed to fail. Walter and Margaret were far from unique in menacing their feoffees and executors with the 'day of doom' or 'dredfull day of Jugement', but threats alone would have little effect until those at risk composed themselves for death. Such clauses and rigorous statutes were no substitute for trust, for reliable executors, and it was on 'the grete love and trust that hath long bene betwene theym and me' that Margaret really relied. The trustworthy heirs and executors were constrained for much of their lives by the dead hand of the past. In all fairness, they faithfully performed most of the burdensome obligations that their parents had heaped onto them.

Heirs moulded their parents' foundations to suit themselves. All Walter's chantries were dedicated to the Virgin or the Annunciation, even that which his mother wanted for St Anne, and Margaret's personal preferences took priority both at Heytesbury hospital and her husband's burial place. Individual taste coloured bequests and foundations and long-term changes are discernible, although the progression is not continuous or direct. Thomas patronised only Austin canons, principally the Arrouasians and Bonshommes, whereas his uncle Robert had patronised them together with other regular orders and had endowed three secular chantries in sharply contrasting locations. Apart from the obits at Bath and Syon abbeys, all later foundations were secular. The hospitals, Walter's school at Heytesbury, and the Syon obit can all be classed as 'forward–looking' benefactions. They can be supplemented by Walter's munificence to Merton College, Oxford and by the bequests of himself and Robert II to the Carthusians. But this neat progression is denied by the wills, where the bequests span almost the whole spectrum. Austin canons, miscellaneous nunneries and Dominican friaries far outnumber Carthusian and Bridgettine houses. Religious houses eclipse in numbers and size of bequest the few hospitals mentioned. Parish churches are also prominent. In short, the range of religious interests remained unchanged, but new foundations – infinitely more expensive than mere legacies – were confined to secular chantries and hospitals. Foundations and bequests alike were concentrated in the Hungerford heartland of north-east

---

[30] WRO, 490/1465d; Devizes Museum, Hungerford Colls., Personal i, fos. 271v, 276.

Somerset and west Wiltshire, but the wills reveal more peripheral interests in Oxford, London, Middlesex and the far west among different testators.

As Professor Rosenthal also found, those commemorated in foundations were normally in the direct line of the founder, especially the male line.[31] Ancestors took precedence over descendants and chantries were smothered with ancestral shields. Apart from Robert I and Geva, whose repeated commemoration testifies to their importance for a parvenu family, later Hungerfords did not normally remember collaterals, even siblings or children. Walter remembered none of his brothers and merely commemorated his children in general terms. Living offspring received education, marriages, estates and bequests, once dead their obits were entered in family service books, but they were not specific beneficiaries from family foundations. The obit of Walter's son Walter (d. 1432) was entered in his father's missal, but he was remembered neither in his father's later foundations nor in his will.[32] Margaret did not remember her three dead sons, nor (except at Syon) her grandson Thomas, nor indeed her own siblings. While men understandably commemorated the male line, ignoring – except heraldically – their maternal ancestors, the women recalled their female progenitors. Thus Joan asked for *her* ancestors to be prayed for, a wish overlooked by her son. Margaret specifically remembered only her father among her Botreaux ancestors, although others unnamed were known to lie at Little Cheverell chantry and Launceston priory (Corn.), but she commemorated not only her mother at Bridgewater (Som.), but her maternal grandparents and uncle. She provided no prayers for her stepmother, nor her father-in-law's second wife, whose own will of 1455 betrays mistrust of both Margaret and her husband.[33] As Walter commemorated only his mother, not his father's first wife, the step was apparently a genuine barrier to family feeling.

The principal beneficiaries were the founders, whose tastes took precedence over all other considerations and even militated against consistency in family piety and benefactions. Hence the multiplication of foundations. Walter could have augmented Robert I's chantries and been commemorated with him, but this cheap alternative was rejected in favour of new foundations. The overlap from generation to generation was remarkably small, even though territorial continuity compelled regular contact with earlier foundations. Just as devoted to the Austin canons as his uncle and in-laws, Thomas patronised Edington, Longleat and Lesnes, not Ivychurch nor Maiden Bradley. None of Robert I's or Thomas's foundations were supplemented by their heirs. The search for personal benefits resulted not just in the prolifera-

[31] Rosenthal, *Purchase of Paradise*, 14–20; compare P. W. Fleming, 'Charity, Faith and the Gentry of Kent 1422–1529', *Property and Politics: Essays in Later Medieval English History*, ed. A. J. Pollard, Gloucester 1984, 51.

[32] V. Leroquais, *Les Sacrementaires et les Missels Manuscrits des Bibliothèques Publiques de France*, Paris 1924, iii, 24.

[33] PRO, PROB 11/4 (PCC 3 Stokton, will of Eleanor, countess of Arundel).

tion of foundations, but also in their duplication, so that there came to be three Hungerford foundations in Salisbury cathedral and two in Farleigh chapel. Robert I lay at Hungerford, sixteenth-century relatives at Heytesbury. Without a single, imposing mausoleum, such as Bisham Abbey (Montagu), Warwick College (Beauchamp) or Tewkesbury Abbey (Despenser), the Hungerfords were commemorated in paltry chantries, where at the dissolution half-forgotten chaplains celebrated daily in tattered vestments from antique mass-books.[34] This striking individuality emerges yet more clearly from the liturgical provisions of these foundations, not discussed here.

Few non-relatives were commemorated at these chantries, but every licence names the monarch of the day. This was an essential inducement for him to permit its endowment.[35] Similarly the commemoration of Dean Goldwell and Bishop Beauchamp at Salisbury and Heytesbury was probably the price Margaret paid for their support. However that may be, neither the reigning monarch nor these ecclesiastics are mentioned in her statutes: privileges granted to smoothe the course of foundation could be conveniently forgotten later.

The principal obstacle to the would-be founder was the necessity for a royal licence to alienate in mortmain. Securing a licence was never a formality. Mortmain has generally been discussed by reference to licences on the patent roll, but such enrolments both overestimate and underestimate the numbers: many enrolments never took effect, many licences went unenrolled, and illegal alienation without licences was common. Thus mortmain cannot be studied purely from the licences, which represent the result of intrigue uncertain of success. Problems in securing licences or the high fines charged forced monasteries to sell donations for ready cash. Licences were not always forthcoming even at a prohibitive price.

In contrast Dr Raban writes:[36]

> Mortmain legislation involved the church in expense and effort. It did not greatly inhibit its freedom of action. There was little to prevent acquisition if the extra cost was judged worthwhile . . . there is no convincing evidence that it had anything other than superficial effect on ecclesiastical participation in the land market.

Dr Raban sets licences to alienate in context, but her context and hence her study is biased in several different ways. It is biased towards the recipients of amortised land; towards ancient Benedictine houses in eastern England before 1400; towards purchases of land by recipients, not gifts by patrons; and towards the success stories recorded in licences and cartularies, rather

---

[34] J. E. Jackson, 'Wiltshire Chantry Furniture', *WAM* xxii, 1885, 322–3.
[35] Wood-Legh, *Chantries*, 311.
[36] S. Raban, 'Mortmain in Medieval England', *P & P* lxii, 1974, 1–26. The next five paragraphs are based on this article and Raban, *Mortmain Legislation, passim*.

than the failures.[37] To Raban a licence is a mark of success, however long it took to secure, despite her evidence of the protracted nature of the licensing process and of intermediate tenure by nominees and feoffees pending the issue of a licence. These devices permitted greater freedom on the land market and enabled licences to be put off until piecemeal acquisitions justified the expense. While these are valid considerations, it is equally likely, indeed more likely, that approval of the desired licences was neither easy nor automatic. To secure any favour, including a licence, a suitor needed access to a monarch and a favourable response to his petition. Hard work and expense, not always successful, was required in the parallel suits for exemption from acts of resumption.[38] Evasion of the licensing regulations became more common in the fifteenth century, but it is not known whether this is due to the crown's growing leniency, as suggested by Dr Raban, or the increasing royal rigour identified by Dr Kreider.[39]

The most striking evidence for royal control of alienation in the fifteenth century is Dr Raban's own graph of licences to alienate in mortmain. Within a long-term decline there are short-term fluctuations corresponding to political changes. The end to the fourteenth-century flood of licences under Henry IV was followed by a trough during Henry V's campaigns abroad. The fifteenth-century peak coincided with Henry VI's majority to 1450. Thereafter licences declined progressively to a low point under Henry VII. It has been shown that Henry VII rigorously restricted the number of licences. Similarly the peak of 1437–50 coincided with lavish and extravagant patronage of all kinds. At this time the proportion of fines charged fell below the levels current immediately before and afterwards. When Henry VI's patronage was curbed in 1450, the number of licences also fell and the proportion of fines increased. Since, however, the actual number of fines was unchanged while the number of licences diminished, there may also have been real restrictions in the issue of licences. We know this to be true of Henry VI's minority, when almost all licences were subject to reasonable fines and the number of new licences reached the lowest level to date. Anxious to preserve the young king's rights intact, the minority council issued licences only in exceptional circumstances despite protests in parliament. After 1470 when the level of fines rose, the number of licences fell, yet the number of foundations increased: evidence not just of resistance to financial penalties, but also of limits to the number of fines available. It is striking that even Edward IV's brother only secured licences as the reward for political

---

[37] E.g. in Raban, *P & P* lxii, 23, when Dr Raban writes that licences to alienate 'indicate the number of churchmen who wished to receive property'. Of course many licences concern donations for which there was no single identified clerical recipient.

[38] B. P. Wolffe, *Royal Demesne in English History*, 1973, 156–7; *Rot. Parl.* vi, 389–90, 430, for All Souls College, Oxford and Monkbretton Priory.

[39] A. Kreider, *English Chantries: The Road to Dissolution*, Cambridge, Mass. 1979, 84. For the rest of the article, see ibid. 71–92; *Raban, Mortmain Legislation*, graphs 4–6.

support.[40] By the turn of the century founders could apparently not obtain licences at any price.

This impression is supported earlier in the century by the Hungerford foundations. They represent a small sample just as biased as that of Dr Raban, but biased towards the patron rather than the recipient, towards donations rather than purchases, and towards the mainstream of late medieval benefactions. Walter was particularly well-placed to secure a licence, yet he waited fourteen years before obtaining one for the Farleigh chantry – a delay hardly to be ascribed to financial motives, since he was already supporting the chaplain. Similarly he found it convenient to establish his Salisbury chantry under the chapter's general licence, but even then had to await an appropriate moment and paid a substantial fine. At Chippenham his chapel was built before he obtained a licence. At Heytesbury the hospital was already operating in 1442, when Walter envisaged an enfeoffment to use until a licence was obtained. Although the feoffees were actually financing the almspeople and this was the time of Henry VI's greatest extravagance, even Walter could not secure a licence before his death in 1449, nor was one obtained for a further twenty-three years. As part of a much wider agreement, Edward IV's brother agreed in 1469 to secure licences for the hospital and Salisbury chantry. As Margaret was prepared to pay the fines, the problem cannot have been financial. The king signed the agreement, yet Gloucester could not meet the twelve-month deadline and Margaret had to wait until 1472. Similarly in another reciprocal indenture of 1470, the king agreed to license Lady Hungerford and Moleyns to amortise land to any religious house of her choice.[41] Such cumulative evidence appears conclusive.

Assuming Walter's influence to be finite and to be deployed sparingly, it is remarkable that he squandered it on licences rather than more tangible assets. The exercise of such influence on behalf of religious corporations represented some sacrifice, for which he was rewarded by Bath priory and Salisbury cathedral with a cut of the proceeds. This price was paid willingly and indeed Salisbury's spire appears a mere pretext for extra payments to the canons residentiary. Other foundations, at Easton, Calne and Longleat, also represented exploitation, since the extra income was not commensurate with the additional burdens imposed. It was hardly in the Church's true interests to plunder the parishes to finance private masses for individual laymen.

Such arrangements suggest that Dr Raban underestimated the importance of delay even to undying religious corporations. They undoubtedly concerned laymen, for whom long delays rendered completion of foundations less likely. Too many heirs refused to complete or even overthrew their parents'

---

[40] M. A. Hicks, *False, Fleeting Perjur'd Clarence*, Gloucester 1980, 150–51. See also the comments by Mr Fleming in Pollard, *Property and Politics*, 39.

[41] Huntington Library MS HAP Box 3, indenture of Edward IV and Sir Oliver Manningham, 13 March 1470. I am indebted to the trustees of the H. E. Huntington Library, San Marino, California for permission to cite this document and for supplying a photocopy of it.

foundations. Surely it was desperation that caused donors, otherwise so careful to ensure the survival of foundations, to resort to impermanent, insecure and illegal enfeoffment of endowments? Licences were a genuine limitation to those making new foundations. No longer exercised through the bureaucratic formalities of inquisitions *ad quod dampnum* and escheators, royal control relied instead on the perusal of applications by kings as capable of assiduous attention to detail as Edward IV and Henry VII. Fifteenth-century kings may have been less concerned about alienations to the Church, but they were acutely interested in patronage and its counterpart in fines or service. Mortmain licences became another form of patronage until the level of alienations again caused concern, perhaps not until the reign of Henry VIII.

TABLE III: Rate of Attrition of Hungerford Foundations.

			Foundation			Dissolution	
		Type	Date	to 1535	1536–39	1546–48
Religious houses:							
Benedictines	Bath	obit	1429		x	
Bridgettine	Syon	obit	1470		x	
Cistercians	Stanley	obit	1331		x	
Augustinians	Edington	obit	1365		x	
	Ivychurch	obit	1336		x	
	Ivychurch	chantry	1321	x		
	Lesnes	chantry	1377	x		
	Longleat	chantry	1408	x		
Trinitarian	Easton	chantry	1336		x	
Secular churches:							
Cathedrals	Salisbury	chantry	1334	?		
	Salisbury	chantry	1429			x
	Salisbury	chantry	1472			x
College	Westminster	obit	1427			x
Hospitals	Calne	chantry	1336	x		
	Heytesbury	almshouse	1442			
Parish churches	Chippenham	chantry	c. 1442			x
	Farleigh	chantry	1429			x
	Farleigh	obit	1428			x
	Farleigh	chantry	c. 1442			x
	Hungerford	chantry	1326			x

Sources: text and chantry certificates.

Many chantries had disappeared by the Reformation. So great was the attrition that three-fifths of the early fourteenth-century chantries had disappeared by the 1540s, when the chantry certificates recorded predominantly recent foundations.[42] Dr Kreider reaches this important conclusion by comparing licences to alienate with the chantry certificates of four counties, including Wiltshire. As he appreciates, this technique involves distortion. Taking the Hungerford foundations as an example, the licences are inflated by the inclusion of chantries at Ivychurch and Longleat, which were not

---

[42] Kreider, 71–86, tables 3.3, 3.4.

founded, and by the use of five licences for two chantries at Farleigh; they are depressed, since obits licensed at Bath and Westminster are not recorded on the patent roll and since foundations at Heytesbury, Farleigh, Syon, Canterbury and Lesnes required no licences.[43] Heytesbury hospital, licensed in 1472 and recorded in the chantry certificates, actually represents five licensed foundations, four of them fourteenth-century chantries. Taking the twenty foundations in table III, two failed at once and another two – Calne and Lesnes – were dissolved respectively in 1442 and 1525. There should thus have remained sixteen (80 per cent) at the Reformation, of which six (30 per cent) were in monastic houses dissolved in 1536–39. Only purely secular chantries survive in the chantry certificates, the eight Hungerford examples representing 40 per cent of the original total, a figure close to the 45.7 per cent surviving from the early fourteenth century found by Kreider.[44] This low proportion results almost wholly from the dissolution of the monasteries. By omitting the dissolution from his calculations, Kreider seriously depressed the number of intercessory institutions active in early Tudor England. He particularly depressed the number of older foundations, since late in the middle ages there was a marked shift from the early fourteenth-century pattern of chantries in monasteries to purely secular foundations. Of the nine monastic foundations of the Hungerfords, two-thirds were of fourteenth-century date. It is no wonder that the chantries were dissolved in 1548, when hundreds or even thousands were abolished a decade earlier. The absence of opposition then is hardly surprising, since most were two centuries old and, as we have seen with the Hungerfords, later generations were preoccupied with their own souls and unconcerned about those of their ancestors. Family tradition played little part in shaping the piety of the individual Hungerford or the distinctive form in which it was expressed.

King Alfred's College, Winchester

---

[43] BL MS Faustina BVIII fo. 12. For what follows, see table III.
[44] This includes the first Salisbury chantry, which may have disappeared much earlier, Salisbury CM, Reg. Hutchins fo. 52.

Religious Life in a Welsh Marcher Lordship: the Lordship of Dyffryn Clwyd in the Later Middle Ages

R. Ian Jack

Although the principality of Wales and the marcher lordships in the four-teenth and fifteenth centuries shared the experiences of the church universal and especially the church in England, there are, particularly in the marcher lordships, some quite distinctive features. These, while detectable, are usually difficult to document in detail.[1] Some of them refer to the wider question of relations between Welsh and English, brilliantly explored by Professor Rees Davies.[2] Others stem from the extraordinary, omnicompetent power wielded by a marcher lord.

The lordship of Dyffryn Clwyd, centred on the castle of Ruthin, is one of the few areas of Wales in the later middle ages where most aspects of everyday life can be explored. The court rolls which have attracted scholarly attention since their rediscovery in the nineteenth century give information far beyond their English counterparts. The royal courts made little impact on marcher lordships and the seignorial courts dealt with criminal as well as civil cases, with Welsh as well as English, with clerical matters as well as lay.[3] Largely unchallenged in secular jurisdiction, the courts of Dyffryn Clwyd faced competition from the diocesan bishop in ecclesiastical causes.

The lordship was in a strong geographical position to limit episcopal control. The deanery of Dyffryn Clwyd was part of the medieval bishopric of Bangor but was separated from the main part of the diocese (Map 1). The island deanery, surrounded by St Asaph's see, was not quite coterminous

---

[1] Cf. Glanmor Williams, *The Welsh Church from Conquest to Reformation*, new edn, Cardiff 1976.
[2] R. R. Davies, 'Race Relations in Post-Conquest Wales: Confrontation and Compromise', *Trans. Honourable Soc. of Cymmrodorion, 1974–5*, 32–56; *Lordship and Society in the March of Wales, 1282–1400*, Oxford 1978.
[3] Cf. R. I. Jack, *Medieval Wales*, 1972, 73, 114–16, 159–60.

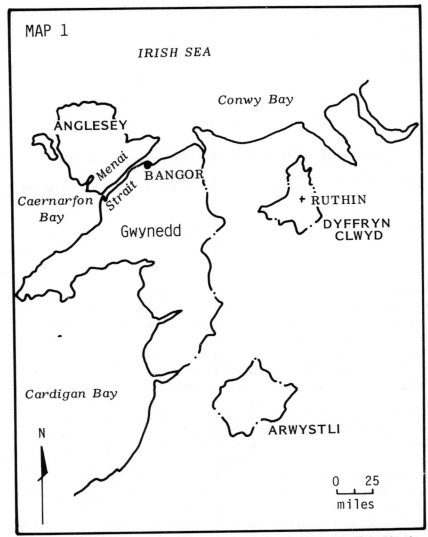

MAP 1

IRISH SEA

Conwy Bay

ANGLESEY

Menai Strait

BANGOR

Caernarfon Bay

Gwynedd

+ RUTHIN

DYFFRYN CLWYD

Cardigan Bay

N

ARWYSTLI

0   25
miles

The medieval Diocese of Bangor, with its isolated deaneries of Dyffryn Clwyd and Arwystli.

with the lordship: the northernmost section of the lordship, centred on the township of Aberchwilar, was part of the Flintshire parish of Bodfari, under St Asaph's jurisdiction, while to the west the deanery included the parish of Llanrhaeadr-yng-Nghinmeirch which formed part of the lordship of Denbigh. But generally speaking, all parochial life in Dyffryn Clwyd was the responsibility of the bishop of Bangor's administration. Since most medieval bishops of Bangor were notorious absentees, these responsibilities were largely discharged by administrative officials of the diocese rather than by the bishop in person.[4]

The outlying deanery was episcopally administered by a dean, official or commissary. This ecclesiastical jurisdiction held courts and maintained a prison, but had a complex relationship with the secular administration. In 1312 a clerk, Cadwgan ap Madog Fychan, was convicted in the lord's court of breaking into Ruthin Castle chapel and stealing two graduals.[5] Under the agreement made between Lord Grey and Bishop Anian in 1286, a criminous clerk could be put in prison only by the ecclesiastical authorities,[6] but the bishop's official refused to admit Cadwgan to the episcopal prison, so Cadwgan was incarcerated in the castle gaol instead. Earlier in the same year 1312 another Welsh chaplain called Dafydd Llwyd claimed benefit of clergy when brought before the lord's court over alleged defamation, and sought trial in the bishop's court instead, but the secular officials insisted on their jurisdiction, the case was heard and the chaplain was amerced 6s 8d.[7] Even more clearly ecclesiastical causes were heard in the lord's court: in 1349 a case between a husband and his father-in-law who was an episcopal chaplain in the lordship, arising from costs in the husband's divorce, was concluded in the secular court, with the chaplain gaining £7 10s 0d in the divorce settlement and the lord receiving £5.[8]

The law was a source of profit as well as principle and there is evidence that the bishop's officials were more zealous in testamentary cases. By chance, the record of the bishop's court of audience held on 6 February 1350 survives, transcribed onto the secular court-roll of the same period. The rector of Llandyrnog, William ap Dafydd, who had been receiver of episcopal revenues in the lordship, had just died. The executors were sued by the bishop for the substantial receipts still due to the bishop from the deceased receiver's last account, and they, unlike Cadwgan ap Madog Fychan in 1312, were put into the episcopal prison pending payment.[9] The more fundamental matter of granting probate seems to have been regularly performed by the episcopal authority, although the evidence is sporadic. In 1495 John Aspull, a graduate and rector of Llanfair, who was acting as the bishop's commissary, proved the will of Ithel Toua of Llanelidan.[10] The notebook of Dafydd Yale, written in the early years of the sixteenth century, contains examples of many documents which do not seem themselves to be actual copies (there are

---

[4] Gwynfryn Richards, 'Notes on the Rural Deanery of Dyffryn Clwyd to 1859', *National Library of Wales Journal* xx (1977–78), 46–84; D. R. Thomas, *The History of the Diocese of St Asaph*, new edn, Oswestry 1908–13, ii, 3, 44–5, 72–134; iii, 343–6.

[5] PRO, Special Collections, Court Rolls, SC2/215/71 m.3r.

[6] National Library of Wales [NLW], B/Misc Vol/27.

[7] PRO, SC2/215/71 m.9d.

[8] PRO, SC2/217/14 m.33r.

[9] PRO, SC2/218/1 m.15r.

[10] Jack, *Medieval Wales*, 142; NLW, Wynnstay 104/61. For Aspull as rector of Llanfair see below 156.

recurrent discrepancies in dates and in names, particularly of the bishops of Bangor) but can be relied upon to give information about plausible situations. Dafydd was much concerned with Dyffryn Clwyd and shows himself proving a will there in 1502. He shows the bishop's official holding Llanhychan church during a vacancy in about 1503, he concocts the episcopal mandate to himself to conduct a visitation of the deanery in 1502 and he records the questions which should be posed to non-exempt clergy.[11]

The consistory court allegedly held by Dafydd Yale in Ruthin as commissary in 1502 may not have met in quite that way (the bishop's name is incompatible with the date).[12] There is no doubt, however, that Fulk Salisbury as episcopal commissary held a full consistory court in 1507 and granted the administration of an estate to two kinsmen of the deceased.[13] Potential tensions between jurisdictions over the estates of testators certainly existed. In 1436 Lord Grey's officials accused the executors of a well-to-do Welsh bondsman of occupying the estate without seignorial licence.[14] On a more general level in the same year, a public proclamation was made throughout the lordship to prohibit all residents of Dyffryn Clwyd from purging themselves in any church in the lordship after accusations of felony had been levelled in the lord's court. The penalty of £10 for disobedience was very heavy and all parochial clergy in the lordship were barred from conniving in the purgation under a similarly harsh penalty.[15] The implication of tension between the two jurisdictions is quite obvious.

The bishop of Bangor also held substantial property in the lordship (Map 2), particularly in the south-east corner where he had interests in almost all the townships of Llanelidan parish. His other lands were near the parish churches of Clocaenog, Llanfair, Llanrhudd, Llanhychan and Llangwyfan. The total rent-roll in Henry VII's reign was £9 6s 6½d.[16] The township of Rhiwbebyll, near Llangwyfan, in the north of the lordship, was entirely under episcopal control and the bishop claimed the right of *arianporth*, a toll on every cart drawn by two horses passing through Rhiwbebyll. This toll was actually levied in the early 1350s at the rate of 4d a cart. When this was challenged by the lord's officials in court in 1354 the bishop was represented by an attorney who conceded that 4d was wrong but counterclaimed that *arianporth* at the rate of 2d had been levied time out of mind.[17] Lord Grey also

---

[11] Cardiff Central Library, MS 2.2 fos. 67d, 71d, 72r, 73d, 77r. For a description of this volume see N. R. Ker, *Medieval Manuscripts in British Libraries II: Abbotsford-Keele*, Oxford 1977, 354–5.

[12] Cardiff Central Library, MS 2.2 fo. 74d.

[13] NLW, Rûg 519. Fulk Salisbury had been commissary in 1492 also (NLW, Crosse of Shaw Hill 8), so it is possible that Dafydd Yale merely hoped to be commissary, just as he hoped to be a poet laureate (Cardiff Central Library, MS 2.2 fo. 69r).

[14] PRO, SC2/222/1 m.1Ar.

[15] PRO, SC2/222/1 m.72r.

[16] Cardiff Central Library, MS 2.2 fos. 16d, 75r; NLW, B/Misc Vol/27 fos. 17r–19r.

[17] PRO, SC2/218/4 m.11d.

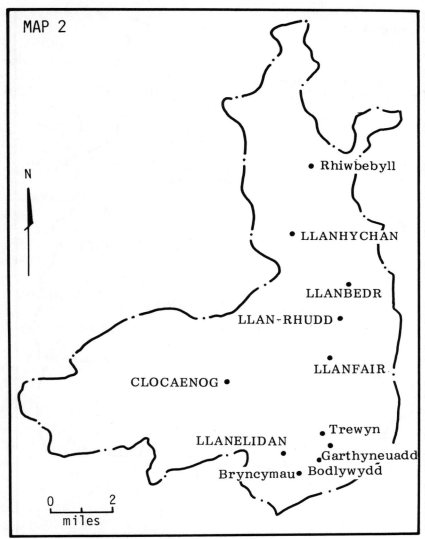

MAP 2

N

• Rhiwbebyll

• LLANHYCHAN

LLANBEDR

LLAN-RHUDD •

• LLANFAIR

CLOCAENOG •

• Trewyn

LLANELIDAN

.Garthyneuadd

Bryncymau• Bodlywydd

0   2
miles

Those townships within the lordship of Dyffryn Clwyd in which the bishop of Bangor held lands in the late middle ages.

had struggles with the episcopal tenants of Rhiwbebyll over the grinding of their grain in 1332–33, when strenuous attempts were made to deny their exemption from suit of the seignorial mill.[18]

The bishop's own temporal administration seems to have been consistently employed. An episcopal bailiff, Iorwerth ab Ednyfed, is known in 1313, a

[18] PRO, SC2/216/13 mm.11r, 11d, 14d.

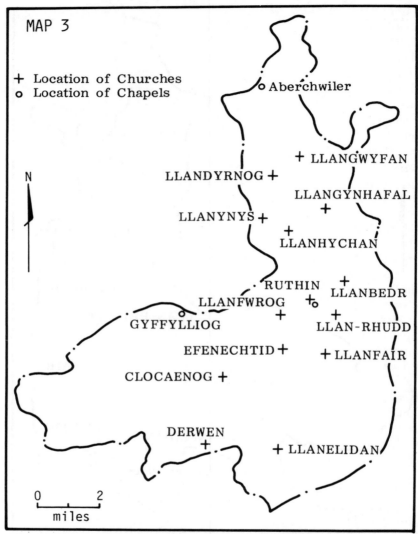

Churches and chapels in the medieval lordship of Dyffryn Clwyd.

steward in 1324 and 1534, a forester in 1341, a bailiff and rent-collector in
1534.[19] A system of courts for episcopal tenants was already in existence in
the thirteenth century and these courts also had jurisdiction over any of Lord
Grey's tenants who transgressed in the bishop's manors as long as the
lordship officials were present and half of the amercements were to be taken

---

[19] PRO, SC2/215/72 m.8d; 216/7 m.1r; NLW, B/Misc Vol/27 fo. 20r; *VE* iv, 416; Browne Willis,
A Survey of the Cathedral Church of Bangor, 1721, 249.

by Lord Grey.[20] The sharing of common pasture between seignorial and episcopal tenants was taken for granted in 1286 and confirmed in 1353 and did not seem to lead to legal problems.

The bishop's court records are lost, like most of the Bangor archives, but an estreat survives from 1498. The court at which this plea over property in Rhiwbebyll was settled was held at Llanhychan, where the bishop had other lands, before Thomas ap Llywelyn Fychan, his sub-steward.[21] Three years earlier, during the vacancy in the bishopric after the death of Richard Edenham in 1494, the lieutenant of the secular steward, on behalf of George Grey, earl of Kent, had held a series of four courts in the episcopal temporalities in Llanfair, Llanhychan, Rhiwbebyll and Llanelidan.[22] These courts were recorded on the lordship rolls and therefore survive: there is every reason to believe that the episcopal administration regularly maintained its own records throughout the late middle ages.

The bishop's presence in the lordship was therefore consistently tangible. Since, rather unexpectedly, the right to present to most of the ecclesiastical livings in the lordship had not been acquired by the Greys, who elsewhere used their advowsons as a normal extension of their landed power,[23] the bishop also had considerable powers of patronage in appointments. The lordship contained fourteen parishes within its hundred square miles and two chapelries (Gyffylliog and Aberchwilar), in addition to the private chapel in Ruthin Castle (Map 3). The following table shows a series of evaluations of the fourteen parish churches from the Valuation of Norwich to the *Valor Ecclesiasticus*.

This table of assessment gives a rough image of the comparative wealth of the rural churches and emphasises the superior importance of Llanynys and Llanfair. Only in the *Valor Ecclesiasticus*, however, does the substantial wealth of St Peter's become apparent and the mere figures do not even hint at the diversity of clerical foundations within the small lordship.

The two institutions of particular interest are Llanynys and St Peter's, Ruthin. Llanynys is an interesting development from a Celtic *clas*. Still in the early fifteenth century it was remembered that the ecclesiastical revenues, in excess of £66, had formerly been divided into twenty-four portions to maintain twenty-four *abad a chlaswyr*.[24] An *abad* or abbot is known by name in 1260, Madog ab Einion ap Maredudd,[25] but in the fourteenth century, under English rule, the chief portioner in Llanynys was called the dean.[26] In 1386

[20] NLW, B/Misc Vol/27.
[21] NLW, Crosse of Shaw Hill 947.
[22] PRO, SC2/223/22 m.9.
[23] R. I. Jack, 'The Ecclesiastical Patronage Exercised by a Baronial Family in the Late Middle Ages', *Journal of Religious History* iii (1964–65), 275–95.
[24] *CPL 1362–1404*, 349; Thomas, *St Asaph* ii, 111; G. R. J. Jones, 'The Llanynys Quillets: a Measure of Landscape Transformation in North Wales', *Trans. Denbighshire Hist. Soc.* xiii (1964), 149.
[25] Jones, 149.
[26] PRO, SC2/215/73 m.3r; 216/1 m.18d; 216/5 m.25r.

Assessed value of parish churches in Dyffryn Clwyd, 1253–1535

	1253	1291	1380	c. 1460	1535
Clocaenog	13s 4d	—	£1 0s 0d	*	£12 0s 0d
Derwen	13s 4d	£4 0s 10d	£2 13s 4d	£4 6s 8d	£10 15s 0d
Efenechtid	10s 0d	—	£1 6s 8d	*	£6 1s 4d
Llanbedr	13s 4d	£4 0s 10d	—	£4 0s 10d	£13 1s 8d
Llandyrnog	£1 0s 0d	£4 6s 8d	£5 0s 0d	£7 13s 4d	£9 19s 6d
Llanelidan	£2 0s 0d	£8 0s 0d	£8 0s 0d	£8 0s 0d	£16 0s 0d
Llanfair	£3 6s 8d	£16 0s 0d	£16 0s 0d	£14 13s 4d	£39 0s 0d
Llanfwrog	13s 4d	£4 0s 10d	£4 0s 10d	£4 0s 0d	£16 13s 4d
Llangwyfan	10s 0d	—	—	*	£7 18s 8d
Llangynhafal	13s 4d	£4 6s 8d	£4 6s 8d	£4 6s 8d	£15 15s 0d
Llanhychan	10s 0d	—	£1 6s 8d	*	£7 17s 6d
Llanrhudd	13s 4d	£5 0s 0d	£5 0s 0d	£3 13s 4d	with Ruthin
Llanynys: rectory	£6 13s 4d	£16 0s 0d	£16 6s 8d	£14 13s 4d	£26 13s 4d
vicarage	—	£4 6s 8d			£8 13s 4d
Ruthin, St Peter's	—	£5 6s 8d	£5 6s 8d	—	£47 12s 0d

* These four parishes were assessed together at £2 in c. 1460.

Sources: 1253, 1291 and 1535 *sub* parish in D. R. Thomas, *The History of the Diocese of St Asaph*, new edn, Oswestry 1908–13.

1380: PRO, Exchequer, King's Remembrancer, Subsidy Rolls, E 179/3/5.

c. 1460: Cardiff Central Library, MS 2.2 fo. 78r (clerical tax assessment in time of James Blakedon, bishop of Bangor, 1453–64).

the churches of Llanynys and Llanfair were appropriated by the bishop, dean and chapter of Bangor and the revenues applied to maintain four chaplains at the cathedral.[27] From 1386 until 1402 the church of Llanynys was held by two unequal comportioners, one receiving two-thirds of the revenue, the other one-third.[28] In 1402 the portions were consolidated and a perpetual vicar was thereafter in charge at Llanynys.[29]

Eleven of the other parish churches were already in the gift of the bishop of Bangor, but Llanrhudd, the original church of the princely *maerdref* of the period before the Edwardian conquest, was appropriated to the new collegiate church of St Peter's, Ruthin on its establishment by John, Lord Grey, in 1310. Thereafter the prior of Ruthin was also rector of Llanrhudd and the first prior in 1310 seems to have been Hugh, the last independent rector of Llanrhudd.[30] The dedication of St Peter's church in Ruthin, established as a chapel of St Meugan's, Llanrhudd in 1286, probably derived from St Peter's well at Llanrhudd.[31] The charter of the marcher lord inverting the importance of the two churches in 1310 made St Peter's collegiate, with seven regular priests under a prior nominated by the lord. One of the priests was to serve as

[27] *CPR 1385–89*, 189–90.
[28] *CPR 1385–89*, 299, 371.
[29] Thomas, *St Asaph* ii, 111; *CPL 1362–1404*, 349.
[30] Thomas, *St Asaph* ii, 116–17.
[31] Thomas, *St Asaph* ii, 121 n. 3.

chaplain in Ruthin Castle. The new house was well endowed, more adequately than the tax assessments suggest, with more than two hundred acres of land, a substantial vaccary, common pasture for more than thirty cows and two bulls, pannage for sixty pigs, a grist-mill on the river Clywedog and the revenues of Llanrhudd church and the castle chapel.[32]

The succession of prior-rectors of St Peter's has not been previously ascertained, because of the scanty information in ecclesiastical and royal records. The not infrequent appearance of the prior in the seignorial court-rolls, however, makes a provisional list possible: it is of importance to assess the patronage of the secular lord to this one significant position in the ecclesiastical life of Dyffryn Clwyd over which he had direct control. The dates shown and the references for them are, in general, merely those of first and last mention.

Priors of St Peter's, Ruthin

Dates	Name	References
1310	Hugh, rector of Llanrhudd	Thomas II 119, 125
1317–21	John de Tilton	SC2/216/1 m.3r; 216/3 m.22r
1323–30	William de Coventry	SC2/216/4 m.10r; 216/11 m.1r
1333	John	SC2/216/13 m.8r
1341–76	Richard (d. 1376)	SC2/217/6 m.15r; 219/11 m.7d
1380	William	SC2/220/1 m.7r
1383	Llywelyn Dyffayn	SC2/220/3 m.6r
1384	William	SC2/220/3 m.7r
1391	Gethin	Newcome, *Gabriel Goodman*, 41
1403–16	William de Sutton	SC2/221/4 m.34r; 221/11 m.7d
1416–33	John Crote	SC2/221/9 m.25d; 222/1 m.56r
1437–8	Robert Blunham	SC2/222/1 mm.79r, 87d
1442	Nicholas Hamond	SC2/222/3 m.14r
1448–52	John Thelwall	SC2/222/3 m.53r; 223/1 m.7d
1455	Robert Hall	SC2/223/1 m.22r
1468–74	John Perte	SC2/223/6 m.1d; 223/9 m.1d

References:

R. Newcome, *A Memoir of Gabriel Goodman, D.D.*, Ruthin 1825.
D. R. Thomas, *The History of the Diocese of St Asaph*, new edn, Oswestry 1908.
PRO, Special Collections, Court Rolls, SC2.

Overwhelmingly the priors were English: only briefly on two occasions in Richard II's reign was there a Welsh prior. Robert Blunham was probably associated with the Grey manor in Bedfordshire, while John Crote's family came from Carlton, also in Bedfordshire. Crote, like other priors, was clearly resident and committed to living in Ruthin. His relations Roger and Robert Crote held burgages in the town in 1450.[33] The second prior, John de Tilton,

---

[32] *CPR 1313–1317*, 178; *Monasticon* vi (3), 1345–6.
[33] PRO, SC2/223/1 m.1d.

rose from the ranks of the chaplains in the house, for in 1313 he was named as parson of Llanrhudd and only in 1317 does he appear as prior.[34] John Thelwall in Henry VI's reign was a member of an increasingly powerful Anglo-Welsh family in the lordship[35] and his successor once removed, John Perte, was the son of a recent arrival in the lordship, Ralph Perte, and had a brother and two nephews in Ruthin by 1474.[36]

Over the first century and a half, the College acquired more land, more pious bequests, more mills. As well as the original mill on the Clywedog, the house had a mill at Rhydonnen on the Clwyd by 1342 and another to the east at Llwynedd by 1350.[37] The endowment of land included a public house in Ruthin bequeathed by Gruffydd ab Einion ab Ednyfed but promptly sold in 1427.[38] By the time of the Dissolution in 1550, although reduced in establishment to only four priests, there were still two bailiffs to collect rents (totalling some £46) and a steward to hold courts (which, along with offerings, produced 6s 8d in revenue).[39]

A remarkable intervention by the no less remarkable Lord Edmund, first earl of Kent, changed the character of the house in 1478. Earl Edmund converted the collegiate establishment into an Augustinian priory of the rare order of Bonshommes. In May 1478 the bishop of Hereford ordained as a priest Dafydd ab Ieuan ap Madog ab Hywel, a Bonhomme already in Ruthin priory[40] and later in the year Thomas Pyle, a Cistercian monk from the Galloway house of Dundrennan (then in some disarray), was given papal permission to stay at the new Bonshommes house at Ruthin for life.[41] The grand design failed: by July 1479 the Bonshommes, including apparently Thomas Pyle, had all abandoned Ruthin priory and the prior (whose identity is not known) had resigned. The pope restored the house to its previous status and confirmed Earl Edmund as patron.[42]

This curious episode was a direct expression of the religiosity of the lord.

---

[34] PRO, SC2/215/72 m.4r; 216/1 m.3r.

[35] *Dictionary of Welsh Biography*, Cardiff 1959, 932.

[36] PRO, SC2/223/8 m.14d; 223/9 m.1d. No one called Perte appears on the rental of the lordship in 1465 (M. Richards, 'Records of Denbighshire Lordships i: the Lordship of Dyffryn-Clwyd in 1465', *Trans. Denbighshire Hist. Soc.* xv (1966), 18–54).

[37] PRO, SC2/217/3 m.1r; 218/1 m.6d.

[38] PRO, SC2/222/1 m.27r.

[39] PRO, Exchequer, Augmentation Office, Miscellaneous Books, E 315/433 fos. 9r, 58r. A handful of estreats from the fifteenth and early sixteenth centuries is all that survives of the courts of St Peter's, Ruthin in the middle ages. They show that the steward was regularly one of the influential Thelwall family: Simon in Henry V's reign, John (not the prior) under Edward IV and Eublo from the early 1480s onwards (J. Y. W. Lloyd, *The History of the Princes, the Lords Marcher and the Ancient Nobility of Powys Fadog and the Ancient Lords of Arwystli, Cedewen, and Meirionydd*, 1882, ii, 297–300).

[40] *Reg. Myllyng*, 160.

[41] *CPL 1471–1484*, 625–6, 698. For Bonshommes, see D. Knowles and R. N. Hadcock, *Medieval Religious Houses: England and Wales*, Cambridge 1953, 179.

[42] *CPL 1471–1484*, 698; D. Knowles and R. N. Hadcock, 'Additions and Corrections to *Medieval Religious Houses: England and Wales*', *English Historical Review* 72 (1957), 69–70.

Lord Edmund is best remembered for his betrayal of Henry VI when he switched allegiance during the battle of Northampton in 1460.[43] But he also displayed considerable independent religious spirit in the course of his half-century at the head of the Grey of Ruthin family. Around the time that he succeeded his grandfather in 1440, Edmund Grey had married Katherine Percy, one of the many children of the second earl of Northumberland.[44] As a wedding present, he gave a copy of Nicholas Love's devotional work, the *Mirror of the Blessed Life of Jesus Christ*, endorsed as orthodox by Archbishop Arundel earlier in the century. The presentation copy was richly illuminated, showing the couple kneeling before the Virgin Mary, each with a prayer-stool and an open book (fo. 12d), while the arms of Grey and Percy were supported by angels (fo. 8d) and there and on fo. 5d, another rich heraldic composition, the motto *Soli deo honor* was repeated.[45]

In middle life, in 1459, Edmund took pilgrim vows of a conventional sort [46] but the telling evidence for an unusually keen interest in religious behaviour comes from Dyffryn Clwyd. The flouting of the canonical requirement for clerical celibacy had long been notorious in Wales: as Glanmor Williams observed, 'this complete dedication to [the priest's] calling, everywhere difficult of enforcement, was less observed in Wales than almost anywhere.'[47] The young Lord Edmund, in his late twenties, toured his Welsh estates in 1444–45[48] and was shocked by the standard of morality of the parochial clergy. On 26 July 1445 Lord Edmund gathered together his principal administrators in the great chamber of Ruthin Castle and examined the rectors of Efenechtid and Llanfwrog '*si venerint in loco suspeccionis vel fornicaverint cum aliqua muliere deinceps infra dominium suum*'. The two priests, Nicholas Reede and John Draper, were enjoined to go and sin no more.[49]

A week later, on 2 August 1445, Lord Edmund and an even larger group of secular officials again held an enquiry in the Castle and similarly examined eight more priests: the rectors of Clocaenog, Llanbedr and Llandyrnog, the vicar of Llanynys, two chaplains and two unbeneficed clergy.[50]

This in itself is notable, but it is more striking that the Grey administration launched a campaign of enforcement. Lord Edmund issued a general warning that no chaplain in the lordship should 'have or hold' a concubine or visit a

[43] R. I. Jack, 'A Quincentenary: the Battle of Northampton, June 20th 1460', *Northamptonshire Past and Present* iii (i) (1960), 21–5.
[44] The date is based on the fact that Edmund and Katherine had at least four children by 1446 (PRO, SC6/1119/4 m.3d, 5 m.7d). Katherine was born in May 1423 (*Collins's Peerage of England*, ed. Sir Egerton Brydges, 1812, ii, 281–2).
[45] National Library of Scotland, Advocates' MS 18.1.7, briefly described in *Trésors des Bibliothèques d'Ecosse*, Brussels 1963, 19–20 and plate 18.
[46] *CPL 1455–1464*, 520.
[47] Williams, *Welsh Church*, 339.
[48] PRO, SC6/1119/4 m.2d.
[49] PRO, SC2/222/3 m.35d.
[50] PRO, SC2/222/3 m.35d.

house of ill-repute.[51] In December 1445, only four months after the general statement, a Welsh priest, Matthew ap Dyk, who had not been examined in July or August, was brought before the commotal court of Llannerch and accused of sleeping with Gwenllian ferch Dyo on 17 October, with Hoen ferch Jollyn ap Ieuan Tussok on 20 October and with many other women on other occasions. The jury found that Matthew had not slept with Gwenllian but had consorted with Hoen.[52] In February 1446 Matthew made fine with the lord, agreeing to pay 40s in two instalments, but continued to be a stormy petrel, refusing to keep the peace, and was accused (unsuccessfully) of carrying a halberd illegally in October.[53]

The moral indignation over concubinage did not abate. Like the fourteenth-century friars,[54] the fifteenth-century administrators of the lordship turned their attack on the mistresses rather than the unchaste priests. In August 1447 a seignorial proclamation was made in all the courts of Dyffryn Clwyd exiling all clerical concubines from the lordship by Michaelmas under pain of 10s, divided two-thirds to the lord, one-third to the bailiff.[55] Such decrees had two faces, one moral, the other financial: this one seems to have operated on both levels. Only five women paid the large sum for the privilege of remaining in the lordship (and therefore possibly with their clerical lovers). Three of the five were not identified as the concubines of individual priests but one of these was Gwenllian ferch Dyo who had been unsuccessfully accused of sleeping with Matthew ap Dyk in the previous year. The two priests named were John ap Dyk (whose 'servant' Margaret ferch Dyk completes a promiscuous group of siblings) and John Draper, rector of Llanfwrog, whose mistress Elen Talbot had clearly survived her lover's confrontation with Lord Edmund in 1445.[56]

The interest of Lord Edmund and his officials in policing clerical morality seems to have abated after 1447. Certainly incontinence continued. Soon after Earl Edmund's death in 1490, for example, Morfedd, the daughter of the rector of Derwen, was the mistress of the vicar of Llanynys, while Moris, the rector of Llanhychan, shared his mistress Gwenllian with an unbeneficed priest, Gruffydd ab Ithel.[57]

There was more to parochial life, however, than sex. A final aspect of religion in Dyffryn Clwyd which repays investigation is the fabric of churches. Rebuilding and adornment of churches affected almost all ecclesiastical buildings in the lordship during the fifteenth century. It is well known that 'the economic recovery in Wales during the second half of the fifteenth

---

[51] The text of the ordinance is not enrolled, but is alluded to in PRO, SC2/222/5 m.14d.
[52] PRO, SC2/222/5 m.14d.
[53] PRO, SC2/222/5 mm.15r, 17d, 18r.
[54] Cf. Williams, *Welsh Church*, 337–8.
[55] PRO, SC2/222/3 m.48d.
[56] PRO, SC2/222/3 m.48d; 222/5 m.21d.
[57] Cardiff Central Library, MS 2.2 fo. 59d.

century which made possible the revival in Welsh poetry also provided the means for a new spate of activity in architecture and the arts which were its handmaidens . . . There was hardly a church in Wales, in however remote or bare a parish, which could not boast some degree of reconstruction or refurnishing' during the Yorkist or early Tudor period.[58] Dyffryn Clwyd is not unusual but the expression of the general impulse there has certain special features.

In church building the style of extension favoured in fifteenth-century Denbighshire is unusual though not unique. To increase space for a growing congregation, the north or south wall of the simple, rectangular, single-aisled church of earlier centuries was partly removed and a second, parallel, nave was constructed with its own pitched roof and gable. Only seven such double-naves were erected in South Wales; in North Wales, there were six in the Principality, seven in Flintshire and the remaining twenty are all in what became Denbighshire. Of these twenty, seven were in Dyffryn Clwyd: Llandyrnog, Llanelidan, Llanfair, Llanfwrog, Llangynhafal, Llanynys and St Peter's, Ruthin.[59] The expenditure on what seems to be an indigenous mason's craft was substantial, but there is little evidence for the means employed in raising the money. In 1352 the lord, Roger Grey, in his old age, had supplied the cart-horses and equipment required for the carriage of unworked stone blocks from a local quarry to build Capel Hwlkyn in the northern township of Aberchwiler[60] and another member of the seignorial family, one of the numerous John Greys, endowed the chapel with 54 acres of land including seven acres adjacent to the chapel.[61] But the fifteenth-century rebuilding of the seven major churches is not documented.

Similarly erected without surviving record is the fine stained glass which is still an outstanding feature of Clocaenog, Llandyrnog, Llanelidan and Llanfair churches. Llandyrnog has a particularly fine east window in the north nave depicting the Crucifixion with figures of saints, including St James of Compostella, while Llanfair's fragments include a portion, reinserted upside down in the south aisle, giving the end of the date 'ccciij'. This can represent only 1403 or 1503 and is presumably what remains of the date 1503 which Sir Stephen Richard Glynne noted when he visited the church in 1849.[62]

[58] Williams, *Welsh Church*, 428–9.

[59] See the list in E. Tyrrell-Green, 'The Church Architecture of Wales', *Trans. Honourable Soc. of Cymmrodorion, 1916–7*, 94–6. I have added St Peter's, Ruthin to Tyrrell-Green's tally.

[60] PRO, SC2/218/3 m.18r. For the site of the vanished Capel Hwlkyn (called Aberchwilar chapel in 1352), see Royal Commission on Ancient and Historical Monuments and Constructions in Wales and Monmouthshire, *An Inventory of the Ancient Monuments in Wales and Monmouthshire IV: County of Denbigh*, 1914, 11 no. 24.

[61] NLW, MS 1600E p. 11f.

[62] S. R. Glynne, 'Notes on the Older Churches in the Four Welsh Dioceses', *Archaeologia Cambrensis* 5th series 1 (1884), 173.

Glynne also noted in the glass of the east window of Llanfair's south aisle part of a legend 'Aspull et pro animabus.. vitreatam fieri fecit'.[63] John Aspull, a member of a family prominent in the lordship, was rector of Llanfair from before 1478 until after 1496.[64] Aspull, moreover, along with two procurators, was held responsible in 1496 for the failure to pay two carpenters, Edward ap Gruffydd and Rhys ap Tudur, for their recent work in the church. The work done in 1496 was substantial, for Edward ap Gruffydd was owed the sum of £3 16s 8d.[65] If this carpentry work was the rood-screen and loft (and F. H. Crossley thought their style contemporary with the glass), then Llanfair's is the only screen not only precisely datable but also ascribable to named Welsh craftsmen. It is singularly unfortunate that the screen was largely destroyed during the 1872 restoration of Llanfair church, but enough of the woodwork, including thirteen tracery heads, survives in the organ chamber to show that the work 'has character' and suggests a screen 'of more than ordinary interest and excellence'.[66]

Llanfair is within a group of southern Dyffryn Clwyd churches in the vicinity of Clocaenog. All the surviving rood-screens in the lordship are in that area – Llanfwrog, Efenechtid, Llanrhudd, Llanelidan, Derwen, Gyffylliog, Clocaenog itself and Llanfair – and on the basis of stylistic similarities at Clocaenog, Llanelidan, Gyffylliog and Llanrhudd, Crossley postulated a 'local centre with its own peculiar forms of setting out and treatment'.[67]

The only wall-painting to survive, the fine, larger than life-size St Christopher in Llanynys church, is likely to date from the first third of the fifteenth century,[68] but the wooden roofs which are so splendid a feature of Llangynhafal, with its angels on the hammer-beams, and St Peter's, Ruthin, inserted in Henry VII's time, after the Greys had ceased to hold Dyffryn Clwyd, are very much part of general Yorkist and Tudor activity.

The later fifteenth century saw a formidable amount of construction, therefore, in stone and in wood. The long, stable reign of Edmund Grey, who held Dyffryn Clwyd for half a century, from 1440 until 1490, clearly encouraged the expression of this religious impulse. Earl Edmund, though careful not to incur unnecessary personal expense, took a keen interest in the moral character of the two dozen or so clergy resident and employed within his Welsh lordship; he was also conventionally pious in his personal and married life but went well beyond conventionality in his abortive attempt to establish Bonshommes in Ruthin, which must have aroused a great deal of

[63] Glynne, 173. A fragment with the name Aspull survives in the church.

[64] PRO, SC2/223/10 m.3r; 224/1 m.10r.

[65] PRO, SC2/224/1 mm.9r, 10r.

[66] F. H. Crossley, 'Screens, Lofts and Stalls Situated in Wales and Monmouthshire, part four', *Archaeologia Cambrensis* xcix (i) (1946), 29–30 and plate facing p. 5.

[67] F. H. Crossley, 'An Introduction to the Study of Screens and Lofts in Wales and Monmouthshire, with Especial Reference to their Design, Provenance and Influence', *Archaeologia Cambrensis* xcvii (ii) (1943), 142.

[68] Cf. L. Parry Jones, *Llanynys Church, Past and Present*, Bangor 1967, 23.

comment and interest throughout the lordship in the 1470s. The fabric of religious life within Dyffryn Clwyd in the later middle ages, viewed through its administration, its social structure, its morality and its buildings, was diverse and vital, with distinctively Welsh elements within the unique jurisdictional framework of the marches, influenced by English ideas and English personnel but creating something *sui generis*, and that *genus* was Anglo-Welsh.

University of Sydney

City and Close: Lichfield in the Century before the Reformation

ANN J. KETTLE

On the whole, city and close remained distinct from, and independent of, each other, and there is nothing to suggest either that the city existed purely to serve the cathedral or that the cathedral was controlled at all by the city.[1]

My intention is to explore the links between the communities of city and close at Lichfield in the century before the Reformation to see if the distinctness and independence which Mrs Owen found at Lincoln were also true for Lichfield. This task is not without its difficulties: Lichfield in the later middle ages must be one of the worst documented of English cathedral cities and the cathedral records before the Civil War are also sparse.[2] If the paucity of material makes it difficult to reconstruct the history of either community, it is even harder to discover the nature of the links between the two. It is this problem of sources which has dictated the concentration on the career in Lichfield of Thomas Heywood, the most important figure in the history of the cathedral in the later middle ages.

The city and the close were small communities: the city had perhaps some two thousand inhabitants at the end of the fifteenth century and the close about one hundred inmates. The number of resident canons had shrunk with the cathedral's revenues from nine in 1417 to five in the 1490s. In addition to the residentiaries and their households, there were twenty-six or so vicars, between eight and twelve choristers, about seventeen chantry chaplains and some servants and office-holders. The vicars lived in houses in the close from the early fourteenth-century and had a common hall from the early fifteenth century. The chantry chaplains, many of whom had previously lived in houses in the city belonging to their chantries, were provided with their 'New

[1] D. M. Owen, *Church and Society in Medieval Lincolnshire*, Lincoln 1971, 46.
[2] *VCH Staffs*. iii, 159.

College' in 1414. The choristers, however, had to wait another century before formal provision was made for them to live in common.[3] The intention behind this encouragement of communal living by the lesser ministers of the church was clearly to maintain and reinforce the separation of the close from the distractions of the city and make it easier for the dean and chapter to control the behaviour of the inhabitants of the close.

The cathedral was separated physically from the city to an unusual extent.[4] The close was surrounded by a stone wall and a moat and linked to the city to the south by causeways; two massive gatehouses guarded the entrances to the close. The inhabitants of the close enjoyed their own water supply and the right to be buried in the cathedral cemetery; both privileges were jealously guarded by the dean and chapter.[5] Although belated provision was made for the spiritual needs at least of visitors to the close,[6] in general the emphasis was on secrecy and exclusion. The statutes and chapter acts of the period stress the need for secrecy and forbid the ministers of the church to involve laymen or outsiders in their quarrels.[7] The gates of the close were shut at eight p.m. in winter and an hour later in the summer months and not opened before seven in the morning, except to carts.[8] Doubtless these regulations were intended to exclude unwelcome visitors such as the plague and suspect women,[9] but they were also directed at the vicars and chantry chaplains, and those returning after closing time were reported by the janitor to the dean and chapter. In 1495 it was necessary for the chapter to draw up a tariff of fines for assaults on the janitor.[10] Although the chapter itself was forced in 1428, after a lengthy dispute, to submit to visitation by the bishop at seven-year intervals, it retained the right to control the behaviour of the minor clergy of the close. This supervision was much resented by the vicars and even resulted in a short-lived strike in 1513 and an unsuccessful attempt to obtain a royal licence of incorporation in 1528.[11]

If the gates constituted an irritation and a challenge to the vicars and chantry chaplains they could also be a protection against too close involvement with the city. In 1436 a dozen Lichfield craftsmen (*villani*, according to the dean and chapter) were accused of trying to break open the gates and laying ambushes for nine named vicars and chaplains. This may not have been simply an isolated outbreak of gang warfare to be dealt with by the appointment of a commission of oyer and terminer, since in 1441 the dean

---

[3] *VCH Staffs.* iii, 156, 159–60, 164–5.
[4] C. C. Taylor, 'The Origins of Lichfield, Staffs.', *Trans. Lichfield and S. Staffs. Arch. & Hist. Soc.* x, 1968–69, 45.
[5] *VCH Staffs.* iii, 143, 150–51, 159, 161.
[6] *VCH Staffs.* iii, 161; LJRO, Chapter Act Book (henceforth CA) iv, fo. 54v.
[7] *VCH Staffs.* iii, 160; CA i, fo. 120v; D. & C. Muniments, Bk of Misc., fos. 76–7.
[8] CA iii, fo. 29; iv, fo. 8v.
[9] CA iv, fo. 63v.
[10] CA iii, fos. 29r–v, 135v.
[11] *VCH Staffs.* iii, 162–4.

and chapter obtained a grant of extensive privileges within the close on the grounds that they had been 'so molested in the precincts of the church that divine service is neglected'. No royal official was to be allowed inside the gates and the dean and chapter were to have the return and execution of all writs and were to be justices of the peace for the close.[12] It has been said of York Minster that 'it would be idle to pretend that the late medieval clergy were able to preserve an oasis of spiritual calm amidst the secular society around them',[13] but at Lichfield strenuous efforts were made by the dean and chapter to isolate the close as far as possible from the distractions of the city across the Minster Pool and to ensure that the ministers of the church lived peacefully and respectably within the precincts and attended to their duties.

The inhabitants of the city could not afford the same exclusive attitude. It is unlikely that many of them were much interested in the affairs of the close; few could have worshipped regularly in the cathedral and in this period no Lichfield citizens founded chantries or obits there. But they could not ignore the importance of the close in their lives. It offered some of them employment as servants and the almost continuous building operations must have provided opportunities for some local craftsmen. The close needed supplies of food and drink, some at least of which must have come from the local market. Pilgrims to the shrine of St Chad and other visitors with business in the church courts needed accommodation and were likely to spend money in the city. The ministers of the church and their servants in search of the entertainment denied to them in the close provided another source of profit for enterprising or accommodating townspeople. The cathedral and its needs must have loomed large in the economy of a small town which had no industry and only a localised trade. It is now recognised that, far from growing 'organically', Lichfield was founded in the twelfth century for the profit of the bishop and it remained technically part of the bishop's manor of Longdon until the Reformation, although during the fifteenth century the government of the town seems to have been shared between the port moot of the borough and the Gild of St Mary.[14] In the later middle ages the bishop and the cathedral clergy intruded into every aspect of the life of Lichfield: economic, religious and social. The major landholders were the vicars who by the 1530s held between 200 and 250 tenements in the city and 185 holdings in the open fields; they were thus probably landlords of at least a third of the town.[15] In ecclesiastical matters the citizens were subject to the peculiar jurisdiction of the dean. The clergy who served the three city chapels were supervised by the dean and chapter and received weekly instruction

---

[12] *CPR 1436–41*, 84; *CPR 1441–46*, 31; CA i, fo. 145v.
[13] G. E. Aylmer and R. Cant, ed., *A History of York Minster*, Oxford 1977, 108.
[14] P. Heath, 'Staffordshire Towns and the Reformation', *N. Staffs. Journal of Field Studies* xix, 1979, 2–5; Taylor, 'Origins', 43, 48; H. Thorpe, 'Lichfield: a study of its growth and function', *Staffordshire Historical Collections* (henceforth *SHC*), 1950–51, 157–71.
[15] LJRO, Evidence Book of the Vicars, *c.* 1535; *VCH Staffs.* iii, 154.

from the subchanter about services.[16] The dean regulated the moral behaviour of the inhabitants of the city through his visitations and his courts in the same way as he supervised the behaviour of the inhabitants of the close.

The social links must also have been strong. It is evident that the clergy who served the city chapels were often from local families and it is likely, though not yet proved, that many of the minor clergy of the cathedral also had family ties with the city. If few of the resident canons had local connections many of them became members of the gild and shared in its social and religious benefits. In addition membership of the gild brought members of the close into contact with the leading citizens of the town and those members of the local nobility and gentry who were regarded as useful patrons and encouraged to enrol in the gild. The register of admissions to the gild contains, at a very rough count, some 11,450 names between 1397, when annual registration began, and 1548 when the gild was dissolved.[17] The number admitted varied considerably from year to year, according to the enthusiasm of individual masters, their attitude to such matters as the admission of single women and posthumous registration of spouses and relatives and also, one suspects, according to the efficiency of the clerks. Between 1400 and 1450 the average number of admissions a year was just over thirty-one. In the second half of the fifteenth century the numbers admitted began to rise and reached record levels of 160 a year on average during the last two decades of the century; the average over the whole half-century was 105 a year. There was a decline in the first decade of the sixteenth century but numbers then began to rise again before inevitably declining in the 1540s; the annual average for the last forty-eight years of the gild's existence was ninety-three admissions. Some 784 names, or nearly 7 per cent of the total admissions, can be identified as those of clergy and at least one in ten of the clergy came from the close. As it is only possible to identify with complete certainty those who were canons and some of the vicars the proportion of cathedral clergy was probably considerably higher.[18] It is clear that there was a continuous and not inconsiderable close presence in an organisation which was increasing rapidly in size, wealth and importance from the mid-fifteenth century. Not only did the number of clerical admissions increase in proportion to the total number of admissions but the character of clerical membership began to change in the 1470s from being predominantly local to include heads of religious houses and other diocesan clergy, secular and religious, who presumably had business in the close. Thus the presence of the cathedral affected the life of the town in another way by widening the connections of its citizens.

[16] *SHC*, 1915, 152; *VCH Staffs*. iii, 154.
[17] The following is based on an analysis of the Register of the Gild, LJRO, D 77/1.
[18] There is a need for a Lichfield equivalent to N. Orme, *The Minor Clergy of Exeter Cathedral*, Exeter 1980.

The influence of the cathedral on the society of Lichfield can be illustrated in another way by examining the career of Thomas Heywood who was connected with the cathedral for nearly sixty years. He was installed in his first prebend in 1433 and progressed through three others before being elected dean in 1457, an office which he held until his death in October 1492.[19] Although he described himself as 'of noble family', his origins are as obscure as the nature of his Oxford degrees. From the obit which he arranged for them we know that his parents were called Nicholas and Alice but an attempt to prove a connection with Heywood in Lancashire and the wool trade is unconvincing and, apart from the fact of his evident wealth, a local connection is just as likely. He was admitted to the gild in 1459 as 'Master Thomas Fisher, al. dict. Heywood, doctor of laws'. The surname Fisher occurs frequently in the gild register, as does that of Heywood, and a William Fisher was master of the gild between 1459 and 1464 but there is nothing else to establish a Lichfield connection.[20]

Thomas Heywood was certainly devoted to the community in which, for whatever reasons, he had chosen to live. Unfortunately no chapter acts survive between 1439 and 1480 so it is impossible to gauge his ability as head of the chapter during the major part of his tenure of the deanship. Some scraps of evidence, however, indicate his concern to maintain the privileges and seclusion of the close. In 1461 he secured the renewal of the 1441 charter guaranteeing the judicial independence of the close and when Sir Humphrey Stanley cut off the close's water supply Heywood had him summoned before the royal council.[21] He also reiterated the regulation that only ministers of the church and members of the households of the canons were to be buried in the cathedral cemetery and statutes made in 1465 ordered the canons to treat the close as a sacred place and not to leave refuse or piles of wood outside their houses.[22] He also made an effort to improve the appearance of the ministers of the church: in 1483 they were ordered to 'reform' their tonsures and make sure that their ears were showing.[23] As well as punishing vicars and chantry priests who left the close without permission and misbehaved themselves in town he took more positive steps to improve their living conditions. He was a generous benefactor to the vicars and repaired their houses and built them an infirmary which contained a chapel and a muniment room. It is perhaps significant that there is no evidence of conflict between the chapter and the vicars during his deanship and he was even admitted to their confraternity. He also improved the 'New College' of the

[19] *Fasti 1300–1541 x, Coventry and Lichfield Diocese*, 6, 30, 43–4, 52.
[20] *BRUO* ii, 897–8; *CPL 1431–47*, 579–80; *CPL 1447–55*, 115; *CPL 1455–64*, 88; H. E. Savage, *Thomas Heywode, Dean*, Lichfield 1925, 7, 10–11; J. C. Cox, 'Benefactions of Thomas Heywood, Dean (1457–1492), to the Cathedral Church of Lichfield', *Archaeologia* lii (2), 1890, 617.
[21] *CPR 1461–67*, 141; *VCH Staffs*. iii, 161.
[22] CA ii, fo. 14; *VCH Staffs*. iii, 161.
[23] CA ii, fo. 11.

chantry chaplains by adding a bakehouse and a brewhouse and supplying the common hall with a stove and a table cloth.[24]

Heywood was, above all, devoted to the church which the close and its inhabitants existed to serve and he did much to improve its appearance. He contributed £40 towards the cost of building a new library and he enriched and beautified the interior of the church with a stone screen at the entrance to the Lady Chapel and stained glass, paintings and panelling in the chapter house. He also bought a new organ and a bell which alone cost £100.[25] He endowed obits for himself and his parents and followed these with two chantry foundations: one in 1466 dedicated to St Blaise and the more elaborate chantry of Jesus and St Anne in 1468. In 1473 he added to the latter foundation a cursal mass, celebrated a week each at a time by the vicars, and extra services on Fridays which were intended to draw lay people into the cathedral for special devotions. He was not content to rely on the popularity of the cult of the Holy Name to draw visitors to his chantry but obtained indulgences from the archbishop of Canterbury and bishops of the southern province in 1473 and from Rome in 1482. Offerings at his statue of Jesus and St Anne brought in a steady income which was used to maintain the fabric of the chapel and of the whole cathedral. The foundation was so popular that in 1487 the chapter set up a fraternity of Jesus and St Anne for men and women of any station in life and made Heywood the first member. Heywood thus put Lichfield at the forefront of liturgical fashion and provided a new attraction for visitors to the cathedral.[26]

Heywood's generosity was not confined to the close and, like bishops and deans before and after him, he seems to have felt some obligation towards Lichfield and, in particular, to the poor of the city. He was not, however, at all original and was content to add to, or reform, existing benefactions. He gave, for example, a pasture in King's Bromley to the almshouses which later took the name of his colleague, Thomas Milley.[27] Nor did he neglect the city chapels which were within his charge as dean: he gave money for repairs to St Michael's and St Chad's and spent £61 on improvements in St Mary's.[28] Any interest in the city chapels was, however, secondary to his main concern for the cathedral as is revealed by an incident in 1461. On the eve of St Katherine's day he sent an inhibition against the celebration of two sung masses in St Mary's in aid of the fabric of the chapel in case they prevented visitors coming to the cathedral to hear mass in St Katherine's chapel. When the inhibition was repeated the following day on the chaplain who was about to celebrate the evening mass in the gild chapel in St Mary's the master of the gild beat the dean's messenger and threatened to make him eat the letter

[24] *VCH Staffs.* iii, 164–5; Savage, *Thomas Heywood, Dean,* 19.
[25] *VCH Staffs.* iii, 165–6.
[26] *VCH Staffs.* iii, 165; Cox, 'Benefactions', 618–20; CA ii, fos. 15v–16; Pfaff, *Feasts,* 77–9.
[27] *VCH Staffs.* iii, 276.
[28] Cox, 'Benefactions', 621.

unless he took it back to the dean, 'saying they wished to have their mass without interruption'. The mass was then held 'in manifest contempt of the dean and his jurisdiction'.[29] It was, perhaps, the jurisdictional aspect which was predominant in Heywood's dealings with Lichfield as can be seen in his reform of 'Our Lady's alms-chest' in 1486. Two canons, John Harwood and George Radcliffe, had each left £20 to be lent to the poor of the city on strict conditions. During his 1485 visitation Heywood discovered that only £13 remained of the fund. Announcing that it 'apperteyneth to owr ordinary cure, to favour and norysshe the thinges that be rightfull, and the thinges that letten the profyt of vertues to correct and amend', he recovered £20 'by laborous and diligent inquisicion and examinacion', made up the missing £7 from his own pocket and then tightened up the administration of the loan chest. The four key bearers, who included the master of the gild and the sacristan of the cathedral *ex officio*, were to say prayers for the souls of Harwood, Radcliffe and Heywood and to swear before the dean and the wardens and six worshipful men of the gild to observe the regulations for the use of the fund; at future visitations the dean was to enquire into the keeping of the regulations and to reform abuses 'to the behofe and profyt of the pore people dwelling in Lichfield'.[30]

The same linking of the cathedral and gild under the jurisdiction of the dean in a common concern for the welfare of the inhabitants of Lichfield can be seen in the supervision of morals which formed part of the 'ordinary cure' of Dean Heywood. The chance survival of a volume of visitation *acta* for the dean's peculiar jurisdiction provides an insight into the realities of daily life in Lichfield in the 1460s and the impact of the dean on the society of the town.[31] The volume, which is in a poor state and is as difficult to read as most such 'repulsive' documents,[32] records the presentment of offenders made to Dean Heywood at his visitations of the city in October 1461, January 1466 and November 1466 and proceedings in his court after the visitations. For some reason the third visitation was very much fuller than the other two. This unevenness, together with the poor state of the document, makes it unsuitable for rigorous analysis and it is certainly not a 'trustworthy basis for statistics'.[33] Something can be learnt, however, from the sort of offences which 'attracted social opprobrium'[34] and were brought to the attention of the dean and the action taken by him. Offenders were 'discovered' to the dean by sworn men from each street or ward. These *jurati* were the respectable members of Lichfield society, mostly members of the gild, and their presentments are a

[29] LJRO, xviii, Dean Heywood's Visitation Book, 1461–66 (henceforth Vis. Bk), fo. 2v.

[30] F. J. Furnivall, ed., *The Gild of St Mary, Lichfield* (EETS, extra series cxiv), 1920, 18–24.

[31] I am grateful to Dr D. B. Robinson for letting me see the draft of an article on the visitation book, which helped me in attempting to decipher it.

[32] G. R. Elton, *England 1200–1640*, 1969, 105.

[33] *Linc. Vis. 1517–31*, xlvi.

[34] F. R. H. Du Boulay, *An Age of Ambition*, 1970, 104.

reflection of public opinion, gossip and neighbourly indignation. It was natural that the dean's attention should be drawn mainly to the misbehaviour of the lower ranks, those on the margin of Lichfield society, but some better-connected citizens do make an appearance in the pages of the volume. John Atkyns, a drover and a member of the gild, was merely accused of adultery with one of his servants in 1461 but in 1466 he was presented for ill-treating his wife and keeping two or three fancy women (*pulcras mulieres*).[35] Two future masters of the gild were presented for quite different offences. John Malyn, who was to become master in 1474, was accused by the parish chaplains of St Mary's of abusing them on Sundays and telling one of them to come down from the pulpit as he could speak better.[36] Sampson Pere, who was master in 1482 and 1483, evidently sowed some wild oats in the 1460s: he was accused of fathering illegitimate children in 1461 and 1466 and it was claimed that he did not care whom he deflowered and that he 'adhered' to so many that he suffered 'a burning in his rod'. One of his women, Alice Browne, was also presented for adultery with a servant of the bishop and was said to pay frequent visits to the monks at Burton.[37]

Public opinion, as reflected in the presentments, was primarily concerned with sexual misbehaviour. Even when men and women were presented for other offences such as not attending church or disturbing their neighbours these were usually associated with sexual offences. Thus Alexander Wotton, who was presented for swearing and not going to church, was also accused of keeping a brothel and Joan Bate, who was presented as a common defamer of her neighbours, was also accused of fornication with three men.[38] The presentments reflect a general suspicion of unattached women, often identified only by their christian names. Such women were suspected of being prostitutes or of running brothels. Joan Grenesall was presented for keeping two women in her house who had come from a London brothel and were common to all.[39] Joan Hardey, who was said to have been made pregnant by John Atkyns, the errant drover, and to have had four children by Roger Hunt, another member of the gild, was presented for having two servants who were common to all.[40] Three professional prostitutes were presented to the dean in 1466: Margery, who lived in the house of Richard Warner, her pimp; Margaret Throstyll, who denied none who came to her and every night made so much noise that her neighbours could get no sleep; and Cecilia, who boasted that she had been known fourteen times by day and night by members of the duke of Clarence's household during a recent visit to

---

[35] Vis. Bk, fos. 4, 22v, 25.
[36] Vis. Bk, fo. 15v.
[37] Vis. Bk, fos. 2, 3v, 21v. For 'burning' see F. G. Emmison, *Elizabethan Life: Morals and the Church Courts*, Chelmsford 1973, 32.
[38] Vis. Bk, fos. 16v, 18, 23v–24.
[39] Vis. Bk, fo. 20.
[40] Vis. Bk, fos. 27r–v.

Lichfield and had made the princely sum of six royals.[41] There were also several women who evidently practised on an amateur basis. Margaret Glover was said to have given birth to a daughter in Coventry and was pregnant again in 1466 but so many men had known her that she could not say who the father was; in court she accused William Sumner, one of the St Mary's chaplains, of fathering both her children.[42] Joanna Cooke acquired a certain notoriety as the widow of Green Hill who acted as a bawd for her daughters but more usually it was the husband who was accused of procuring.[43] Servant girls were a constant temptation and the majority of men presented for fornication or adultery were accused of misbehaving with their own or other people's servants. Thomas Hull was presented in 1461 for making no less than three of his mother's servants pregnant.[44]

It must have been difficult to avoid the prying eyes of neighbours in such a small community and sometimes public disapproval resulted in direct action. Mariot Irish was taken from the bed of Robert Beckett by neighbours, and Robert Hyens who was discovered committing adultery in the house of Adam Taylor was thrown out in the morning by Adam's wife.[45] What Professor Du Boulay calls 'the fear-driven anger of the married woman' was a force to be reckoned with:[46] John Norley was found by his wife committing adultery in the house of one of the town's most notorious procurers and had his head broken by her in three places.[47] If ill-treated wives were not always willing to take such violent action, their neighbours could present their errant husbands at the dean's visitation. John Holmon was accused of ill-treating his wife by not sleeping with her, refusing her food and making her work on feast days.[48] The fear and suspicion of married women can perhaps also be detected in the frequent presentments of couples suspected of not being married or having wives or husbands elsewhere and of married women behaving suspiciously while their husbands were absent.[49]

The group which found it most difficult to avoid prying eyes and censorious gossip were the local clergy. Nine were accused of fornication, four of fathering illegitimate children, and others were presented for riotous or suspicious behaviour, card-playing or neglect of their cures.[50] Two offenders stand out from the ordinary run of clerical fornicators: William Sumner, a chaplain of St Mary's, was not only accused of being the father of Margaret

---

[41] Vis. Bk, fos. 15v, 16v, 26v.
[42] Vis. Bk, fo. 26.
[43] Vis. Bk, fos. 21, 27.
[44] Vis. Bk, fo. 2v.
[45] Vis. Bk, fos. 17v, 22v.
[46] Du Boulay, *Age of Ambition*, 107.
[47] Vis. Bk, fo. 22.
[48] Vis. Bk, fo. 23.
[49] E.g. Vis. Bk, fos. 3v, 16v, 17, 25.
[50] Vis. Bk, fos. 3v, 17v–18, 21–2, 23r–v, 27r–v, 31; cf. P. Heath, *The English Parish Clergy on the Eve of the Reformation*, 1969, 115–18.

Glover's two children but also of neglecting his duty of ringing the fire and service bells in order to play dice and of behaving improperly by wearing piked shoes, flowing hair and a cheerful face.[51] William Heyth was presented for not wearing his habit or tonsure or conversing in a proper clerical fashion and was also said to neglect his duties as a gild chaplain in favour of his cure in the close.[52] As might be expected the close and its inhabitants do not often figure in the volume but the story of Thomas Coke, one of the cathedral clergy, illuminates the relationship between close and city on one level. He was presented in 1461 for fornication with two women; one of them was then married and living in Coventry or Nuneaton but was said to visit his chamber in the close as before. The other had lived in the house of a notorious pimp but left 'in debt to many'; she then stayed in the house of Matilda Andrew for a fortnight before moving, with two gallons of ale, into Thomas' chamber in the close where she was seen by Matilda who was taking beer to the room of another priest.[53]

How did Heywood react when presented with this collection of ruined servant girls, shameless prostitutes, bigamous husbands and fornicating chaplains? In quite a large number of cases, including one of incest, no further action is recorded. This may be due to the nature of the record or it may be that those involved were not interested in defending their good names and the dean not anxious to pursue the matter. He was, however, concerned to follow up cases concerning marriage. When the validity of a marriage was in doubt those involved were ordered to produce acceptable written evidence of their marriage: alleged witnesses were not sufficient. In one case the man died before the hearing but the woman was still required to produce her marriage lines (*litteras nuptiarum*). In several of these cases the personal interest of the dean is clear: Thomas Wryght confessed to marrying Joan Hewster while her husband was still alive when summoned to the house of the dean. In July 1466 an estranged couple were called before the dean in the cathedral: Helen Hyndman said she would not live with her husband because he was a dice player and had wasted their goods. Heywood ordered him not to gamble and to treat his wife honestly on pain of three whippings.[54] Married women living apart from their husbands were ordered to return to them, in some cases repeatedly.[55] In appropriate cases of fornication the dean would also use the threat of marriage in an attempt to end irregular unions. Thus William Pereson and the woman he lived with as his wife were made to promise publicly before the dean to marry if they slept together again, and Thomas Hull was made to give up two of his three servant girls on pain of

[51] Vis. Bk, fos. 21, 26.
[52] Vis. Bk, fos. 17, 23.
[53] Vis. Bk, fo. 4.
[54] Vis. Bk, fos. 16v, 18, 19v, 20v, 21v, 23v.
[55] Vis. Bk, fos. 17, 19v, 22r–v.

marrying within a month if he resumed relations with either of them.[56] The concern of the ecclesiastical courts to defend the marriage bond is now well-established but Heywood seems to have shown a remarkable personal interest in this aspect of his jurisdictional role.

Those who stood accused by public fame had the right to attempt to re-establish their good name by purgation. In Lichfield, as elsewhere, the majority of those who chose to go to purgation had little difficulty in finding enough compurgators, although it was sometimes less easy for women and the court was sympathetic to their problems: one woman was allowed three attempts at purgation and another who had recently moved was allowed to produce three of her six compurgators from the street where she had formerly lived.[57] It has been pointed out that purgation was not a reliable indication of guilt or innocence but a means by which those threatened by gossip could restore their public reputation, 'a useful means of avoiding conflict and maintaining social harmony', and Heywood was probably expected to operate the system in this way.[58] He could, however, show his individuality in the imposition of penances and other penalties on those unable to purge themselves and on occasion he was lenient. The sentence of public penance and whipping against Thomas Wylson was commuted because he had recently married and his wife was not aware of his misbehaviour and the sentence of whipping on his mistress was also commuted because she was expected to give birth within the next fortnight.[59] In the case of a deranged woman who was presented for scattering the stubs of holy candles around the streets the court fees were remitted because of her poverty.[60]

Heywood seems to have exercised his jurisdiction in Lichfield in a paternalistic fashion, showing a concern both to satisfy public opinion and to restore public harmony through the system of presentment, purgation and penance. None of this was unusual but what is perhaps distinctive was Heywood's emphasis on the links between city and cathedral. Offenders were sometimes cited before the dean in person in the close; public promises to marry were made in the cathedral; public penance was sometimes shared between the cathedral and one or more of the city chapels and financial penalties were often divided between St Mary's and the fabric fund of the cathedral or the dean's alms. This emphasis on the interconnection of city and close came at a time when there was possibly some questioning of the efficiency of the church courts and when the gild was taking over more of the government of the city. The gild ordinances of 1387 had emphasised the religious and charitable

---

[56] Vis. Bk, fos. 2v, 24v.
[57] Vis. Bk, fos. 22, 24v, 27.
[58] On purgation, see R. H. Helmholz, 'Crime, Compurgation and the Courts of the Medieval Church', *Law and History Review* i, 1983, 13–20; R. Houlbrooke, *Church Courts and the People during the English Reformation, 1520–1570*, Oxford 1979, 45–7; R. M. Wunderli, *London Church Courts and Society on the Eve of the Reformation*, Cambridge, Mass. 1981, 41–8.
[59] Vis. Bk, fo. 19v.
[60] Vis. Bk, fo. 24.

obligations and benefits of membership; any brother openly defamed of adultery was to be admonished by the master and wardens and expelled if he did not mend his ways.[61] In contrast, Sir Humphrey Stanley's ordinances in 1486 placed on the master and his 48 brethren the responsibility of dealing with disturbers of the peace such as night-walkers, rioters, prostitutes and scolds.[62] In the case of harlots parenthetical lip-service ('the ponisshment of the Church reserved') was paid to the rights of the dean but the times were evidently changing and possibly indifference to the close and its affairs was being superseded by a growing resentment of economic dependence and jurisdictional subordination as the gild and its lay patrons took over control of the city. This may be badly documented speculation but it is clear that Thomas Heywood during his long tenure of the deanship endeavoured to continue both the seclusion of the close and the benevolent intrusion of the dean into the society of the city.

University of St Andrews

---

[61] Furnivall, *Gild of St Mary*, 6–7.
[62] Furnivall, 13; cf. Wunderli, 61, 94, 102.

Archbishop Thomas Bourgchier Revisited*

F. Donald Logan

The appearance in 1957 of an edition of the register of Thomas Bourgchier, archbishop of Canterbury (1454–86), filled a large gap in the sources available to ecclesiastical historians of the fifteenth century.[1] Coming exactly ten years after the publication of the last volume of the register of Archbishop Henry Chichele (1414–43),[2] the publication of Bourgchier's register meant that the principal surviving official records of the two longest pontificates in the primatial see of Canterbury during the fifteenth century – indeed, during the late middle ages – were at the historian's disposal.

Thomas Bourgchier's tenure of the archbishopric of Canterbury spanned the crucial years in the political history of the fifteenth century. While historians have been anxious to pin a dynastic rose on Bourgchier, F. R. H. Du Boulay in his introduction to the register wisely advised caution and saw the archbishop as 'a mediator, probably by temperament and almost by profession'[3] and as 'a political primate content to crown the current victor'.[4] Like most archbishops, Bourgchier left the Canterbury administration, both diocesan and provincial, to well-trained canon lawyers, who formed the core of the ecclesiastical bureaucracy in fifteenth-century England.[5] It is to the work of this bureaucracy that the register bears witness: litigation, licences, appointments, correspondence, institutions, commissions, administration of vacant sees, and, indeed, the keeping of the register itself. The person of the

---

* The author would like to record his gratitude to Miss Helen Powell, Assistant Librarian, The Queen's College, Oxford, for her kind assistance in making available material in her keeping.

[1] *Reg. Bourgchier.*
[2] *Reg. Chichele.*
[3] *Reg. Bourgchier*, xx.
[4] *Reg. Bourgchier*, xxxiii. As a royal councillor he is described as 'a man skilled in delicate missions', Griffiths, *Henry VI*, 727.
[5] J. R. Lander, *Government and Community: England, 1450–1509*, 1980, 126.

archbishop appears seldom and only briefly – as if for cameo performances – on the high stage where convocation was played out and where archbishops spoke with popes and kings.

The register's editor noted its incompleteness.[6] Much is missing from the middle years of the pontificate, especially commissions and bulls. Records of only three out of thirteen convocations held are in the register at Lambeth. There are notable *lacunae* in testamentary commissions and in the institution records. Loss or neglect could explain these gaps, but here surmise must replace hard evidence.

This paper reports the appearance of a considerable amount of material from the period of Bourgchier's pontificate in a fifteenth-century formulary book. It is not suggested here that this material fills the many gaps in the register or that all of this material would have been placed in the register. This formulary book, however, does add to our knowledge of the Canterbury administration and, particularly, of the archbishop's court of Audience.

The importance of formulary books has long been acknowledged.[7] Quite simply, they were books which contained forms for use in ecclesiastical or secular matters. The registers of writs which were used in the royal chancery are examples of the latter. Most of the formularies now extant pertain to ecclesiastical affairs. But too sharp a distinction should not be insisted upon: the so-called Snappe's Formulary, a formulary principally pertaining to the ecclesiastical courts, contains thirty forms concerning Oxford University.[8] Other examples could be given. The ecclesiastical courts, to a large extent using a procedure by written documents, spawned many formularies, drawn up by practitioners, quite often notaries public, mainly for the purpose of providing themselves with a ready 'file' of forms for their future use. Most formulary books are comprised of forms taken from actual cases; sometimes these forms contain the names of persons and places and precise dates, but more often these are submerged into an all too frequent *et cetera*. For the historian formulary books provide a valuable source to complement court *acta*, where they exist, and to fill in the gaps, however incompletely, where they do not exist. In addition, they occasionally provide documents of a more general historical interest.

Manuscript 54 in The Queen's College Library, Oxford, is a late fifteenth-century formulary book which contains forms pertaining to the ecclesiastical courts and other material as well. This is not the place for a full description of its contents.[9] Suffice it to say for now that it contains forms relating to elections, a treatise on charters, a series of Cambridge sermons, the statutes,

---

[6] *Reg. Bourgchier*, xxiii–xxv.

[7] For formulary books see C. R. Cheney's remarks and the literature cited in *Notaries Public in England in the Thirteenth and Fourteenth Centuries*, Oxford 1972, 46–50.

[8] *Snappe's Formulary*, ed. H. E. Salter (OHS lxxx), 1924.

[9] For a description see Henry Coxe, *Catalogus codicum MSS qui in Collegiis Aulisque Oxoniensibus hodie adservantur*, 2 vols., Oxford 1852, i, *Coll. Reg.*, 8–9.

customs and a procedural treatise of the court of Arches, and a summary of almost the whole of the *Liber Sextus* of Boniface VIII; yet the vast bulk of this large codex (438 folios) is comprised of forms used in the church courts. These forms pertain to many courts – the court of the archdeacon of Ely, the Norwich consistory, the court of the archdeacon of Colchester, the London consistory, the court of Arches and the archbishop of Canterbury's court of Audience. This list might suggest the career route of a Cambridge-trained canonist. Although the forms, written down as it appears at one time, cluster about the last two decades of the fourteenth century and the period of the fifteenth century virtually coterminous with Bourgchier's archiepiscopate, the manuscript itself must be dated to the 1480s: the latest datable reference is to the years 1482 to 1486.[10]

I

From the long pontificate of Bourgchier only two provincial constitutions have been hitherto noted.[11] Both came from the convocation of 1463, and they dealt with arrests in sacred places by laymen and with the dress of the clergy.[12] One further constitution appears in the Queen's College formulary book. In addition, a further piece in the jigsaw puzzle concerning Bishop Reginald Pecock has now come to light as has a case strikingly illustrative of the problems surrounding benefit of clergy in the late fifteenth century.

First, the new-found constitution. On 3 April 1481 the prolocutor of the lower clergy produced *inter alia* two petitions. The lower clergy requested relief from the violation of their immunity from arrest and trial by secular authorities; they also asked the higher clergy to establish certain feastdays in the calendar of the province: the Visitation of the Blessed Virgin and the feasts of Saints Osmund, Frideswide and Etheldreda.[13] The minutes of convocation merely noted that the higher clergy wished to discuss these matters and that, since the hour was late, convocation would continue its business on the next day. And there the records fall silent on these two petitions, but we now know that something was done about the second petition and that the issue of benefit of clergy persisted.

Convocation did reach a positive decision concerning the new feasts: while the business of convocation was prorogued from 6 June 1481, the archbishop, '*nostri prouincialis concilii robore et decreto suffulti*', issued a constitution granting the request.[14] Dated at the archbishop's manor at Knole on 13 July 1481, it

---

[10] Oxford, Queen's College MS 54, fos. 356v–357. Hereafter cited only by folio number.

[11] *Reg. Bourgchier*, xxxi.

[12] *Reg. Bourgchier*, 108–11.

[13] *Reg. Bourgchier*, 134–6; also Wilkins, *Concilia* iii, 612–13.

[14] Fos. 341r–v; for the text see Appendix A. For convocation (i.e. provincial council) see Irene J. Churchill, *Canterbury Administration*, 2 vols., 1933, i, 360–79; Dorothy B. Weske, *Convocation of the Clergy*, 1937; E. W. Kemp, *Counsel and Consent*, 1961, particularly chaps. 4 and 5; C. R. Cheney, 'Legislation of the Medieval Church', *EHR* l, 1935, 193–217.

was addressed to Thomas Kempe, bishop of London, as dean of the bishops of the province of Canterbury, to communicate its contents to the other bishops.[15] Following very closely the text of Archbishop Chichele's constitution (4 January 1416) which had established the observance of the feasts of Saints George, David, Chad and Winifred,[16] that of 1481 established the feast of the Visitation as a double feast (i.e., the antiphons were repeated in full before and after each psalm) according to the Sarum use, to be observed on 2 July with an octave and *'cum regimine chori'* (with senior clerics ruling the choir). Although this feast had been first established by Pope Boniface IX in 1389 to seek the Virgin's intercession to end the Great Schism and its observance had been further ordered by the council of Basel in 1441 – again to bring unity to the church – the English church (or, rather, the province of Canterbury) responded only now in 1481 to the decree of Pope Sixtus IV, who 'virtually re-established the feast' in 1475 to seek the Virgin's aid against the Turks.[17] Moreover, this constitution introduced the feasts of St Osmund on 4 December, St Frideswide on 19 October and St Etheldreda on 17 October; these feasts were to be observed *'cum regimine chori'* and with nine lessons. St Osmund had been recently canonised (1457), and his feast was to be that of his deposition rather than his translation.[18] It is interesting to note that an earlier petition of the lower house of convocation (19 October 1434) had asked for the introduction of the feast of St Frideswide into the calendar of Canterbury province and that no action had been taken at that time.[19] On the same day on which the archbishop sent this mandate to the bishop of London he also sent a mandate to his commissary general in the diocese of Canterbury, ordering him to see that the feasts were observed in his own diocese.[20]

About the matter of clerical exemption from secular prosecution no decretal is known to have been issued at this time, but the Queen's College formulary book contains a perhaps not unrelated form dated 4 September 1481; it immediately precedes the decree on feastdays and, hence, might arguably be related to the petition of the lower clergy which refers to the

---

[15] On 15 December 1481 Thomas Milling, bishop of Hereford, wrote to the archbishop that he had executed the archbishop's mandate (*Reg. Millyng*, 74).

[16] *Reg. Chichele* iii, 8–10; William Lyndwood, *Provinciale (seu Constitutiones Angliae)*, Oxford 1679, 103; Wilkins, *Concilia* iii, 376.

[17] See Pfaff, *Feasts*, 40–46. York did not introduce the feast until 1513 (Pfaff, 41). For the problem in England where other feasts of significance fell within the octave of the Visitation see the letter of Pope Sixtus IV in *CPL 1471–84*, 90–91. For the introduction of feasts into England see C. Wordsworth and H. Littlehales, *The Old Service Books of the English Church*, 1904, 190–93.

[18] For the ruling in choir and for double feasts see *The Use of Sarum*, ed. W. H. Frere (2 vols., Henry Bradshaw Soc.) Cambridge 1898–1901, i, 27–33, 248–51. For St Osmund see *The Canonization of Saint Osmund*, ed. A. R. Malden, Salisbury 1901.

[19] *Reg. Chichele* iii, 256.

[20] Fo. 346.

question of criminous clerks.[21] The compiler, quite uncharacteristically, reproduced this document in its entirety and without the '*et ceteras*' that were so often used. It is a commission from Archbishop Bourgchier to a Master John Lee, master of 'our college' at Maidstone concerning two allegedly criminous clerks.[22] John Cowley, a London mercer, and Rober Chamberleyn, a London shipman, had related to Archbishop Bourgchier that they had been falsely accused of the following charges: on 8 February 1472 in the parish of St Margaret's, Rochester, by force and arms (viz., with swords, daggers and knives) they had stolen from Thomas Fitzwilliam, a gentleman from Lincolnshire, a number of articles, valued at £6 6s 2d, as well as £49 10s 4d in money.[23] They had been indicted and tried before the king's justices in the secular court, where they had been convicted. Because they were clerics, they had been handed over to the archbishop for imprisonment, and, hence, Cowley and Chamberleyn had been placed in the archbishop's jail at Maidstone. They claimed now that they were innocent of the charges and should be allowed to purge themselves and be freed. Thus, on 4 September 1481 – five months after the petition of the lower clergy – Bourgchier ordered the master to have announced in the parish church in Rochester that anyone opposing these two clerks or their purgation should appear before the master in his college in Maidstone at a date of the latter's choosing. The master was told to proceed to a purgation with ten priests or clerks swearing. If the purgation were successful, the two men were to be delivered from the archbishop's jail.

Two London 'businessmen', clerics possibly only by reason of having received clerical tonsure at some perhaps half-forgotten time, having been convicted in the royal courts of serious theft, had set in motion the ecclesiastical machinery for their release. What convocation had been asked to do was to reintroduce an older procedure which would permit a clerk, seized by the secular authorities, to claim clerical exemption and to be tried in the ecclesiastical courts, unlike Cowley and Chamberleyn, who had been tried in the secular courts, there convicted, and then sent to the church for imprisonment. The allowing of purgation in this case – ten clerks, who would swear to the credibility of the accused – meant that the judgement of the king's court could in practice be vitiated. This case exemplifies the usual procedure at this time, described by Dr Gabel.[24] Convocation had complained about aspects of this procedure in 1460 and the lower clergy had complained in

---

[21] For the text of the form see fo. 340v. For an introduction to this question see Leona C. Gabel, *Benefit of Clergy in England in the Late Middle Ages*, Northampton, Mass., 1928–29. For more particular reference to Bourgchier's pontificate see *Reg. Bourgchier*, xxxii–iii.

[22] The parish church at Maidstone had been made into a college in 1395. John Lee was master from 1470 to 1494 (*VCH Kent* ii, 232–3).

[23] Thomas Fitzwilliam was probably the man by this name from Louth, Lincs., mentioned frequently in the patent rolls at this time (*CPR 1476–85*, 630).

[24] Gabel, chap. 2.

1463 and in 1471.[25] Some amelioration was promised by Edward IV in a charter of 1462,[26] but it seemed to have had little effect.[27] The Cowley-Chamberleyn case and its insertion in full in our formulary book witnesses the continuing concern with the issue of the *privilegium fori*.

Reginald Pecock, the maverick bishop of Chichester, and Lollard books both feature in another form in the Queen's College formulary book.[28] Although undated, this form clearly comes from the later 1450s and almost certainly from March 1458. The compiler placed above this form the heading, *MONICIO CUM CITACIONE CONTRA STUDENTES IN LIBRIS DAMPNATIS*. The exact nature of this *monicio* will be returned to shortly, but, for now, the contents. The monition is addressed by Archbishop Bourgchier to all the rectors (with or without care of souls) of the province and to preachers at Paul's Cross (i.e., the preacher's cross in the churchyard of St Paul's Cathedral). Bourgchier stated that it had come to his attention that there were souls within his province who were studying dangerous books. These books were of two kinds: (i) books composed in English by Reginald Pecock, 'our brother bishop of Chichester', which have already been examined and condemned as suspect of error and heresy and against which further action was about to be swiftly taken,[29] and (ii) books of the Bible in English, clearly a reference to Lollard scriptures.[30] Those who possessed books of either sort were to be warned, no matter who they were, that within twenty days they must hand over such books either to the archbishop or to one of the other diocesan bishops of the province under pain of excommunication. If they did not, then a fortnight later they would be declared suspect of heresy. After a further fortnight, if they still had not handed over their books, they would be considered as heretics and would be cited to appear to explain the cause of their rebellious behaviour.

This document fits into the Pecock saga sometime in the years 1457–59, when action was being taken by royal and church officials against him. Two

[25] See *Reg. Bourgchier*, xxxii.
[26] *Reg. Bourgchier*, 102–7; Wilkins, *Concilia*, iii, 583–5.
[27] Further clerical complaints were made in 1483, and Richard III confirmed the charter of Edward IV in 1484 (Wilkins, *Concilia* iii, 614, 616).
[28] Fos. 341v–342v. For the text see Appendix B.
[29] The most recent study of Pecock is the excellent reassessment by R. M. Haines, 'Reginald Pecock: A Tolerant Man in an Age of Intolerance', *SCH* xxi, 1984, 125–37. See also, E. H. Emerson, 'Reginald Pecock: Christian Rationalist', *Speculum* xxxi, 1956, 235–42; A. B. Ferguson, 'Reginald Pecock and the Renaissance Sense of History', *Studies in the Renaissance* xiii, 1966, 147–65; V. H. H. Green, *Bishop Reginald Pecock: A Study in Ecclesiastical History and Thought*, Cambridge 1945; E. A. Hannick, *Reginald Pecock, Churchman and Man of Letters: A Study in Fifteenth Century Prose*, Washington 1922; E. F. Jacob, 'Reginald Pecock, Bishop of Chichester', *Proceedings of the British Academy* xxxvii, 1951, 121–53, which now appears in his *Essays in Later Medieval History*, Manchester 1968, 1–34; and J. F. Patrouch, *Reginald Pecock*, New York 1970.
[30] On Lollard bibles see Margaret Deanesly, *The Lollard Bible and Other Medieval Biblical Versions*, Cambridge 1920, especially chap. 14; J. A. F. Thomson, *The Later Lollards, 1414–1520*, Oxford 1965, especially 242–4; and Anne Hudson, 'Some Aspects of Lollard Book Production', *SCH* ix 1972, 147–57.

clues help us further to define the date of the archbishop's letter. First, he called Pecock 'bishop of Chichester', an office he held till his resignation probably in the autumn of 1458 and certainly by early in 1459. Likewise, the archbishop stated that he had already examined the English works of Pecock and found them suspect of error and heresy and that he was about to proceed further against them. Pecock spent much of late 1457 explaining his position on points of theology (e.g., Christ's descent into hell, salvation outside the church, the inerrability of the church and general councils). In early October the king's council asked Bourgchier to appoint assessors to examine Pecock's works; they were to report to a special tribunal. This tribunal – its actual composition is obscure – met for the first time on 11 November. Ten days later Pecock appeared before the tribunal and again a week later (28 November), when, faced with the alternatives of recantation or of being handed over to the secular arm for burning, he recanted. This document would fall between the trial of November 1457 and the resignation a year or so later. For a further refinement of the dating we should compare this monition with a letter sent by Bourgchier on 9 March 1458 to the bishop of London for dissemination to the suffragans of the Canterbury province.[31] In this letter Bourgchier said that he had condemned the very same kinds of books mentioned above, and he now ordered the bishops of the province to make inquiries about the names of those having such books, to warn the faithful in their dioceses, and to send him a report by 21 May next. At Ely Bishop Grey held inquiries on 6–8 April, warnings were read in all the churches of the diocese, and, in a letter of 14 May, he reported to Bourgchier that no one was found possessing the forbidden books or holding erroneous or heretical views.[32] Unlike the monition in the formulary book, which was addressed to all the clergy of the province, this letter of 9 March 1458 was sent only to the bishops; yet the words used to describe the condemned books – which, the archbishop told the bishops he had ordered to be burned – are almost identical. All of this suggests a date for the monition near to the date of the letter to the bishops, i.e., early in March 1458.

One might ask by what right Archbishop Bourgchier directed this monition to the subjects of his suffragan bishops. The key to the answer to this question is the word *querela*: the archbishop said he was responding to a complaint (*querela*) from many people which came '*ad auditum*'. It is clear that Bourgchier was acting here in his audience and was exercising jurisdiction because the matter had been brought to him *per modum querelae*, a jurisdiction

---

[31] It was enregistered in the episcopal register of William Grey (Cambridge Univ. Libr., Ely Diocesan Records, G/1/5, fos. 106r–v). The bishop of London had sent Bourgchier's letter to Grey on 10 March. For Grey see R. M. Haines, 'The Practice and Problems of a Fifteenth-Century English Bishop: The Episcopate of William Gray', *Mediaeval Studies* xxxiv, 1972, 435–61, and 'The Associates and *Familia* of William Gray And his Use of Patronage while Bishop of Ely (1454–78)', *JEH* xxv, 1974, 225–47.

[32] A copy is in Grey's register, fo. 106v.

traditionally held by archbishops of Canterbury. Too fine a distinction should not be insisted on between judicial and administrative decisions reached by the archbishop in his Audience. This monition, then, was a document issued non-judicially from the archbishop's Audience.

II

The court of Audience of the archbishop of Canterbury was, as its name suggests, the court where business was brought *coram nobis*.[33] It was in origin the archbishop's personal court, the oldest kind of ecclesiastical court, a tribunal in which the archbishop personally made decisions, administrative and judicial. Just as courts devolved from the *curia regis*, so too courts devolved from the *curia archiepiscopi*. Among these were (i) the consistory court of the diocese of Canterbury, (ii) the court of Canterbury (i.e., the appellate court for the province of Canterbury, known popularly from the late thirteenth century as the court of Arches), and (iii) the prerogative court of Canterbury with jurisdiction in testamentary matters.[34] After these courts peeled away from the personal court of the archbishop, the court of Audience still remained. It had jurisdiction *iure ordinarii* over the archbishop's subjects in the diocese of Canterbury and its peculiars. Moreover, it exercised jurisdiction over the subjects of the archbishop's suffragans *iure legationis*. The archbishops claimed this latter right by reason of the decretal letter of Pope Alexander III, *Cum non ignoretis*, which can be dated to the years 1174–81, possibly 1174–75: it allowed the archbishop *as legate* to hear cases brought to him by his suffragans' subjects whether they came to him by way of appeal or by way of complaint.[35] In 1282 the suffragan bishops of the Canterbury province complained *inter alia* that the court of Canterbury could hear neither *querelae* of their subjects nor appeals that bypassed their courts.[36] Archbishop Pecham replied that he could do this by two-fold authority, which he had by custom and by law. The two-fold authority, not explained, must surely have referred to his authority as metropolitan and as legate. The experts to whom the dispute was referred allowed that the archbishop could hear complaints

---

[33] For the Audience see Churchill, *Canterbury Administration* i, 470–99; Felix Makower, *The Constitutional History and the Constitution of the Church of England*, 1895, 461–2; and Brian Woodcock, *Medieval Ecclesiastical Courts in the Diocese of Canterbury*, Oxford 1952, chap. 1 *passim*.

[34] The devolution of the prerogative was a very late development (see Churchill i, 412–19). In Bourgchier's time prerogative cases seem to have been deputed individually to judges for probate and administration.

[35] For the dating of this decretal letter see Anne Duggan, *Thomas Becket: A Textual History of His Letters*, Oxford 1980, 107. The text (Jaffé no. 11665) can be conveniently found in Churchill (i, 425, n.). That the archbishops could hear appeals *iure metropolitico* was not questioned by his suffragans.

[36] The texts of this material can be found conveniently in *Councils and Synods*, ed. F. M. Powicke and C. R. Cheney, vol. ii, pt. ii, Oxford 1964, 923, 926, 928, 931, 933–5. For commentary see Churchill i, 427–30, 470–71; F. W. Maitland, *Roman Canon Law in the Church of England*, 1898, 117–20; and Decima Douie, *Archbishop Pecham*, Oxford 1952, 206–13.

iure legacionis but that he could not commission his official of the court of Canterbury to do so. The opinions of the experts were embodied in a letter to Pecham, which may not have been widely circulated.[37] In any case, the archbishop's Audience was to hear cases coming to it both by way of appeal and by way of complaint throughout the fourteenth and fifteenth centuries, and, when in 1532 Archbishop Warham replied to the Petition of the Commons, he simply asserted that the archbishops of Canterbury and York have had for four hundred years the papal privilege of citing before them subjects from their provinces in cases concerning appeals and complaints.[38]

It is not clear how the Audience differed in practice from the Arches except that it seems that the Audience did not, as a rule, hear tuitorial appeals (i.e., double appeals, one to the Roman court on the substantive matter and another to the Arches to protect the appellant's interests pending appeal).[39] Furthermore, the Arches was a permanently situated court, sitting from the late thirteenth century in London, usually in the church of St Mary-le-Bow; the Audience, on the other hand, seems to have followed the archbishop and it sat where he was. Suitors in the Audience had to have been prepared to travel.

Very few of the medieval records of the court of Audience of the archbishop of Canterbury are known to be extant. A volume from Robert Winchelsey's archiepiscopate (1294–1313) survives[40] as do fragments of act books from Archbishop John Stratford's Audience, particularly for the years 1340–43 and 1347–48.[41] In addition, there are gleanings from the archbishops' registers concerning the court of Audience. The material in the Queen's College formulary book relating to this court substantially increases the quantity of our sources. Over twenty-six folios contain forms pertaining to the court of Audience, almost all from the period of Bourgchier's pontificate. They reveal the court in action, exercising jurisdiction in a variety of cases, making judgements, demanding obedience, fulminating sanctions, absolving the repentant, etc. It must be remembered, however, that these are forms in a formulary book, not *acta* from an act book. The compiler was not keeping a record: he was merely collecting forms found personally interesting to him.

---

[37] A marginal note in Pecham's register claims that the letter was never sealed or sent and was lost for twelve years in the archives, yet a copy was enregistered at Worcester in 1282 (Churchill i, 430).

[38] H. Gee and W. J. Hardy, *Documents Illustrative of English Church History*, 1896, 167–8.

[39] Miss Churchill found two examples of tuitorial appeals when tuition was sought in the Audience, both from the years near 1400 (i, 494); the present writer has found no other examples.

[40] London, Lambeth Palace Libr., MS 244.

[41] See C. Donohue and J. Gordus, 'A Case from Archbishop Stratford's Audience Act Book', *Bulletin of Medieval Canon Law*, n.s. ii, 1972, 45–59, and R. M. Haines, *Archbishop Stratford*, Toronto 1986, pp. 90, 93, 385–6. Excerpts can be found in C. E. Woodruff, 'Notes from a Fourteenth Century Act Book of the Consistory (*sic*) Court of Canterbury', *Archaeologia Cantiana* lx, 1928, 53–64, from which one might wish to conclude that all cases came from the diocese of Canterbury.

Thus, names and dates are generally suppressed, and we are left with the unhelpful *et cetera*. Although one would prefer to have the full form in every instance, the inability to date individual forms merely means that we are unable to date them to specific dates in Bourgchier's pontificate. There is no suggestion that institutional changes were occurring in the archbishop's courts at this time. Hence, instead of a number of miniatures we have a wide-lens picture. What does this picture show?

It shows the archbishop acting by legatine authority. Although there are a number of explicit references to the archbishop so acting, there is no such explicit reference in the only general commission to an auditor of the Audience in this formulary book – the appointment (undated) of Master Thomas Winterborne.[42] Yet, when the archbishop commissioned two lawyers to hear a marriage case, that case was said to have come to the Audience *'iure legacionis nostre'*.[43] Also, in an inhibition dated 9 November 1481 the archbishop indicated that he was acting in his Audience by legatine authority.[44] Moreover, in a commission to an auditor to act for a very limited period of time Bourgchier authorised him to continue cases in the Audience *'nostre legacionis aut metropolitano iure'*.[45] Should one see in these latter words a distinction between cases coming to the Audience by way of complaint and, hence, heard by right of the legateship and cases coming by way of appeal and, hence, heard by metropolitan right? Although this hazy distinction with its roots in the decretal letter of Alexander III continued to be made, the evidence from the forms shows that in almost every instance the party who brought a case to the Audience brought a *querela* and sought a remedy. The plaintiff is called the *'pars actrix et querelans'*, and the defendant is called the *'pars rea et querelata'*. In one instance the plaintiff was called *'pars querelans siue appellans'*.[46] The impression is clearly given that little distinction was being made in practice between an appeal and a complaint.[47]

Since there was no official in the Audience – only an auditor – all documents from the court proceeded in the name of the archbishop, who would simply state that a particular case had come to his Audience where it was being heard before his auditor. These documents proceeded routinely from the Audience in the archbishop's name. Only two auditors – Master

---

[42] Fo. 355.

[43] Fos. 351r–v.

[44] *'Nos igitur qui iure legacionis nostre et prerogatiue ecclesie nostre Cantuariensis obtentu uniuersas causas singulorum subditorum suffraganeorum nostrorum que per appellacionem uel querelam ad nostram audienciam peruemunt audire possumus et debemus sicuti qui uices domini nostri pape in hac nostra prouincia gerere comprobamur . . .'* (fo. 353v).

[45] Fos. 351v–352.

[46] Fos. 357r–v.

[47] In an inhibition from the archbishop's Audience to the bishop of Norwich (Walter Lyhert) and his commissaries, dated 4 May 1458, reference is made that the case came to the audience by way of appeal (fos. 308v–309). Also, there is an undated demand for a *processus* to be sent by the commissary of the bishop of Worcester in an appeals case (fo. 357v). These are the only references in the formulary book to cases coming to the Audience by way of appeal.

John Stokes and Master Thomas Winterborne – are known to have held that office during Bourgchier's long pontificate. The commission appointing Stokes appears on the first folio of the archbishop's register and, although undated, was given in 1454.[48] The commission appointing Winterborne is to be found, undated, in the formulary book.[49] A comparison of the two commissions reveals no difference in the powers deputed to the two men. They could hear all cases traditionally coming to the Audience – criminal and civil – and could impose correction and penance when necessary; they could remove clerks from ecclesiastical positions; they could fulminate censures. Each man was appointed to act as the archbishop's commissary as well as his auditor.

Two additional commissions also appear but they are limited in scope. In one instance, two doctors of law were commissioned to hear a specific divorce case in Coventry and Lichfield diocese and were given powers to compel reluctant witnesses, to reach a definitive sentence, and to use ecclesiastical censures.[50] In another instance, a commission was given to continue and prorogue all cases coming to the Audience, particularly from 5 June to 18 July – year not given – in the parish church of L.[51] Thus, the use of judges-delegate by the Audience continued into the fifteenth century.

The court of Audience, from its origins, was peripatetic: it followed the archbishop from one place to another. Business was conducted *ubicumque in nostris ciuitate, diocesi aut prouincia Cantuariensi fuerimus*. During Bourgchier's pontificate these traditional words continued to be used, but there is no evidence one way or the other to show that the words were still literally true or that the court had become more or less permanently settled in London. When Winterbourne was auditor – and dean of St Paul's – he held a session of the court in the dean's house.[52] In another, tantalisingly abbreviated form a certain Richard was warned that he must solemnise his marriage to Joan Nightingale or appear in the church of the Blessed Virgin in L., W. diocese, to explain himself.[53] The implication here is that the court was sitting in that church. One is strongly tempted to identify this church as the church of St Mary in Lambeth, Winchester diocese – the same church where the Audience is known to have sat in Archbishop Morton's time[54] – rather than a church in the provinces where the archbishop was appearing personally, perhaps on

---

[48] *Reg. Bourgchier*, 2. For Stokes, see *BRUO* iii, 1782.
[49] For the commission see fo. 355. For Winterborne see *BRUO* iii, 2060–61.
[50] Fo. 351r–v.
[51] Fos. 351v–352.
[52] Dated 16 December 1476 (fos. 370v–371v).
[53] Fos. 343v–344.
[54] The only reference to proceedings in the Audience in Morton's register concerns a case heard in this church. I am grateful to Dr Christopher Harper-Bill, who is preparing Morton's register for publication by the CYS, for calling this reference to my attention.

visitation, or where he had sent judges to hear Audience cases.[55] Itinerant or fixed? *Quaestio stat.*

The matters brought before the Audience reflect the general variety of cases heard in the church courts: marriages, testaments, contracts, defamations, tithes, benefices, adultery, simony and the rest. The actual complaints could have arisen from any wrong, real or imaginary, felt by a party: a judgement was unfair; an excommunication was imposed wrongly; a lower court lacked jurisdiction; a bishop had instituted someone else to the benefice claimed by the plaintiff; a person had been cited to a place too far and a time too soon. And so it went, and cases came to the Audience.

The court accepted a *querela* (or an *appellatio*) by sending an inhibition to the person or persons complained about: no further action should be taken against the plaintiff and any judgement should be held in abeyance. For example, an inhibition came from the archbishop, while at Knole on 9 November 1481; it inhibited the commissary of the bishop of Norwich as well as the instancer in the lower court from doing anything prejudicial to two women from Clare in Suffolk: the commissary and the instancer were ordered to appear in the Audience ('*ubicumque . . .*') to show reason why the two women should not be absolved *ad cautelam* from the excommunication imposed by the commissary.[56] In another case, the parties were ordered not to contract or solemnise marriage.[57] When an unhappy cleric complained that the bishop of London and the archdeacon of London had instituted another cleric to his benefice, the Audience heard his complaint and inhibited bishop and archdeacon from doing anything to the prejudice of the plaintiff.[58] Mention here of absolution *ad cautelam* underlines the fact that an excommunicate had no standing in court and, hence, for him to prosecute his appeal it was necessary that he be absolved *ad cautelam* (for safety's sake).[59]

---

[55] Bourgchier's register contains no records of visitations during his pontificate, but Professor Du Boulay published as an appendix, from a Canterbury MS, an account of Bourgchier's visitation of Christ Church Canterbury on 25 August 1484 (*Reg. Bourgchier*, 457–60). The Queen's College formulary book refers to three dioceses visited by the archbishop. Dates are missing and initial letters are used for the dioceses in two cases: dioceses C (fo. 362v), L (fo. 363) and Salisbury (fos. 362r–v, 363r–v).

[56] Fos. 353–4.

[57] Fo. 356.

[58] Undated, it belongs to the years 1482 to 1486 (fos. 356v–357).

[59] Two forms for absolution *ad cautelam* in the formulary pertain to St Paul's Cathedral, London. In the first, undated, licence was given to Archbishop Bourgchier to Master J.D. to absolve *ad cautelam* the canons of St Paul's from any sentence of suspension, excommunication and interdict, if they had incurred such penalties and if they might be absolved by the archbishop (fo. 346). Master J.D. might have been John Derby, canon from 1443–68, often mentioned elsewhere in the formulary. The second form relates that in 1456–57 Master Thomas Winterborne, the archbishop's chancellor and auditor of causes, absolved Master W.B., president of the chapter during the vacancy of the deanery, from any sentence of suspension or excommunication incurred by him as an executor of the testament of the late dean, Master Thomas Lisieux (fo. 346v). Lisieux died in 1456. W.B. could have been William Brewster or William Briggeford, although neither is known to have been a master (*Fasti 1300–1541 v, St Paul's London*, 6, 50–51).

A citation, if not already contained in the inhibition, then followed. The person or persons complained against were cited to appear in the Audience generally on a specific date. The court officer responsible for presenting the citation was called a *mandatarius*. His work was not always easy. Occasionally, as in one instance in the Norwich diocese, the *mandatarius* was maltreated: the citees *'causa et occasione eiusdem citacionis male perperam iniuste diuersimodo tractarunt atque uariis contumeliis et tribulacionibus afflixerunt seu saltem sic tractari et affligi mandarunt et fecerunt'*.[60] The *mandatarius* was not always able to locate the citee as in the case of the master of a hospital in L. diocese, against whom a complaint had been made by the founders that he was not fulfilling the terms of the foundation.[61] Also, the *mandatarius* could find himself cited to appear in the Audience to explain how he had executed the citation.[62]

If he had not been successful in serving the citation personally to the citee, the court then resorted to a citation *viis et modis* (i.e., a citation made by public announcements which should predictably reach the citee's attention). Proctors would normally then be appointed, although parties might choose to act on their own behalf. The court, however, in one case when it insisted on the personal appearance of a defendant averred that *'legalior est persona et melius nouerit in dicto querele negocio quam eius procurator dicere ueritatem'*.[63] And, of course, the court could insist on the personal presence of the parties. One form – how often it was used one really must wonder – reveals a proctor confessing to the court that his client did not have a just case: in fact, it was hopeless.[64] Occasionally the plaintiff did not prosecute his case in the Audience, and consequently the auditor demanded the plaintiff's appearance on penalty of dismissal of the case. This happened in the case of a woman of Canterbury diocese who took a case to the Audience, secured inhibition and citation, but failed to proceed with her appeal.[65] In another case the auditor remitted the matter to the official of the archdeacon of Coventry because the allegedly wronged party had failed to appear in the Audience and his proctor had agreed to dismissal of the case.[66] The auditor might even cite such a party to appear for the fixing of costs.[67]

After citation and appearance the case proceeded by the plaintiff issuing his positions and the defendant by responding. Relevant documents were needed from the lower jurisdiction from which the case had come. Officials of these jurisdictions were not always quick to obey. In an interesting marriage case which proceeded by appeal from the court of the archdeacon of Lincoln

[60] Fo. 348.
[61] Fo. 343r–v.
[62] Fo. 347v.
[63] Fo. 348v.
[64] Fo. 348.
[65] Fo. 357r–v.
[66] Fo. 359r–v.
[67] Fo. 347r–v.

to the consistory of the bishop of Lincoln to the archbishop's Audience the auditor ordered the lower courts to send the processes to the court by a specific date.[68] Similar demands for documents were made to the dean and chapter of Wells, the commissary of the bishop of Worcester, and the abbot and archdeacon of Westminster, although in this latter instance there was more deference shown, probably because of the abbey's exempt status.[69]

The response of the defendant to the charges, if not made personally or by proctor, could be made by notarised deposition. The notary would be instructed to examine the defendant and to transmit the responses by letters close.[70] Similarly, when witnesses could not appear personally in the Audience – this is not surprising in a peripatetic court – notaries were instructed to put the witnesses under oath, examine them secretly and separately, take their depositions and transmit them sealed, closed and notarised to the court. The number of witnesses deposed could have been limited as, for example, in a tithes case between a rector and a vicar, where no more than twelve witnesses were allowed for each of the parties.[71] Physical disability of witnesses could have prevented their personal appearance: '*propter senium corporum debilitatem et infirmitatem ac alia impedimenta*' the auditor allowed depositions to be taken in the local parish church on 20 February next with return by 27 April.[72]

Barring non-prosecution or out-of-court settlement cases went to judgement, the one aspect of the ecclesiastical courts about which we know the least, and the evidence in the Queen's College formulary book does little to enhance our knowledge. The scraps are few. An appeal from the Lincoln consistory in a marriage case was not sustained in the Audience and was remitted to the Lincoln consistory.[73] In another defamation case the judgement was against a certain chaplain of Exeter diocese, and it was declared that he had incurred major excommunication, which should be publicly announced.[74] In yet another defamation case the party found at fault was cited to appear to show reason why the sentence should not be executed.[75] An unfortunate layman was required to lead the procession into his parish church on a specified Sunday, alone, shoeless and carrying a candle worth one penny; the reason for his penance was to be publicly announced; while he knelt before the altar, he was to recite five times the *Pater* and the *Ave* and once the Apostles' Creed; and, finally, he was to offer the candle to the priest.[76]

---

[68] Fos. 359v–360.
[69] Fos. 343v, 357, 357v–358.
[70] Fos. 349v–350.
[71] Fo. 350.
[72] Fo. 350r–v.
[73] Fos. 365v–366.
[74] Fos. 364v–365.
[75] Fo. 364v.
[76] Fo. 367.

The court, at every stage, enforced its authority through warnings and threats of censure and through censures themselves. Failure to appear when cited and failure to obey any mandate of the court, including the court's judgement, left the offender liable to the full force of the church's spiritual penalties and, even, to imprisonment by the secular arm. From the forms in the Queen's College formulary book five stages appear in this process. First, a simple warning was issued: obey the court's order under pain of excommunication, and, if you refuse to obey, appear to show cause why excommunication should not be imposed.[77] Second, excommunication was decreed by the court, particularly at the instance of the other party.[78] Third, denunciation of the excommunicate followed, but he might first be called to show reason why there should be no denunciation.[79] Denunciations were made in the excommunicate's parish church and often in the neighbouring parishes. Matters did not always go as planned or ordered. For example, a certain notary public, although excommunicated and later absolved from the excommunication, was subsequently denounced as excommunicate at Paul's Cross through the machinations of an enemy; a public correction was ordered.[80] Fourth, the excommunication was aggravated, and, again, the excommunicate might be cited to appear to show reason why it should not be aggravated.[81] The aggravation meant a widening of the social ostracism: an aggravated excommunicate should be avoided, and the faithful should not associate with him – like the rebellious executor of a testament from Rochester diocese – *'seruiendo, loquendo, stando, sedendo, ambulando, salutando, hospitando, commedendo, bibendo, molendo, coquendo cibum, panem, aquam, uel ignem ministrando aut aliquo humanitatis solacio preterquam in casibus et personis a iure permissis'*.[82] Fifth, after the passing of forty days as an excommunicate – aggravation was not required – he was liable to arrest by the secular arm, and, again, he might have been given a term in the Audience to show cause

---

[77] A certain Richard of the city of London, was ordered to restore conjugal rights to his wife, and the preacher of God's word at Paul's Cross and three London rectors were ordered to warn him publicly so that the warning would come to his attention (fos. 342v–343).

[78] For example, '*W.T., Exoniensis diocesis nostre Cantuariensis prouincie propter suas contumacias in non parendo certis monicionibus licitis et canonicis auctoritate nostra sibi ad instanciam G.B. legitime factis et contractis sentencia maioris excommunicacionis extitit innodatus pariter et inuolutus*' (fo. 350).

[79] In one case, a man who had incurred excommunication by order of the court for having 'familiar conversation' with a woman was ordered to appear to show cause why he should not be denounced as an excommunicate (fos. 364r–v). In another form several priests were ordered to announce an excommunication on Sundays and feastdays at solemn Masses when a multitude of people would be present, and this was to be done as often as the instancer so required (fos. 364v–365).

[80] Fo. 359. In another case the auditor discovered that his order for a denunciation in London was being thwarted by a certain F.G., whom he cited (fo. 361v).

[81] An executor of a testament refused to obey the auditor's mandates, was warned, excommunicated, denounced, and cited to appear to show cause why '*dicta sentencia si in eadem perseuerauerit pertinaciter contra eum aggrauari non debeat*' (fo. 356).

[82] Fo. 345v.

why this should not happen.[83] Writs issued from the royal chancery as a matter of course against such obdurate excommunicates signified by the bishops of England.

These steps had the correction of the erring party and his reconciliation through absolution as their purpose. At any stage absolution could be requested and, oaths having been given to obey the court, absolution would be given. It was enough in many cases where the penalty had been imposed for non-appearance that the person's proctor swear his obedience to the court in the future.[84] If arrest had taken place, the archbishop requested the release of an excommunicate later absolved.[85] Absolution showed that the 'medicine' of excommunication had been effective.

The court of Audience during Bourgchier's pontificate – from the glimpses we have of it – was operating in full vigour, applying the canon law to the cases brought before it, being ably manned by university-trained lawyers, and doing its part to keep the wheels of the ecclesiastical administration moving smoothly. No hint here of high piety, merely the daily workings of a large institution.

Emmanuel College, Boston, Massachusetts

APPENDIX A

Constitution of the Canterbury province establishing the feasts of the Visitation of the Blessed Virgin, St Osmund, St Frideswide and St Etheldreda, dated 13 July 1481 (Oxford, Queen's College MS 54, fo. 341r–v).[a]

Thomas miseracione diuina etc. uenerabili fratri nostro Thome dei gracia Londonensi episcopo salutem et fraternam in domino caritatem.

Ineffabilis et inperscrutabilis potencie dominus cuius altitudo prudencie nullis inclusa limitibus, nullis terminis comprehensa, recti censura iudicii celestia pariter et terrena gubernans, cunctos eius ministros magnificans altis decorat honoribus et celestis efficit beatitudinis possessores.

Et si Deum in sanctissima uirgine Maria, unici filii dei humani generis redemptoris genitrice, sanctis Osmundo episcopo, Fredeswida et Etheldreda

---

[83] A man from Lincoln diocese was given a fortnight to oppose the suing of a royal writ for his capture (fo. 357). For this general procedure see F. D. Logan, *Excommunication and the Secular Arm in Medieval England*, Toronto 1968.

[84] Examples of this can be found on fos. 344r–v, 346v.

[85] Two men from Lincoln diocese who found themselves imprisoned as a consequence of the royal writ *de excommunicato capiendo* successfully sued for absolution, and the archbishop requested a writ for their release (fo. 360r–v).

[a] *Heading in MS*: Mandatum ad publicandum constitucionem siue decretum.

uirginibus meremur, ut orbis affatus ipsaque gracie desuper concesse experiencia, rerum cunctarum interpres optima, attestantur, hinc [fo. 341v] est quod nos qui Dei laudem in sanctis suis, quibus gloriosus existit, in nostra prouincia Cantuariensi cupimus ampliari procerum et regni incolarum ad hoc ortatibus excitati, confratrum nostrorum et cleri dicte nostre prouincie ducti conciliis, quinymmo et nostri prouincialis concilii robore et decreto suffulti, antiquorum patrum pium erga sanctos[b] Dei deuocionis affectum prosequentes, festum uisitacionis sancte Marie gloriosissime uirginis antedicte sub more duplicis festi secundum usum ecclesie Sarum cum pleno seruicio sexto nonis Iulii cum octauis que celebrentur cum regimine chori, festaque sanctorum Osmundi episcopi secundo nonis Decembris, Fredeswide xiiii^{mo} kalendis Nouembris et Etheldrede sextodecimo kalendis Nouembris cum regimine chori et nouem leccionibus, decreto per totam prouinciam nostram Cantuariensem antedictam et per uniuersas ecclesias eiusdem suis temporibus de expresso consensu confratrum nostrorum et cleri antedicti uolumus, statuimus et precipimus annis singulis perpetuis futuris temporibus deuote et solenniter celebrari.

Uobis uenerabili fratri nostro tenore presencium mandantes et firmiter iniungentes quatenus festa predicta singulis annis decetero ut profertur suis temporibus deuote et solenniter celebretis et per uestras ciuitatem et diocesim faciatis modo premisso deuote et solenniter celebrari, uolumus eciam et mandamus quatenus uestris confratribus et coepiscopis nostris et ecclesie nostre Cantuariensis suffraganeis omnibus et singulis per literas uestras auctoritate nostra ac dicti concilii iniungatis et mandetis, quibus et nos modo consimili iniungimus et mandamus quod ipsorum singuli eadem festa sicut premittitur singulis annis deuote et solenniter celebrent et per suas ciuitates et dioceses modo premisso perpetuis temporibus futuris faciant deuote et solenniter celebrari. Et quid feceritis in premissis ac quomodo et sub qua forma presens nostrum mandatum executi fueritis nos citra festum sancti Michaelis archangeli proxime futurum distincte certificetis per literas uestras harum seriem habentes sigillo uestro sigillatas. Mandantes eciam singulis confratribus nostris quod et ipsi singillatim quatenus presens mandatum nostrum ipsorum ciuitatis et diocesis concernit nos citra festum natalis domini proxime futurum per literas suas modo consimili certificare non omittant sub pena incumbenti[c] tam uobis quam ipsis si contra factum fuerit canonice infligenda.

Datum in manerio nostro de Knoll sub sigillo archiepiscopatus nostri xiii^{mo} die mensis Iulii anno domini etc. lxxxi^{mo} et nostre translacionis anno uicesimo septimo.

---

[b] antiquorum . . . sanctos *scripsi*; cf. *Reg. Chichele* iii, 9, where it is misread; Lyndwood, *Provinciale* 103; Wilkins, *Concilia* iii, 376.

[c] *MS adds*: vel sic sub pena que incumbit. *This was meant as an alternative reading.*

APPENDIX B

Mandate from Archbishop Bourgchier to the clergy of the Canterbury province concerning the English books of Reginald Pecock, bishop of Chichester, and books of the bible translated from Latin into English, undated but c. *March 1458* (Oxford, Queen's College MS 54, fos. 341v–342v).

Thomas etc. dilectis filiis uniuersis et singulis rectoribus, et curatis et non curatis, quibuscumque per nostram prouinciam Cantuariensem et necnon cuicumque uerbum Dei ad crucem sancti Pauli Londonie predicante siue predicaturo salutem, graciam et benediccionem.

Inter solitudines [fo. 342] nostris humeris incumbentes cura solerti reuolimus ut ea que causam prestant erroris extirpare et in uiam ueritatis reinducere errantes ipsosque lucrifacere Deo sua nobis cooperante gracia ualeamus. Cum itaque multorum querela ymmo euidencia facti quod dolenter referimus nostrum deduxerit ad auditum quod nonnulli nostre prouincie Cantuariensis plus sapere conantes quam oportet libros habentes diuersorum operum non solum confratris nostri Cicestrensis episcopi in uulgari anglico compositos quos coram nobis exhibitos et per nos examinatos tanquam errorum et heresum suspectos quantum ad usum suspendimus et dampnauimus, contra eos tamen iuxta potestatem nobis desuper attributam et iuris exigenciam cum omni celeritate accomoda ulterius processuri, sed alios e latino in anglicum ex sacra scriptura traductos siue translatos in ipsis libris student et laborant, sanctorum patrum sanccionibus, dictis et decretis que alma mater ecclesia hactinus approbant spretis pariter et neclectis, quo sic[a] in ecclesia anglicana presertim in prouincia nostra Cantuariensi talia murmura, cediciones seccionesque et scandala sunt exorta ut, si non oportunum hiis remedium celerius apponatur, ecclesia predicta erit – quod Deus avertat – enormiter sanciata, quocirca uobis communiter et diuisim committimus et mandamus firmiter iniungentes quatinus moneatis peremptorie et in genere omnes et singulos nostre Cantuariensis prouincie subditos libros huiusmodi in sua custodia habentes cuiuscumque status, preeminencie, gradus, ordinis, sexus uel condicionis existant sub penis infrascriptis quos nos eciam tenore presencium sic monemus quod infra uiginti dierum spacium a tempore monicionis uestre quinuerius nostre continue numerandorum quorum uiginti dierum sex pro primo, sex pro secundo et reliquos dictorum uiginti dierum pro tercio et peremptorio termino ac monicione canonica eis et eorum cuilibet assignamus et prefigimus ac sic per uos assignari et prefigi uolumus et mandamus libros antedictos omnes et singulos nobis aut confratribus nostris coepiscopis, locorum diocesanis, nostre prouincie Cantuariensis reuelent, exhibeant et tradant realiter et cum effectu sub pena maioris excommunicacionis quam in singularum libros antedictos habencium et

---

[a] *MS*: fit.

illos, ut premittitur, non reuelancium, exhibencium et tradencium personas eorum contumacia mora, culpa et necligencia atque predicta monicione canonica precedentibus ferimus et promulgamus exnunc prout extunc et extunc prout exnunc in hiis scriptis.

Et si, quod absit, infra dictos uiginti dies libros memoratos habentes, sicut premittitur moniti, eos reuelare, exhibere et tradere[b] nobis uel confratribus nostris antedictis non curauerint lapsisque dictis uiginti diebus infra quindecim dies extunc immediate sequentes, sicut premittitur, reuelare, exhibere et tradere distulerint, preter excommunicacionis sentenciam qua eos uolumus striccius ligari pena suspicionis quod sunt fautores heretici prauitatis eos uolumus et decernimus debere notari.

Demum uero dictos quindecim lapsis diebus per alios [fo. 342v] quindecim expectati libros memoratos nobis aut dictis nostris confratribus reuelare, exhibere et tradere postposuerint, distulerint aut recusauerint, eos extunc tanquam hereticos et catholice fidei subuersores[c] censendos et reputandos esse decernimus prout eo casu tenore presencium reputamus et censemus. Contradictores uero et rebelles, si quos inueneritis in hac parte, peremptorie citetis seu citari faciatis quod compareant etc. quintodecimo die etc. causam sue reclamacionis et rebellionis, si quam habeant, in debita iuris forma dicturos et allegaturos facturosque etc. Et quid in premissis feceritis etc.

[b] et tradere *scripsi*.
[c] *MS erronee*: submersores.

Church, Nationality and Revolt in Late Medieval Buda

Martyn C. Rady

Medieval Buda was founded in the late 1240s by German refugees from Pest. In 1241 their town, which lay exposed and unfortified on the westernmost limit of the Great Hungarian Plain, had been sacked by the invading Mongol forces of Batu Khan. The German community had survived the assault but six years later, on receiving rumour of an impending second attack, the bulk of its inhabitants fled across the Danube for the greater safety of the Buda hill opposite. There they stayed, occupying the central portion of the hill which they henceforth referred to as the 'New Mount of Pest'. From Pest, the Germans brought their civic seal and charter granted them by King Béla IV in 1244.[1] Without royal objection, they carried on as if the new settlement enjoyed all the freedoms previously given to Pest. The centre of the German settlement became the Church of Our Blessed Lady (the present-day Matthias or Coronation Church), which was at this time one of the many royal *Eigenkirche* to be found in the middle part of Hungary's Danube basin.[2]

It was once thought that the Pest Germans were the first inhabitants of the Buda hill. Recent archaeological and topographical investigations indicate, though, that a Hungarian village had been set up previously on the hill's northern part. Excavations here have yielded heavy soot deposits and the remains of rough stone barricades: the legacy of the Mongol attack in 1241.[3] The material needs of this small indigenous community are known to have been met by a weekly market held on Saturdays. The selection of this day suggests the market's, and so probably the village's, twelfth-century origin.[4]

---

[1] Dezsö Csánki and Albert Gárdonyi, *Monumenta diplomatica civitatis Budapest 1148–1301*, Budapest 1936, 41–3; a translation of the 1244 charter may be found in Ágnes Ságvári (ed.), *Budapest: The History of a Capital*, Budapest (Corvina) 1975, 78–9.

[2] Miklós Jankovich, 'Buda környék plébániának középkori kialakulása és a királyi kápolnák intézménye', *Budapest régiségei* xix, 1959, 57–98.

[3] Katalin Gyürky, 'Buda településének kezdete a régészeti adatok alapján', *Archaeológiai értesítö* xcix/1, 1972, 44.

[4] Erik Fügedi, 'Közepkori magyar városprivilégiumok', *Koldul barátok, polgárok, nemesek* (Collected Essays), Budapest 1981, 307.

Spiritual care was administered by the Church of Mary Magdalene which later claimed to have exercised a parochial authority from its foundation, the date of which remains uncertain. On its north-western boundary, the Hungarian village bordered a Slovak village known as Tótfalu which shared its market and church.[5]

Despite the destruction of the Mongol attack in 1241, the Hungarian village was able to recover. During the 1240s, it received a new population influx and first began calling itself 'Buda'.[6] In this way, it remained at first quite distinct from the neighbouring 'New Pest' German settlement. Even long after the absorption of the 'Buda' community, a confusion of nomenclature persisted in regard to the hilltop town. Throughout the later middle ages, it might be variously referred to as the *'Novus Mons Pesthiensis'*, *'Castrum Pesthiense'*, *'Castrum Budense'* and *'Mons Budensis'*.

The migration of the Pest Germans to the Buda hill was accompanied by the planning, construction and fortification of a completely new town which spread out to encompass the older Hungarian village. The entirety of the hilltop was encircled by walls; the area enclosed divided into groundplots and roadways. In this massive building programme, the Hungarian village was uprooted to make way for the proposed network of streets.[7] The whole enterprise had the active support of King Béla IV (1235–70) and was possibly undertaken on his behalf by a consortium of Pest Germans acting in the capacity of royally appointed *locatores*.[8] At the same time, the growing town attracted to it a host of immigrants who fast populated not just the fortified area but spilled out beyond the walls to create new suburbs. In the tide of construction and immigration, almost all trace of the older Hungarian settlement disappeared.

Yet the original Hungarian village still managed to give rather more than just its name to the new town. Although the village vanished, its institutions did not. The Saturday market continued to be held and is clearly referred to in a document of 1332. By the early fifteenth century, though, this market had been downgraded in importance and reduced to little more than a few stalls actually within the portals of the nearby town gateway – then not surprisingly called the Saturday Gate (the present-day Vienna Gate).[9]

---

[5] Erik Fügedi, 'Megjegyezések a budai vitáról', *Századok* xcviii, 1964, 777; András Kubinyi has sought the origins of the Saturday Market and Magdalene Church in the Tótfalu settlement: 'Topographic Growth of Buda up to 1541', (ed.) *Commission Nationale des Historiens Hongrois, Nouvelles Études historiques*, i, Budapest 1965, 140–41.

[6] *Monumenta diplomatica civitatis Budapest*, 39.

[7] Gyürky, 44; Erzsébet Lócsy, 'Középkori telekviszonyok a budai várnegyedben', *Budapest régiségei* xxi, 1964, 191–206.

[8] Elemér Mályusz, 'A mezővárosi fejlödés', (ed.) György Székely, *Tanulmányok a parasztság történetéhez Magyarországon a 14. században*, Budapest 1953, 142.

[9] Imre Nagy, *Codex diplomaticus Hungaricus Andegavensis* ii, Budapest 1881, 586; Karl Mollay, *Das Ofner Stadtrecht: Eine deutschsprachige Rechtssammlung des 15. Jahrhunderts aus Ungarn*, Budapest 1959, 114.

Likewise, the Magdalene Church survived and continued to maintain a close relationship with the Hungarian population of the town. And indeed, it was on the open space beside Mary Magdalene's that the eventual successor to the Saturday market was held: the Friday market. This was specially reserved for Hungarian traders and compares thus with the German Wednesday market held by Our Blessed Lady's.[10] The Hungarian church and its neighbouring market provided the nucleus of medieval Buda's Hungarian quarter which extended across the northern part of the walled area. Both institutions also served the largely Hungarian community outside the walls. During the 1250s, though, the Church of St Peter the Martyr was constructed to help minister to the Hungarians living in the town's north-eastern suburb and a small market grew up beside it.[11]

Nevertheless, it would be wrong to suppose that Buda, as it emerged during the later middle ages, was a town consisting of two communities, Germans and Hungarians, entrusted with largely similar rights and freedoms, and with national churches each in turn enjoying an equal status. From the very first and right up until the 1430s, the commanding nationality group within the town was the German one. Even though the Germans as a whole formed only a minority of the town's population,[12] their supremacy was built into not just the town's government but its ecclesiastical organisation as well.

In late medieval Buda, the town's governmental and judicial apparatus was administered by a twelve-man council or *Rat* headed by the judge or *Richter*. Attached to this body was a notariate under the supervision of the town's scribe. Both the judge and the scribe had to be Germans. When the annual municipal elections were held, the citizens were asked 'to appoint from out of their number a judge, whomsoever they wish, and he should be a German and of German descent'. Similar requirements attended the election of the scribe. As for the twelve councillors of the *Rat* it was laid down that, 'By old custom and ancient law the Germans should elect ten men to the council and the Hungarians two'.[13] This last provision may be confirmed by the surviving council lists which indicate that up to the 1430s the bottom two or three places only were occupied by Hungarians.[14]

[10] Mollay, *Stadtrecht*, 137.
[11] András Kubinyi, *Die Anfänge Ofens* (*Giessener Abhandlungen zur Agrar- und Wirtschaftsforschung des Europäischen Ostens* lx), Berlin (Duncker u. Humblot) 1972, 41.
[12] Quite what was the ratio of Germans to Hungarians remains uncertain and wisely no serious attempts have been made towards an estimate. Buda's population during the fifteenth century has been calculated variously at 8,000 and 12,500–15,000.
[13] Mollay, *Stadtrecht*, 67–70.
[14] A list of Buda's judges and councillors during the medieval period is included as an appendix in Martyn C. Rady, *Medieval Buda: A Study of Municipal Government and Jurisdiction in the Kingdom of Hungary*, East European Monographs no. 182, Boulder 1985.

The unequal relationship evident between Germans and Hungarians within Buda's municipal government had its counterpart in the town's ecclesiastical organisation. From the time of their settlement on the Buda hill, the Church of Our Blessed Lady had functioned as the Germans' church. Probably at first, its priest was elected by the citizens of the town although this right was soon assumed by the council.[15] Until the mid-fifteenth century the priests of Our Lady's were of German descent and its services conducted in German. For their part, Mary Magdalene's and St Peter's ranked as the Hungarians' churches. Yet these last two were considered not equal in status to Our Blessed Lady's but, instead, subservient to it. The parish district of Our Lady's, so its priests maintained, encompassed not just the German quarter of the town but reached out across the entire walled area and over the suburbs. Within this district, the Hungarians' churches were held to be interlopers 'newly founded by the inhabitants (*homines et hospites*) of the suburbs within the parish of Our Blessed Lady's'. As such, they were regarded as filial churches and accordingly obliged to make annual symbolic payments to the mother-church. Nevertheless, by special concession, Mary Magdalene's and St Peter's were able to exercise a limited parochial authority over the town's Hungarians but, it was stressed, only because these 'do not understand the German language which the parish priests (of Our Blessed Lady's) publicly speak'. Similarly, by permission of Our Lady's, the Hungarian community of the town chose its own priests.[16]

Mary Magdalene's in particular resented the claims put forward by Our Blessed Lady's. The priests of the Magdalene Church always maintained that theirs was 'a parish church, having its own distinct bounds and subject to none nor tied to the Church of Our Lady'. Right up until the fifteenth century, its representatives were involved in continual and useless litigation around this issue with the priests of Our Lady's who, for their part, claimed Mary Magdalene's to be 'a daughter-church and chapel within the parish district of Our Blessed Lady's'.[17] Some attempts have been made to explain this dispute by reference to the terms of the Magdalene Church's foundation.[18] Originally, so it has been argued, while Our Lady's was still an *Eigenkirche* and before the arrival of the Pest Germans, Mary Magdalene's had been established as its daughter-church and entrusted with care of souls over the indigenous population on the northern part of the Buda hill. This may well be. It should, though, be noted that many contemporaries considered the superior status of Our Blessed Lady's to derive not from any *a priori* legal

[15] Mollay, *Stadtrecht*, 67.
[16] Xystus Schier, *Buda sacra sub priscis regibus*, Vienna 1774, 105–6, 112; (ed.) A római magyar történeti intézet, *Monumenta Romana Episcopatus Vesprimiensis* ii, Budapest 1899, 383–4; *Monumenta diplomatica civitatis Budapest*, 383–4.
[17] Schier, 105–7.
[18] Erik Fügedi, 'Megjegyezések a budai vitáról', *Századok* xcviii, 1964, 777.

right but instead from the simple fact that the Germans were the town's more powerful nationality. In this respect, it is certainly significant that similar forms of ecclesiastical organisation are found in other central European towns of mixed population where one nationality group was regarded as politically dominant. Here, the towns of Old Prague, Cracow, Kassa (Košice) and Eperjes (Prešov) are the most obvious examples.[19]

The ecclesiastical organisation of medieval Buda served, however, as rather more than a pale reflection of the political *status quo*. For the presence within the town of distinct national churches plainly reinforced some early form of national self-consciousness and, in so doing, deepened divisions. Both Our Blessed Lady's and Mary Magdalene's served as the focal points of their respective German and Hungarian communities. Accordingly, both became closely associated with other institutions also specifically tied to one of the town's two nationalities. This development made itself felt not just in the location of the town's two markets – upon which we have already remarked – but also in the arrangement of its guilds and confraternities.

It was during the late fourteenth and early fifteenth centuries that Buda's first guilds were formed. In many cases, though, these were organised according both to their members' craft and to their nationality. To a degree, the presence of two markets, one for Hungarians and the other for Germans and each held on separate days of the week, had as its inevitable consequence the division of the guilds along national lines. Thus, besides a German butchers' guild, there was in Buda a Hungarian butchers' organisation which plied a separate trade on the square beside the Magdalene Church.[20] Likewise, we may read of guilds of Hungarian tailors and coopers and one of German skinners. Just as the location of the town's two markets was greatly determined by where the respective Hungarian and German churches stood, so also were the various guilds identified with either the Germans' Church of Our Lady or the Hungarians' Magdalene Church. The German skinners' guild described itself thus as 'pertaining to the altar of the Blessed Andrew the Apostle in the parish church of Our Lady'. For its part, the Hungarian tailors' guild enjoyed a special relationship with the Magdalene Church and made regular payments to its Holy Spirit side-chapel. The German butchers similarly provided for the upkeep of Our Lady's.[21]

The emergence of separate confraternities for each of the two nationalities of Buda and their close association with one or other of its churches extended beyond the town's craft organisations. By the early 1430s, the leading

---

[19] R. D. P. Hieronymus Pez, *Scriptores rerum Austriacarum* ii, Leipzig 1725, col 628; György Székely, 'Towns and Languages in East Central Europe', *Reports of the XIV International Congress of the Historical Sciences* ii, New York (Arno Press) 1977, 1006–21.

[20] Hungarian National Archive (Budapest), *Collectio antemohacsiana*, Dl 15196.

[21] *Ibid.*, Dl 50564, Dl 25268; Archive of the Great Library of the Reformed Church Diocese Beyond-the-Tisza (Debrecen), R1110/134; Béla Bevilaqua Borsody, *A budai és pesti mészáros céhek ládáinak okiratai* i, Budapest 1931, 169.

Germans of the town had set up their own exclusive society called, after one of the altars in Our Blessed Lady's, the Corpus Christi German Brotherhood. Later materials attest to the substantial wealth possessed by this organisation. In Nuremberg alone, it held assets estimated at 2,250 gold gulders and rents worth 75 gulders a year. In 1526, on the eve of the Turkish attack, the Brotherhood deposited no less than 5,000 Hungarian florins for safe-keeping in Nuremberg.[22] Although it always purported to be a charitable organisation, the Corpus Christi Brotherhood was closely identified with German domination of the town. For this reason, it soon became a focal point for the criticisms of Buda's Hungarian 'opposition'.

Throughout the thirteenth and fourteenth centuries, the Germans maintained a firm grip on town government and thus ensured that the 'old custom and ancient law' which sanctioned their control became no dead letter.[23] Power within the council was shared by a small group of about ten German families, many of which were interrelated. All these families possessed a quite substantial wealth and heavily invested in land and leases. The economic superiority of these top patrician families extended to Buda's German citizenry as a whole. Generally, the Germans proved wealthier than the town's Hungarians. Long-distance trade and many of the crafts remained almost exclusive German preserves.[24] Again, it was mainly Germans who occupied Buda's more fashionable residential quarters while the more numerous Hungarians filled the suburbs where house prices were much cheaper. At a time when the acquisition of citizenship, and thus the right to vote in civic elections, depended upon being 'a man of property from among the well off',[25] the greater financial resources possessed by the Germans reinforced their control of municipal institutions.

During the late fourteenth and early fifteenth centuries the social composition of town government experienced a significant alteration. As a consequence of mortality and feudalisation, the old patrician families disappeared from government. Simultaneously, the granting of staples to Hungary's western border towns reduced Buda's share of the realm's international trade and, by so making it a less attractive location for merchant firms, worked against the creation of a new and wealthy mercantile élite. The transfer of the royal court to Buda in the early years of the fifteenth

[22] Bavarian State Archive (Nuremberg), *Urkunden des sieben-farbigen Alphabets*, no. 4001; *ibid.*, *Akten des sieben-farbigen Alphabets*, no. 48.
[23] For this and much of what follows: Rady, 87–109; András Kubinyi, 'A budai német patriciátus társadalmi helyzete családi összeköttetései tükrében a XIII. századtól a XV. század második feléig', *Levéltári közlemények* xlii, 1973, 203–64; *idem*, 'Soziale Stellung und Familienverbindungen des deutschen Patriziats von Ofen in der ersten Hälfte des 14. Jahrhunderts', *Archiv für Sippenforschung* xxxvi, 1970.
[24] István Szamota, *Régi utazások Magyarországon és a Balkán-Félszigeten 1054–1717*, Budapest 1891, 93.
[25] Mollay, *Stadtrecht*, 67.

century further compounded these developments by drawing off into its patronage network the more ambitious and successful of the town's German families. Nevertheless, Buda continued to function throughout this period as a major manufacturing centre and local distribution point for cloth and fashioned goods. The arrival of the court increased the demand for these commodities as well as for foodstuffs. All these changes had the result of reducing the wealth and number of those German councillors who lived by long-distance trade and gave instead a new economic advantage to the town's guildsmen. This the guildsmen rapidly translated into political terms and, after a bloodless rising in 1402, succeeded in taking a larger share of council places. Sometime before 1420, one of their number even received appointment as judge.

But precisely because the council was now filled by craftsmen and poorer short-haul merchants, the degree of German economic ascendancy over the town's Hungarians diminished. This development was furthered by the arrival in Buda of Hungarian hangers-on from the court and the emergence of groups of Hungarian craftsmen – particularly metalsmiths – with a wealth commensurate and sometimes exceeding that of their German counterparts in the council. Yet, despite the changed economic relationship between the town's two nationalities, the Hungarians were still obliged to retain an altogether inferior role within town government. German councillors remained in the overwhelming majority; the judge was always one of their number. This imbalance soon gave way to frustration and violence.

In view of what we have already seen, it is not surprising that the first stirrings of Hungarian protest should have been directed against the German ecclesiastical hierarchy. In July 1436, visitors from nearby Pressburg (modern-day Bratislava) reported back to their town council that a certain 'George Litteratus has caused great unhappiness among the priesthood and particularly to the priest of Our Blessed Lady's. He would like Our Blessed Lady's to be the chapel and filial church of Mary Magdalene's. Along with his Hungarian supporters he wants to confiscate those luxuries which people have left to Our Lady's and especially those most valuable treasures which have been given to the Corpus Christi Brotherhood. He is plotting all sorts of incredible things.'[26] Obviously though, George's expressed intentions were inspired by rather more than religious concerns. By threatening the status of Our Blessed Lady's and attacking the Corpus Christi Brotherhood, George was directly challenging German political supremacy in the town. Significantly also, George's principal supporters came from amongst Buda's better-off Hungarian craftsmen and the resident nobility: those groups whose upward advance was blocked by German control of the municipal council.[27]

---

[26] László Gerevich (ed.), *Budapest története* ii, Budapest 1973, 71.
[27] Hungarian National Archive, *Collectio antemohacsiana*, Dl 12990; Jenö Szücs, *Városok és kézmüvesség a XV. századi Magyarországon*, Budapest 1955, 290.

The principal German citizens of the town were not slow to respond. In an attempt to preempt the growing Hungarian opposition, they secured in 1437 the election of a wealthy Hungarian judge who by marriage and business connections had aligned himself with the town's Germans.[28] The next year, and possibly as a result of German intrigues, George was ousted from the leadership of the Hungarian faction.[29] But these measures provided only a temporary relief. In 1438 a countrywide xenophobia, set off by the election of King Albert as Holy Roman Emperor, spread through its resident nobility into Buda and exacerbated still further national tensions there. In the mean time, the Hungarians had found for themselves a new leader in Johann the Silversmith: 'a man of no small standing nor insignificant in the town'.[30] By May 1439, the leaders of the German community clearly felt that more decisive action was needed. Accordingly, they kidnapped Johann and had him secretly murdered in the Town Hall. His corpse they dumped in the Danube. Unfortunately for the Germans, their crime was soon discovered and a spontaneous rising broke out. Reading between the lines of the various chronicles, it would appear that the rioters consisted in the main of poorer Hungarians from the suburbs.[31] Although some of these may have indulged in some opportune looting, all accounts are agreed that it was the town's German minority which was the main target for their violence. German shops and homes were singled out for destruction; their occupants for slaughter. The Hungarian judge, upon whom the Germans had earlier pinned their hopes, was also pursued and obliged to seek out the safety of the palace.[32] Peace was only restored by the entreaties of one of the Hungarian magnates and the discovery that the Germans had nothing left worth taking.

Despite its evident violence, the revolt can scarcely have lasted more than a few hours. Nevertheless, it did capture international attention. News of the events in Buda called especially into question Albert's qualifications for leading the proposed European crusade against the Turks. Albert was accordingly obliged to give out that the rising had been but a very local affair and that his power-base in Hungary remained unaffected.[33] This was a clearly optimistic assessment. The Hungarian nobility were able to employ the revolt as additional evidence that Albert's German advisers were unwelcome in the kingdom and force their dismissal on these grounds.[34]

---

[28] Elemér Mályusz, 'Budai Farkas László', *Tanulmányok Budapest múltjából* xv, 1963, 153–87; András Kubinyi, 'A budai német patriciátus', 247–50.

[29] *Quellen und Forschungen*, Vienna 1849, 230.

[30] J. G. Schwandtner, *Scriptores Hungaricarum veteres ac genuini* i, Vienna 1746, 237–8.

[31] *Ibid.*; Gaspar Heltai, *Chronica Az Magyaroknac Dolgairol*, Kolozsvár (Cluj) 1575, fo. 77v; György Székely, 'A Huszitizmus és a magyar nép', *Századok* xc, 1956, 577.

[32] R. Liliencron, *Die historischen Volkslieder der Deutschen von 13. bis 16. Jahrhundert* i, Leipzig 1865, 368.

[33] Rozprawy Akademii Umiejetnosci wydziat Historyczno-Filozoficzny, Serya II, Tom xii, Cracow 1899, 315–16.

[34] Aeneas Sylvius, *De viris illustribus* (*Bibliothek des litterarischen Vereins in Stuttgart* i, 1843, 68).

Within Buda itself, the shock of the revolt compelled the German citizens to come to terms with the leaders of the Hungarian opposition. By April 1440 the town's constitution had been completely revised. The presence of two separate national communities was formally admitted and representation in the council divided equally between Germans and Hungarians. Henceforward also, appointments to the rank of judge were to be shared, with Hungarians and Germans taking it in turns to fill this office.[35] The surviving council lists show that the new arrangements for town government endured without interruption until 1529. It goes, of course, almost without saying that the newly-appointed Hungarian representatives consisted entirely of middle class and noble elements and that the urban poor were deliberately excluded from the settlement.

But it was not just Buda's constitution which was adjusted after the revolt of 1439. The recognition of two separate but equal national communities within the town had implications also for the relationship between the Germans' and Hungarians' churches. Discussions about a more equitable form of ecclesiastical organisation were fast entered into and certainly completed by February 1440.[36] The document given out at the conclusion of the negotiations attests to the eagerness felt by 'the citizens and members of both communities' to set aside 'the hatreds, squabbles and diverse discords of the past years'. It was agreed that henceforward the Germans' church of Our Blessed Lady would no longer claim to be the sole parish church of the town and would release the Hungarians' churches from their filial obligations. From now on, there would be three parish churches in Buda: Our Blessed Lady's, Mary Magdalene's and St Peter the Martyr's. Each would hold an equal status and three parish districts of roughly comparable size were duly elaborated.[37] Despite a subsequent attempt by the priest of Our Blessed Lady's to have this decision reversed, the newly defined parish boundaries remained unaltered until the Turkish occupation of the town in 1541.

In his recent study of class and conflict within the late medieval German town, Professor F. R. H. Du Boulay has drawn the conclusion that, 'the German town risings occurred because a few important people were treated as outsiders. When they had won their point and got into the council-chambers they no longer needed the backing of the poorer classes and quickly ignored them.'[38] In short, it was the unrepresentative nature of town government and the exclusion from it of people who felt they deserved a place there which brought about the periodic explosions of urban violence. Even in Buda, where national tensions greatly determined the character of urban conflict, the revolt of 1439 may be perceived to have its origin in much the

---

[35] Elek Jakab, *Kolozsvár történetének oklevéltára* I, Buda 1870, 280–85.
[36] Elemér Mályusz, 'Budai Farkas László', 164.
[37] Archive of the Esztergom Primatial Chapter, *Arch. Eccl. Vetus*, no. 46 (Hungarian National Archive, Section U, Df 249009).
[38] F. R. H. Du Boulay, *Germany in the Later Middle Ages*, 1983, 151.

same sort of thwarted ambition. The participation of the poor in the rising and their exclusion from the political settlement which followed again suggest close parallels to the processes Professor Du Boulay has outlined. What makes Buda unusual, though, is the role played by the town's churches in distinguishing the two parties in the conflict. Far from being agents of social reconciliation, Buda's churches reflected the injustices and divisions of the existing order and in so doing sharpened them. But precisely because church, government and nationality were such interrelated institutions, once a new constitutional formula had been decided upon for the town, its churches could not remain unaffected. The old thirteenth-century ecclesiastical structure had thus to be remodelled in accompaniment and the Hungarians' churches formally granted the status they had for so long demanded.

Lancastrian Bishops and Educational Benefaction

JOEL T. ROSENTHAL

The data for this paper are not hard to come by. Neither do they contain any great surprises. The Lancastrian episcopate comprises a group of sixty-six men, many of whom are at least moderately familiar figures to students of late medieval England. Some of the bishops have been the subjects of individual studies and biographical endeavours, and even the least of them have been coolly embraced by a number of collective and prosopographical studies.[1] This is, therefore, a well travelled landscape by the standards of fifteenth-century history. What problems there are lie rather in the realms of interpretation. What do we make of the data; towards which conclusions about the bishops, the transfer of their wealth, their pursuit of fame as expressed by their gifts to educational institutions, and their concern for the social role and glamour of education are we steered by our investigation? What premises are verified, what generalisations about late medieval society and at least one of its élite groups reinforced or modified by this look at aggregated behavioural patterns and testamentary gift giving?

By the Lancastrian episcopacy I refer to the sixty-six men appointed to the seventeen English sees between the accession of Henry IV in 1399 and the

---

[1] For the basic biographical material see *BRUO* and *BRUC*. The data on the education of the bishops is discussed in my *The Training of an Elite Group: English Bishops in the Fifteenth Century* (*Transactions of the American Philosophical Society*, n.s. lx, 5), 1970, 12–19. For a recent and similar treatment of the bishops (with some duplication because of chronological overflow), Helen Jewell, 'English Bishops as Educational Benefactors in the Later Fifteenth Century', *Church, Politics, and Patronage*, 146–67. I wish to acknowledge Dr Jewell's cheerful help when the coincidence of our interests became known.

first deposition of Henry VI in 1461.[2] To investigate their record as patrons of education seems a reasonable line of inquiry, since we know that the bishops themselves were by now predominantly men with Oxford and/or Cambridge backgrounds and that it was the lack of higher formal education that had come to be the exception, rather than the rule. In fact, among these men, higher university degrees were considerably more common than were (just) first degrees. To rely on Emden's biographical registers – and since their publication no one has suggested that we do anything else – only ten (or even fewer) of the sixty-six bishops were without the benefit of a recorded involvement with one of the universities.[3] Of these non-academic bishops, some were regulars and presumably still unlikely to get their higher educational training beyond the cloister, while one other – William Booth, bishop of Coventry and Lichfield (1447–52) and archbishop of York (1452–64) – was a 'graduate' of the inns of court.[4] Of the remaining fifty-six or sixty or so men, almost half (26, which is 39 per cent of all the bishops) had degrees or at least some graduate training in theology, almost as many (21: 32 per cent of their total) had formal university work in civil law or canon law or both, only nine had not gone beyond their studies in the arts faculty, while John Arundel, bishop of Chichester (1459–77), was a university trained doctor of medicine.

In aggregate these are impressive educational and intellectual credentials. They show that the higher clergy were apt to be among the intelligentsia of the realm, to some extent, and that the intelligentsia of the realm were apt to be found, to some extent, among the higher clergy. They suggest that whatever their level of spiritual zeal and dedication, and whatever their facility as civil servants, diplomats, and ecclesiastical administrators, the bishops had no trouble assuming the mantle of advanced, formal learning. From a different perspective, one we can term the demographic or life-cycle view, these data remind us of how many years of an episcopal (or pre-

---

[2] Dates of provision and death are those given by *HBC*. The one bishop not considered is the obscure Lewis of Luxemburg, bishop of Ely (1438–43). The principle of inclusion adopted here means that survivors of Richard II's episcopate are not considered (unless translated by Henry IV or Henry V), and therefore in a few cases the first Lancastrian bishop did not take office until the reign of Henry V: Stephen Patrington only became bishop of Chichester in 1415, John Catterick of Coventry and Lichfield in 1415 and of Exeter in 1419, and Philip Morgan of Ely in 1426. But at the other end, five Lancastrian appointments lasted well through and even beyond the Yorkists: Thomas Bourgchier at Canterbury (1450–86), John Hales at Coventry and Lichfield (1459–90), Thomas Kempe at London (1448–89), Richard Beauchamp at Salisbury (1450–81), and William Wainfleet at Winchester (1447–86).

[3] Bishops without university training include William Heyworth of Coventry and Lichfield (1420–47), Thomas Langley of Durham (1406–37), John Wakering of Norwich (1416–25), Nicholas Bubwith of London (1406–07), Salisbury (1407), and Bath and Wells (1407–24), William Strickland of Carlisle (1400–19), and Alexander Tottington of Norwich (1407–13). The regulars included John Low of Rochester (1444–67: he was probably a D.Th.), Philip Repingdon of Lincoln (1405–19: a Lic.Th. or D.Th., former abbot of Leicester), Robert Mascall of Hereford (1404–16: an Oxford Carmelite, probably a D.Th.), and John Stanbury of Hereford (1453–74: an Oxford Carmelite and a D.Th.).

[4] A. Compton Reeves, 'William Booth, Bishop of Coventry and Lichfield, Archbishop of York', in his *Lancastrian Englishmen*, Washington 1981, 265–362.

episcopal) life were spent in training, in preparation for professional service and, ultimately, for major ecclesiastical (and secular) responsibility. Such a point can also be expressed in a more concrete numerical sense: four or eight or twelve years of university work, or even more, though frequently not spent continuously, and often, no doubt, at least partially *in absentia*. It is also true in a proportionate or relative sense: one-sixth or one-eighth or one-tenth, etc., of a lifetime within and devoted to the institutions and arcana of formal higher education and training. Our bishops had mostly come through such a long *cursus honorum*, sometimes begun when they were very young, often continuing until they were well into their twenties and thirties or beyond. Since the university years seem to constitute an exceptionally vivid chapter of the total life experience, we shall be examining a group of men whose ties and bonds, to their colleges, to their universities, and to each other, may have long outlasted their years of common life and academic training.

There is considerable material from the fifteenth century, mostly relating to Oxford, attesting to the strength of the 'old boy' connection, or at least to the university's desire to invoke and capitalise on such a connection.[5] But to what extent did youthful training and academic service and residence lead to educational patronage and benefaction, beyond and apart from the probability of simple favouritism while the bishop was alive and on active duty? There is obviously some correlation. But just as obviously, it is an imperfect or partial correlation, as anyone knows who has tried to raise funds from fellow alumni. Furthermore, in a society with positive values attached to education, we know that great patrons of formal learning were not necessarily those who had attended or been attached to the beneficiary institution. It would be cynical to do more than hint at the possibility of an inverse relationship, no doubt, but at least we must accept the need for aetiological caution. There is no simple causal chain between attendance at a university, a subsequent career of high achievement (often dependent to some considerable degree upon university training and university contacts), and eventual gift giving or benefaction to the *alma mater*. Biographical data are not fixed stars. Furthermore, in a study of collective behaviour we should keep an eye upon as many members of the group as possible, and not allow ourselves to be dazzled by the occasional flash of lightning. To assess episcopal support for education we must balance the quantitative evidence with the qualitative, and we should think in terms of how many failed to respond as well as of the positive polarities and eccentricities of benefaction and foundation.

We can delineate several largish categories within which almost all the relevant activity is contained. Since the universities are not only our most interesting educational institution but the most readily studied, it is reasonable to begin with the benefactions to Oxford and Cambridge and their

---

[5] For a glimpse at the petitions, reminders, begging letters and pious entreaties, from Oxford to the *alumni* who went on to become bishops, see *Ep. Ac. Ox.*

subunits. A second category consists of *all other* educational institutions and establishments, regardless of level or location. Then come the bequests, gifts, and benefactions to individuals, either specified by name or as belonging to some general category. Lastly, and not as directly relevant but worth our passing reflection, is what we might call the role of individual examples, of episcopal 'role-modelling'. Since our approach begins at the top, we must be careful not to over-estimate the tide of the activity under consideration. However, by beginning with the universities we begin against the background of an experience more or less shared by the bulk of the bishops, one that to some degree united them at a common site (or sites, though the overwhelming proportion were Oxford men), as well as within a common educational structure. For aspiring and talented young men of the church, Oxford and Cambridge served as the controlled, visible neck of the national hour-glass, lying between the grass-roots world of villages and towns and that loftier plateau of the higher church and its episcopal thrones.

It is also pleasant to begin at the top because there is some immediate gratification. Among our bishops were three founding fathers: Henry Chichele, of All Souls, Oxford, Richard Fleming, of Lincoln College, Oxford, and William Waynfleet, of Magdalen College, Oxford. Their stories are familiar ones and we need not linger at great length.[6] Each man and each college's tale offers its peculiar variation on the standard medieval theme of *de novo* foundation and creation. We can follow each enterprise from its (often modest) conception through the inevitable maturation of the first idea, through the need to meet and to cover the mounting financial obligations – and covering a time span usually a good bit longer than that originally envisaged – and ultimately through to a successful and happy ending. Each bequest was explicitly designed for the advancement of learning, each college intended simultaneously as a haven and a nursery. Though these examples indicate what a strong will, lavish finances, and helpful and highly placed friends could accomplish, our three founding fathers set a standard of dedication and of magnificence that no others among their episcopal peers sought to emulate.

Beyond the founders are two lesser if still appreciable groups of friendly bishops. The first is comprised of some half-dozen or so men who were major benefactors, either of a particular college, or of several colleges, or of the university as a corporation. There were such men as Archbishop Bourgchier, who spread his benefactions to each university. Both Oxford and Cambridge

---

[6] For All Souls, E. F. Jacob, 'The building of All Souls College, 1438–43', in *Historical Essays in Honour of James Tait*, ed. J. G. Edwards, V. H. Galbraith, and E. F. Jacob, Manchester 1933, 121–33, and *VCH Oxford* iii, 173–9. For Lincoln College, *VCH Oxford* iii, 163–6, and Andrew Clark, *Lincoln College*, Oxford 1898, 1–9: Fleming's own gifts were quite modest. For Magdalen College, *VCH Oxford* iii, 193–207, and R. Chandler, *Life of William Waynflete*, 1811. In summimg up the educational mission of these colleges, J. A. F. Thomson remarks that 'this intellectual counter-attack probably did more to defeat Lollardy in the university than the repressive measures of Archbishop Arundel had done' (*The Later Lollards, 1414–1520*, Oxford 1965, 212).

received £100 for the establishment of a loan chest, and there were additional gifts to All Souls.[7] Bishop Carpenter was primarily a patron of Oriel. He bestowed some small tenements upon the college, gave some gifts of cash, and in 1452 purchased Bedel Hall and presented it to Oriel.[8] Roger Whelpdale touched a number of Oxford colleges with his generosity; among the beneficiaries were Queen's College, Balliol College and the theology scholars in the university.[9] Walter Lyhart maintained twelve scholars at Fishwick Hostel, a dependency of Gonville Hall, Cambridge. He eventually bought the Hostel and gave it to the Hall, and he also left benefactions to Oriel and Exeter Colleges at Oxford and to Trinity Hall, Cambridge.[10] Edmund Lacy was but one of a number of bishops of Exeter who preserved the link between the diocese and the college by a string of endowments and gifts.[11] Richard Clifford could well have figured among our founders, for the £1,000 he left to London College, Oxford, was certainly substantial. However, the money was never invested in land and when the sum was expended (at a distribution rate of £40 *per annum*) the institution just faded away.[12] Such fatuous behaviour, especially with their money, is unusual among these men.

In addition to such men and their lavish gift giving, there is the larger group who made donations and bequests of a more modest type. Nicholas Close of Carlisle gave books to King's College, Cambridge. His service to Henry VI had already involved work on the original college statutes, so he had been a friend from the very beginning. Robert Fitzhugh donated books to the libraries of each university.[13] John Bottlesham left all his law books (both canon and civil), plus £20, to Peterhouse, of which he had been master, and he also specified cash bequests to other colleges and to the university as a whole. John Rickinghale gave his books to Clare Hall, Cambridge. Thomas

---

[7] Graham Pollard, 'Medieval Loan Chests at Cambridge' *BIHR* xvii, 1939–40', 113–29. The money did not reach Cambridge until about 1520, when the will of the Archbishop's nephew and executor, Sir Thomas Bourgchier (d. 1513) was proved. The chest *vocabitur cista Thome Bourgchier* (Leland L. Duncan, ed., 'The Will of Cardinal Bourgchier, Archbishop of Canterbury, 1486', *Archaeologia Cantiana* xxiv, 1900, 244–52). For other such gifts, especially in a projected Audley-Chichele chest, Strickland Gibson, ed., *Statuta Antiqua Universitatis Oxoniensis*, Oxford 1931, 323–4, and *Reg. Chichele* i, lvii.

[8] C. L. Shadwell and H. E. Salter, eds., *Oriel College Records* (*OHS* lxxxv), 1926, 136–9. Also, Roy M. Haines, 'Aspects of the Episcopate of John Carpenter', *JEH* xix, 1968, 11–40, and Anthony Wood, *History and Antiquities of the Colleges and Halls in the University of Oxford*, ed. J. Guth, 1786, 124–25.

[9] *Reg. Chichele* ii, 237–40. The books include such standard treasures as Augustine's *City of God* and Gregory the Great on Ezekial, as well as his *Moralia*.

[10] Francis Blomefield, *Topographical History of the County of Norfolk*, Lynn, 5 vols., 1739–75, iii, 536 and John Venn, ed., *The Annals of Gonville and Caius College*, Cambridge 1904, 39.

[11] Charles W. Boase, ed., *Registrum Collegii Exoniensis* (*OHS* xxvii), 1894, liii–liv (and lxx for gifts from Bishop Beaufort). For Lacy's efforts to compose an office for the feast of St Raphael, *CPL 1427–47*, 246–7.

[12] Hastings Rashdall, *The Universities of Europe in the Middle Ages*, ed. F. M. Powicke and A. B. Emden, Oxford 1936, iii, 482–4, as part of an appendix on 'lost colleges at Oxford'.

[13] *Reg. Chichele* ii, 540–41.

Brouns left money to subsidise the exhibitions of six boys to study grammar and sophistry at Oxford.[14]

In quantitative terms the proportion of Lancastrian bishops who ranked as benefactors of the universities was reasonable, if not high. But we should remember how little comparative material there is for fifteenth-century group behaviour, at any social level. No matter how we rate the level of benefaction, to whom else could the universities turn? The secular aristocracy in the fifteenth century had almost nothing to do with either Oxford or Cambridge. The kings – apart from Henry VI's immoderate enthusiasm for King's College, Cambridge – were generally able to restrain themselves. Neither Henry VI's father nor his grandfather had very much recorded interest, at least not beyond a desire to purge Oxford of its Lollard contagion and then to use its purified resources to further the causes of bigotry and persecution elsewhere in England. But if our purpose here is to go beyond a tally of who, how much, and to whom, and to move towards some general reflections, we have some further aspects of benefaction and patronage to discuss.

At best, our list of benefactors covers slightly less than half of the episcopate. Many a bishop with a long and distinguished academic career, as well as with more than adequate personal and diocesan revenues, left no recorded benefaction of the sort we are seeking, no subsidised memorial to self. Old academic ties often counted for little in the final disposition. Nothing was forthcoming from such men as William Barrow, bishop of Carlisle (1423–29), though he had once been Chancellor of Oxford and held a doctorate in canon law. Nor was Robert Gilbert of much help, though his career included such academic distinctions as an M.A. and a D.Th., and such academic service as membership on a commission against Wycliffite errors and the role of official petitioner for more benefices for graduates. At least Marmaduke Lumley extended his generosity elsewhere, though neither the memory of a stint as Chancellor of Cambridge (1425–27) nor a longer period as a student at Trinity Hall plucked at his purse strings. The universities talked a great deal in the fifteenth century of the difficult plight of their graduates and of the pressing need for more resources and buildings. But they could only reach a fraction of their most likely and receptive audience, and our list of once-active academics who were *not* benefactors could be lengthened considerably.

Higher education was focused and centralised. Were provincial loyalties stronger, either for the diverse places of one's youth or for the institutions of those towns and churches the men had encountered during the course of a long ecclesiastical career? What can we say for our bishops as patrons of

---

[14] For other examples, H. E. Salter, ed., *Registrum Annalium Collegii Mertoniensis* (*OHS* lxxvi), 1923, 119–20, 140, 144, 186, and 522. Walter Skirlaw made some academic bequests: James Raine, ed., *Testamenta Eboracensia* i (Surtees Society iv), 1836, 308–11.

educational institutions at the primary and secondary level, mainly in the provinces and way-stations of their earlier days? How does the rate or incidence of such benefaction compare with that touching the universities?

The picture turns out to be much the same as it was regarding the universities, at least in the number of bishops involved. Some twenty or two dozen of the bishops were patrons, in some fashion, of local educational institutions: almost the exact number as we found when we looked at Oxford and Cambridge. Again, there were a number of founding fathers, somewhat more in fact than for the universities, including Chichele (once again), whose new collegiate foundation at Higham Ferrers was to have a staff of about twenty four, including a grammar master and a choir master.[15] Strickland of Carlisle founded a chantry at St Andrews, Penrith, in 1395, and he 'directed that the priest should teach the children church music and grammar'.[16] John Kemp founded a college for chantry priests and a grammar school at his birthplace in Wye, Kent.[17] Waynflete eventually founded Magdalen School in Oxford, intended as a preliminary step for promising youngsters on their way to his university college, on the Winchester–New College or Eton–King's College model. He also founded a more traditional college at Wainfleet, Lincolnshire.[18] John Carpenter was 'regarded as a second founder' of the college at Westbury, Gloucestershire.[19] Otherwise the bequests were usually on the minimal side: books, small 'scholarship' funds, an odd chantry provision that included some educational or song-school duties. Both in quality and quantity these donations and foundations were almost invariably well below those given to the universities – not much of a testimonial to any deep ties bridging the decades between the promising young cleric and the venerable episcopal figure, nor much indication of a desire to channel resources towards a particular provincial institution.[20] Neither sentimentality, the possibility of (post-humous) social control, nor pet projects are much in evidence.

---

[15] *VCH Northamptonshire* ii, 177–9. Chichele talked of how gratifying it was to found a college in the place of his baptism. *Reg. Chichele* i, li–lii, and E. F. Jacob, *Archbishop Henry Chichele*, 1967, 87–90.

[16] C. M. L. Bouch, *Prelates and People of the Lake Counties: A History of the Diocese of Carlisle, 1133–1933*, Kendal 1948, 110.

[17] *VCH Kent* ii, 235–6. All of the thirteen fellows of the college were to be either scholars or doctors of theology and members of Merton College, where Kemp had been a fellow (1395–1407) and bursar (1403–04).

[18] R. S. Stainer, *Magdalen School* (*OHS*, n.s. iii), 1940, 2–25. For the grammar school at Wainfleet, *VCH Lincolnshire* ii, 483–4. And for Waynflete's role in the 'resuscitation' of Eton College, *VCH Buckinghamshire* ii, 169–70.

[19] *VCH Gloucestershire* ii, 108. He began to endow and build (or rebuild) in 1447. In 1463, when bestowing the advowson of Clifton parish church, he stipulated that the Dean and Chapter were to find a master to teach grammar to those connected with the church 'and (to) any other person whomsoever comes to him, without any charge'.

[20] For an attempt to find and measure such attachments, J. T. Rosenthal, 'The Fifteenth Century Episcopate: Careers and Bequests', *SCH* x, 1973, 117–27.

Some of the bishops who gave in this localised fashion were also men who gave to their universities, as did Chichele, and Waynflete, the only founders at two levels. Many bishops, not surprisingly, were inclined to give to their own cathedral churches, and books were among the frequently transferred paraphernalia. But it is hard really to see such books as being singled out in a unique fashion for their educational potential, and not many men other than the college founders went as far as Nicholas Bubwith of Bath and Wells, who rebuilt his cathedral library as well as worked to stock it.[21] Rather, books and associated items were just another tangible category in the whole web of a reciprocal relationship linking the living with the dead and comprising one part of a table of equivalents between worldly goods and spiritual services. Only few of the book collections that changed hands contained much out of the ordinary, either in terms of the number or identity of the volumes. John Stafford died as archbishop of Canterbury, but he left his books to Wells Cathedral, where he had presided for nineteen years. Robert Hallum was bishop of Salisbury for ten years (1407–17), and the bequest of his books to that institutional recipient seemed a natural transaction. He gave no testamentary signs of nostalgia for Oxford, of which he had been chancellor (1403–06), nor of Exeter College, where he may have resided while earning a B.A. and then a doctorate in both canon and civil law. A paper of this sort would be remiss not to tally this kind of activity and gift giving, but we should be under few illusions about its avowed links with educational purposes or educational institutions. We can assume that all the bishops possessed books, but we have seen no indication that all of the bishops were patrons and benefactors by our standards.

Personal bequests for educational purposes, in contrast to institutional ones, were almost non-existent. What we do find are bequests for certain categories of recipients, to support and further their educational opportunities. A fair number of bishops left funds to send boys of their diocese or cathedral chapter or old college network to a university: aiding poor scholars was an agreeable form of social work, comparable to helping poor (and virtuous) maidens find marriage portions, or helping underwrite the repair of roads and bridges. Such charity might yoke local patriarchal sentiments – usually more marked by their absence than by their expression – with support for the university. William Alnwick had been bishop of Norwich and then of Lincoln: the residue of his estate was to be used to send poor scholars of both dioceses to either university. One of Carpenter's bequests to Oriel was specifically intended for a poor scholar from Worcester diocese.[22] Sometimes such bequests stipulated that the money was to be divided or

---

[21] C. M. Church, 'Notes on the Buildings, Books, and Benefactors of the Library of the Dean and Chapter of the Cathedral Church of Wells', *Archaeologia* lvii (2) 1901, 201–28. For the bishop's will, *Reg. Chichele* ii, 298–301.

[22] Wood, *History*, 124.

distributed among poor scholars already at the university: Lyhart's residue, and £20 in Whelpdale's will, went in this fashion. Bekington spoke of 'ten honest priests without sufficient exhibition . . . especially of my diocese', and poor boys from his own chapel were to have first chance at the money.[23] Otherwise there was little regard for the needs of individuals, even relatives and the younger members of the episcopal *familia* or the children of such men and women. John Catterick's testamentary gift of all his books in both laws, to a nephew, was almost unique.[24] At the other extreme the high born Thomas Arundel left his books to such men as Edward, duke of York, and Philip Morgan, successively bishop of Ely and Worcester.[25] The conclusion here is that bishops were mostly lofty and remote figures. Their testamentary benefactions towards education, such as they were, rarely reached down to the level of individuals, and any impulses to foster local education were better satisfied by institutional commitments, though there were certainly few enough of those. Perhaps great men did not think in terms of particular boys and girls, any more than they did of the long-abandoned sites of their own early training and careerism. If money were spent at all, it was apt to go to the higher levels, to those university colleges that would collect and hone the intellectual and spiritual élite of the future, rather than to children individually or to their pedestrian educational points of origin.

The tone here is becoming rather negative. This should be qualified. We have already said that in a collective study of this sort expectations must be tied to reality (as defined in large part by empirical data). It is of no use to decide, *a priori*, that all bishops *should* participate in some form of activity and then to attack those who fail to meet our standard. Any form of voluntary activity in which somewhere between one-quarter and one-half of a statistically significant group participates is probably to be seen as a popular, well-supported activity. After all, we began with the universe of Lancastrian bishops, not one of patrons and benefactors. They neither reached their office because of past prominence nor future proclivity towards educational benefaction. Neither was such prominence so much a matter of course that those who failed to make a philanthropic mark were apt to be castigated by their contemporaries. No particular career or biographical thread that we can identify serves as a sure guide regarding who would give, let alone as to how generously or to what sort of category or recipient.

In some instances we can wonder about the discrepancy or dissonance between intellectual activity on the part of a particular bishop and an inclination to support the educational superstructure of the day, a hint

---

[23] F. W. Weaver, ed., *Som. Med. Wills, 1383–1500*, 205. There are additional bequests to Winchester College, Oxford. For Bubwith, *Som. Med. Wills, 1501–30*, 327.

[24] *Reg. Chichele* ii, 178. Whelpdale also left bequests within the family: *Testamenta Eboracensia* iii, 66.

[25] C. Eveleigh Woodruff, ed., *Kent* Sede Vacante *Wills* (Kent Archaeological Society, Records Branch, iii), 1914, 81–5.

perhaps of the sort of inverse relationship we referred to above. We have bishops who were authors of note and acquisive collectors of books and manuscripts – the artefacts of high culture – and who were also active and generous benefactors. We have others with intellectual contributions of their own to make but who were still not particularly inclined to redistribute their wealth for what seems to us to be such a proximate and related purpose. Edmund Lacy was a minor author and a moderate patron of Exeter College. Reginald Pecock, an important but heterodox author, naturally left nothing to anyone: his imprisonment and obscure death must have reduced him to poverty, nor was his own library likely to have been a popular memento. But even in his years of prominence there is no indication that he thought of the universities as the bodies to be entrusted with his intellectual or pedagogical legacy. Stephen Patrington probably helped assemble the material used by Thomas Netter in the *Fasciculi Zizaniorum*: however, Patrington left no relevant educational bequests. Philip Repingdon left manuscripts, including some of his own works, to Lincoln Cathedral: a stormy but powerful and prolonged academic career ended here with educational but not with academic gifts. Nor were those few bishops who were important figures in the early days of English humanism major actors in the flickering drama we are trying to watch. William Grey of Ely, a major figure in fifteenth-century humanism, was a significant friend of Balliol College, especially its library, but no one just concerned with his formal institutional benefactions would be certain to spot him as an important transitional figure in English intellectual history.[26] This is also true, to a lesser extent, for such real if minor friends of the new learning as Adam Moleyns and George Neville.[27] If they were role models, leading by example and inspiring a few to take a new interest in the literary culture of Italy and the Burgundian world, they looked in the main neither to Oxford nor to Cambridge for students and protégés. Nor did they seek to found grammar schools in which to cultivate their new vines. If the old vintage was not to their taste, these early humanists and patrons of humanism were mainly content to pass the cup.

The conclusion to this survey and assessment is that it is hard to draw a conclusion. Many years ago I learned in Robin Du Boulay's seminar that it is fascinating to follow the data relating to fifteenth century history, but hazardous to lead them. More recently I have worried, on a related topic,

---

[26] Weiss, *Humanism*, 86–96: his Oxford gifts are discussed, 94–5. Also Roy Haines, 'The Associates and *Familia* of William Gray and his Use of Patronage while Bishop of Ely (1454–78)', *JEH* xxv, 1974, 225–47.

[27] A. C. Reeves, *Lancastrian Englishmen*, 203–63, and Weiss, *Humanism*, 71–83 (for a chapter on Bekynton, Clement, Hales, and Moleyns). For Neville, J. Tait, 'Letters of John Tiptoft, Earl of Worcester, and Archbishop Neville to the University of Oxford', *EHR* xxxv, 1920, 570–74. For Neville as a useful practical friend of Lincoln College, Clark, *Lincoln College*, 21–3 and Weiss, *Humanism*, 141–8.

about how we should assess the calculus of collective behaviour.[28] From one corner, an episcopate that in a half-century produced three founders of Oxford colleges, some half dozen or so founders of large chantry colleges with educational mandates, several dozen benefactors of Oxford and Cambridge, and many men who gave smaller provincial and diocesan gifts of an educational nature is hardly an anti-intellectual or a disinterested one. Some of the bishops, at least, remembered how they had risen in the world, and they wanted to help enlarge that institutional framework so others too could rise, 'unembarrassed by cure of souls or pecuniary troubles', as Fleming said regarding Lincoln College.[29]

But from another angle there is the inescapable impression that what we have here is a behavioural or social norm about which a few men cared a great deal, a fair number cared a bit, and many cared not at all. Accordingly, the contributions of the first group greatly raise the mean for gift giving and benefaction. Why did so many men, with higher education as part of their own professional and careerist credentials, fail to give anything? And though the records can never be held to be complete and wholly accurate, we are looking at well-charted territory and the chances are that little significant activity has escaped modern inquiry without a trace. Many an episcopal will is a total cypher regarding our union of philanthropy and educational or intellectual pursuits.[30] Were some of our bishops in reaction against too many institutions, against the letter that warred with the spirit? An intriguing idea, but hardly a likely one, given the men under consideration and the course of their prior careers. The final evaluation, for a laconic world, probably just has to lie in the empirical tallies. No matter how important any voluntary activity is adjudged to be, only a certain percentage of any group or universe ever support it. After all, the educational establishment *does* seem to have been growing in the Lancastrian period.[31] For a population to increase, not everyone has to have a baby every two years. To improve a society's rate of agricultural production, not everyone has to work in the fields. Similarly, for educational institutions to prosper, not everyone, not even all the highly educated and university-trained bishops, has to be a significant patron and benefactor. Evidently, among the Lancastrian bishops

---

[28] J. T. Rosenthal, 'Aristocratic Cultural Patronage and Book Bequests, 1350–1500', *BJRL* lxii, 1982, 522–48.

[29] Clark, *Lincoln College*, 2.

[30] For some wills that contain nothing of concern to this particular pursuit, *Reg. Chichele* ii: the wills of Robert Mascall (106), Stephen Patrington (133), Richard Young (165–6), Richard Clifford (224–5), Philip Repingdon (285–6), William Barrow (433–4), Philip Morgan (530–31), and William Gray (bishop of London and then of Lincoln) (544–6) are all without educational bequests – though some of these men gave during their lives and in other ways.

[31] Nicholas Orme, *English Schools of the Middle Ages*, 1973, 194–223, for a general assessment of the fifteenth century, and especially 194: 'It is here (in the fifteenth century) and not in the age of the Reformation, that the *great movement* really begins. . . .' (my emphasis). Also, A. F. Leach, *The Schools of Medieval England*, 1915, 235–76, for a similar if less grounded view.

enough were so moved, so attracted by a sense of thanksgiving, by a desire for fame and chantry prayers, and perhaps, on occasion, even by a love of books, of the classroom, and of the academic cloister.

State University of New York at Stony Brook

The Lancastrian Bishops

The dates are from provision or election, as given in *HBC*. Only English sees are given: no reference is made to prior episcopal experience, usually in Wales.

The Episcopal Appointments of Henry IV

Arundel, Thomas	Canterbury, 1399 (Canterbury, 1396–97)	d. 1414
Strickland, William	Carlisle, 1400	d. 1419
Bottlesham, John	Rochester, 1400	d. 1404
Clifford, Richard	Bath & Wells, 1400: Worcester, 1401: London, 1407	d. 1421
Bowet, Henry	Bath & Wells, 1401: York, 1407	d. 1423
Mascall, Robert	Hereford, 1404	d. 1416
Young, Richard	Rochester, 1404	d. 1418
Beaufort, Henry	Winchester, 1404 (Lincoln, 1398–1404)	d. 1447
Repingdon, Philip	Lincoln, 1404	res. 1419
Walden, Roger	London, 1404 (Canterbury, 1397–99)	d. 1406
Bubwith, Nicholas	London, 1406: Salisbury, 1407: Bath & Wells, 1407	d. 1424
Langley, Thomas	Durham, 1406 [York, 1405–06]	d. 1437
Tottington, Alexander	Norwich, 1406	d. 1413
Peverell, Thomas	Worcester, 1407	d. 1419
Hallum, Robert	Salisbury, 1407 [York, 1406–07]	d. 1417

The Episcopal Appointments of Henry V

Courteney, Richard	Norwich, 1413	d. 1415
Chichele, Henry	Canterbury, 1414	d. 1443
Catterick, John	Lichfield, 1415: Exeter, 1419	d. 1419
Wakeryng, John	Norwich, 1415	d. 1425
Lacy, Edmund	Hereford, 1417: Exeter, 1420	d. 1455
Chaundler, John	Salisbury, 1417	d. 1426
Patrington, Stephen	Chichester, 1417	d. 1417
Ware, Henry	Chichester, 1418	d. 1420
Morgan, Philip	Worcester, 1419: Ely, 1426 [York, 1423–24]	d. 1435
Kempe, John	Rochester, 1419: Chichester, 1421: London, 1421: York, 1425: Canterbury, 1452	d. 1454
Fleming, Richard	Lincoln, 1419 [York, 1424–25]	d. 1431
Heyworth, William	Lichfield, 1419	d. 1447
Whelpdale, John	Carlisle, 1419	d. 1423

Polton, Thomas	Hereford, 1420: Chichester, 1421: Worcester, 1426	d. 1433
Langdon, John	Rochester, 1421	d. 1434
Spofford, Thomas	Hereford, 1421	res. 1448

Episcopal Appointments. Early Henry VI (1422–1435)

Barrow, William	Carlisle, 1423	d. 1429
Stafford, John	Bath & Wells, 1424: Canterbury, 1443	d. 1452
Gray, William	London, 1425: Lincoln, 1431	d. 1436
Alnwick, William	Norwich, 1426: Lincoln, 1437	d. 1449
Rickingale, John	Chichester, 1426	d. 1429
Neville, Robert	Salisbury, 1427: Durham, 1438	d. 1457
Lumley, Marmaduke	Carlisle, 1429: Lincoln, 1450	d. 1450
Sydenham, Simon	Chichester, 1429 [Salisbury, 1426–27]	d. 1438
Fitzhugh, Robert	London, 1431	d. 1436
Brouns, Thomas	Worcester, 1433: Rochester, 1435: Norwich, 1436 [Chichester, 1429]	d. 1445
Bourgchier, Thomas	Worcester, 1435: Ely, 1444: Canterbury, 1452 [Ely, 1436–37]	d. 1486

Episcopal Appointments. Middle Years of Henry VI (1436–1450)

Gilbert, Robert	London, 1436	d. 1448
Wells, William	Rochester, 1436	d. 1444
Aiscough, William	Salisbury, 1438	d. 1450
Praty, Richard	Chichester, 1438	d. 1445
Beckington, Thomas	Bath & Wells, 1443	d. 1465
Carpenter, John	Worcester, 1443	res. 1476
Low, John	Rochester, 1444	d. 1467
Moleyns, Adam	Chichester, 1445	x. 1450
Lyhart, Walter	Norwich, 1446	d. 1472
Waynflete, William	Winchester, 1447	d. 1486
Booth, William	Lichfield, 1447: York, 1452	d. 1464
Kempe, Thomas	London, 1448	d. 1489
Beauchamp, Richard	Hereford, 1448: Salisbury, 1450	d. 1481
Close, Nicholas	Carlisle, 1450: Lichfield, 1452	d. 1452
Boulers, Reginald	Hereford, 1450: Lichfield, 1453	d. 1459
Pecock, Reginald	Chichester, 1450	res. 1457

Episcopal Appointments. Late Henry VI (1451–1461)

Chedworth, John	Lincoln, 1451	d. 1471
Percy, William	Carlisle, 1452	d. 1462
Stanbury, John	Hereford, 1453	d. 1474
Grey, William	Ely, 1454	d. 1478
Neville, George	Exeter, 1456: York, 1465	d. 1476
Booth, Lawrence	Durham, 1457: York, 1476	d. 1480
Arundel	Chichester, 1459	d. 1477
Hales, John	Lichfield, 1459 [Exeter, 1455–56]	d. 1490

N.B. [   ] indicates an appointment proposed but never effected, or else quashed.

Marian Oxford and the Counter-Reformation

ELIZABETH RUSSELL

The Catholic Church Militant which, in 1563, confirmed the decrees of the Council of Trent was, for the first time, recognising that a lasting breach and a possibly perpetual schism had destroyed the unity of Christendom. As Dermot Fenlon has pointed out, the Council of Trent marked 'the collapse of the eventful, but neglected movement in the Catholic church to avert the Counter-Reformation'. The 'spirit of militant authority' which in the end triumphed at Rome was an admission of defeat.[1] In 1553, this defeat had not yet been acknowledged in Rome. It would, therefore, have been foolish and unconstructive for Mary Tudor to have acknowledged it in England. When Mary emphasised to Pole and the papacy that England was troubled by heretics and schismatics, she was making an important distinction between the two. Heretics, if unrepentant, were beyond the reach of the church's salvation and mercy: schismatics, if not too grossly alienated by harsh policies on such matters as the resumption by the church of alienated church lands, could be persuaded back, without reconversion, to the unity of Christendom. Neither Mary nor the Roman church intended to fight schismatics as if they were a perpetual enemy. That would have been an attitude of the Counter-Reformation. It would also have suggested that an English breach with Rome of twenty years had raised a permanent impediment to reconciliation, and that the Protestantism preached under Edward VI had, in a few short years, turned what had begun as a diplomatic rupture with Henry VIII into a state of permanent heresy.

Mary has frequently been much blamed for not discovering the Counter-Reformation.[2] She was bent instead on revitalising English Catholicism as it

---

[1] D. Fenlon, *Heresy and Obedience in Tridentine Italy: Cardinal Pole and the Counter-Reformation*, Cambridge 1972, ix, 22–3. See also Scarisbrick, *Reformation*, which was published after this article was written. My thanks are due to Professors T. G. Barnes, D. Hirst and Conrad Russell for their help with this essay.

[2] A. G. Dickens, *The English Reformation*, 1964, 280–82. D. M. Loades, 'The Enforcement of Reaction 1553–1558', *JEH* xvi, 1965, 54–66, 66.

had been for centuries in England, thus preserving and building on the notion that England was a Catholic country that had always known how to be properly Catholic, and that the nation and the crown need not therefore be too concerned to impress the Papacy by an unquestioning devotion and obedience: England could reject the missionary zeal of the Jesuits, be largely indifferent to the debates that were taking place at Trent, and cling to its own long-established Catholic rituals and dogmas. Mary could afford to be the heir of Edward I, Edward III and Henry V.[3]

For the reconversion of schismatics and the avoidance of new heresy, Mary placed her trust primarily in two weapons, preaching and sound education. It is not then surprising that the queen looked particularly upon the University of Oxford as the cradle of her long-term plans, not only for effective reconciliation with Rome, but, more important, for the effective and permanent re-establishment of Catholicism in England. If good preachers made good Catholics, then good universities made good preachers. In the mix-sixteenth century, Oxford, with its strongly conservative flavour and its slow reception of radical intellectual ideas, was ideally suited to Mary's purposes.

In assuming that there is a causal connection between Mary's involvement with Oxford and the University's overwhelmingly Catholic stance, both during her life-time and for several decades beyond, it is necessary to accept that the surviving evidence is more suggestive than conclusive. It must also be admitted that the nature of the surviving evidence is biased in many ways. Unobtrusive dissent would make little mark on the university records, and silent dissent none. The type of evidence which makes the story of religious conflict in the universities in the later part of Elizabeth's reign so vivid simply does not exist. The period of large collections of private papers, personal recollections and reflections post-dates Mary's reign. This is not peculiar to the University, but seems to be true of all types of source material for the period.[4] Mary's relationship with Oxford presents a hen and egg problem. Did the University respond well towards her because she was benevolent to their interests, or vice-versa? Or was the process mutual? Why did Mary not succeed at Cambridge to anything like the same extent?[5] Should one

---

[3] F. M. Powicke, *The Thirteenth Century*, Oxford 1953, 674–7; 25 Ed. III cap 4 (Statute of Provisors); K. B. McFarlane, 'Henry V, Bishop Beaufort and the Red Hat, 1417–1421', *EHR* lx, 1945, 316–48.

[4] Conrad Russell, *The Crisis of Parliaments*, Oxford 1971, 218–19.

[5] H. C. Porter, *Reformation and Reaction in Tudor Cambridge*, Cambridge 1958, 101–7, slightly modifies this picture of the weakness of Cambridge Catholicism. P. Collinson, *The Elizabethan Puritan Movement*, 1967, 129–30, stresses the vitality of Oxford Protestantism under Elizabeth. The broad picture of Oxford as more Catholic and Cambridge as more Protestant still stands, however. The distinction in geographical intake between the two Universities, though a tempting explanation of their differences, can, by Mary's reign, be over-emphasised. Both Universities had such a multiplicity of local links that they were likely to blur any overall regional bias. See Victor Morgan, 'Cambridge University and The Country 1560–1640', in *The University in Society*, ed. L. Stone, Princeton and London 1975, i, 183–245.

attribute the predominant conservatism of Oxford and the predominance of reformers in Cambridge before Mary's accession to the geographical distribution of their students, to the activities of a few prominent men, or to mere chance?

Both universities had suffered the same rough handling under Henry and Edward, but it was apparent at her accession that of the two Oxford was the more likely to find Mary's policies congenial. The University of Oxford expressed its relief at a return to a recognisable and stable order in a letter to Mary, dated 28 June 1554,

'Recently, when the study of letters lay almost extinct, when the good state of all depended on a doubtful and exiguous hope, who then did not fear for the uncertain outcome of fortune, who did not groan, and indeed with anguish? Some were forced to defer their studies; first one group and then another were tossed hither and thither with each fluctuation, nor did any certain order long survive its proposing.'[6] Such attitudes, once established, can, in part, be self-perpetuating. But the loss of favour both Oxford and Cambridge suffered when their dominant religious view was out of fashion argues that there was some true independence of mind involved. This was particularly true from the reign of Elizabeth onwards, when university posts first became coveted prizes in the national patronage network. Mary interfered singularly little in the election of Oxford college fellows and heads of houses. Oxford's conservative stance in the face of much manipulation and interference under Elizabeth is, then, perhaps even more remarkable. It is clear which queen showed more respect for the liberties, statutes and privileges of both the University and the colleges.

On 20 August 1553, Mary wrote to both Universities, giving them instructions to keep both the ancient University and College statutes 'inviolabley', as was decreed by the wills of their founders and her progenitors, and to ignore all ordinances 'made, set forth or delivered by any visitours or others' since the death of Henry VIII. In the same letter, she described what she saw as the Universities' function in contemporary Catholic society:

> Wee therefore knowing it our bounden dewtie to almightie god, bi whose onlie goodnes wee acknoledge our selfe callyd and placid in the roiall estate of this realme, to travers by al the waies wee maye that his glorie and Hollye will being trulie declarid to all our subjects, he maye of all sorts in there severall vocations be reverentlie fearyd, servid and obaid, have thought good for a beginning to wisshe that thexamples hereof maye first beginne in our Universities, where yong mene and alsorts of students, ioyning godly conversation with ther studies in learning maye after as well by ther doings, as by there preachyng instruct and confirm the rest of our subiects, bothe in the knoledge and

[6] PRO, SP 11/4 fos. 46 r–v. See below p. 216. My translation.

feare of almightie god, in ther dewe obedience towards us, our laws, and all other there superiors, and in ther charitable demainour towards all men.[7]

In the State Papers, the rough draft of this letter, in what appears to be Petre's hand, survives with corrections.[8] Some are trifling, but others remove threats of coercive action by the Crown from the letter. The threat to 'purge our Universities where yought being brougte up' has been erased, as has the order to the Chancellors, heads of houses and those under their care to observe the statutes 'uppon payne of forfytur of your and other offices'; 'ordeyne' has been crossed out, with much else that is unintelligible because incomplete, to leave standing: 'wee therfor have thought good to will and require you'. The whole tone of the letter has been deliberately lightened, to produce a clear and straightforward message which takes obedience for granted. The queen intends to leave the Universities to their old familiar ways, removing from them the very severe threat that Protestantism had created to their lands and their very autonomy, and trusting to their unforced co-operation in return. Such co-operation was essential if teachers and preachers of the true religion were to be provided for Catholic England. Oxford responded promptly. By 10 October 1553, the University Grace Book records that those to be admitted masters of arts at the next comitia are to be admitted to Congregation on condition that they swear to observe all the ancient statutes of the University which apply to them.[9] This was decreed by authority of Congregation.

Acceptance of Mary's instructions was, of course, neither total nor complete. However, among heads of houses, only the President of Magdalen, Walter Haddon, saw fit to resign in 1553 as a result of Mary's accession. Later there

---

[7] BL Add. ms 32, 091, fo. 145r–v. Letter to Oxford, a copy. Cited by R. H. Pogson, 'Reginald Pole and the Priorities of Government in Mary Tudor's Church', *HJ* xviii, l, 1975, 3–20, 14, to whom I owe this reference.

[8] SP 11/1, fos. 20r–21v. F. G. Emmison, *Tudor Secretary*, 1961, 163–4 and n. credits Petre with being both the initiator and the corrector of this letter, because the draft is in his hand. Petre had been an Edwardian Visitor of Oxford in 1549 and 1551. His rôle on both occasions is ambiguous. It seems fairly clear from SP 11/1 that at the time the Marian letters to the University were sent, Petre was not infrequently acting as Mary's secretary (a point which Emmison allows, *Tudor Secretary*, 162).

[9] Oxford University Archives, Register of Congregation and Convocation, 1535–63, N.E.P./ supra/Register I (Register I.8.), fo. 138. I would like to acknowledge my debt to the late Dr W. A. Pantin and to his successor as Keeper of the University of Oxford Archives for their permission to consult this and other material in the Archives, including the typed transcript of Register I, Oxford University Archives, Typed transcript of Register of Congregation and Convocation, 1535–63, N.E.P./supra/Register I, which is the source of the majority of the references to Register I quoted here. The oath which was demanded was not merely *pro forma*, as the newly created masters would only be admitted into Congregation provided they were present at the next meeting of Congregation. On the strength of feeling about the Protestant threat to college lands, see a conference between (with others) Cox, bishop of Ely and John Feckenham, former abbot of Westminster, Strype, J. *Annals*, Oxford 1824, i (2), 529. I owe this reference to William Barr.

were other changes among them. At All Souls, John Warner resigned the Wardenship in January 1556, retiring to a rectory in Middlesex until restored as Warden by the Visitor, soon after Mary's death. Since he had been Vice-chancellor in 1554, it is difficult to be sure exactly what caused his departure. It is possible that it was simply the fruit of internal strife in the college. William More of Exeter, Richard Cox of Christ Church (who became bishop of Ely in 1559) and Ralph Skinner of New College were the only three heads of houses in Oxford deprived at Mary's accession.[10]

Reginald Pole's Visitors visited the University in the summer of 1556 by Pole's legatine authority. Pole was not elected Chancellor until 26 October 1556, and the Oxford visitation was part of a general visitation of the whole English church. Mary herself appears to have been the original instigator of the national Visitation. Pole's Visitors deprived one Oxford head of house, Hugh Weston, rector of Lincoln. It seems that his deprivation was not primarily for religion, since he immediately appealed against it to Rome. He had been involved in the disputations with Cranmer, Ridley and Latimer, and left a Catholic will. He was probably deprived for immorality, since he lost his deanery at St George's, Windsor a year later, on grounds of adultery. The Visitors had been directed to search out not only heretics or those reading heretical books but also those of infamous reputation. Weston probably came into the latter category.[11]

The accession of Mary did, of course, produce an exodus of convinced Protestants from the University. And doubtless many who remained were glad enough to be able to avail themselves of Pole's general dispensation to the University, which was sent in March 1555, to mark the reconciliation with Rome.[12] The pressure of events alone seems to have been sufficient to persuade some convinced Protestants that they should leave Oxford; others left under pressure from college or University Visitors. Jewel, after some initial hesitation, and after, in his rôle as University Orator, writing a letter of congratulation to Mary from the whole University, went abroad in 1554,

[10] *BRUO 1501–40*, 607–8. Reg. I.8 fo. 143v 15 April 1554. Mason, as Chancellor of Oxford, informed Convocation by letter that he had chosen Warner to succeed Marshall as Vice-Chancellor. Warner was appointed by Convocation to keep yearly accounts of Mary's benefaction, July 1554, Reg. I.8., fo. 144v and on 7 September 1554 he was appointed by Convocation to make a ruling on the stipend of Holm Cultram, one of the three ex-monastic rectories that comprised Mary's gift to the University, Reg. I.8, fo. 147r. See also PRO, SP 15/8 fos. 195r–196v, Seth Holland to Pole, 'Whitsun Even', 1558, and R. H. Pogson, 'Cardinal Pole, Papal Legate in Mary Tudor's Reign' (Cambridge Ph.D., 1972), 346–7. I would like to thank Dr Pogson for permission to read and quote from his thesis. On heads of houses see G. D. Duncan, 'The Heads of Houses and Religious Change in Tudor Oxford, 1547–1558', *Oxoniensia* xlv, 1980, 226–34, 230–34.

[11] *BRUO 1501–40*, 616–17. For the Visitors' *Articuli Interrogandi* see Bodleian ms Twyne 7, fos. 155r–157r; another copy is in ms Twyne 2, fos. 84r–85r. For Mary as the instigator of the Visitation, see BL Cotton ms Titus C vii, fo. 120v, no date, c. Nov.–Dec. 1554. I owe this reference to Dr Pogson.

[12] Copy in ms Twyne 7, fo. 147v (p. 88) dated in a mixture of papal and ancient Roman dating.

when it became clear what direction events were taking.[13] Three fellows of Oriel are thought to have left Oxford for religious reasons during Mary's reign though the exact reasons for their departure are unspecified.[14] New College, though predominantly conservative, lost two Fellows at the time of Pole's visitation, and at All Souls, Richard Bullingham and William Whittingham went into exile. At Magdalen, nine Fellows were ejected by the commissaries for Gardiner, the College Visitor, and the College remained a source of trouble for some time.[15] Their President, Owen Oglethorpe, who was re-elected after this visitation and had been in and out of office for some time, resigned, and was replaced by the Catholic Arthur Cole.[16] Trinity and St John's, both being Marian foundations, caused no touble until Elizabeth's accession.

Apart from Magdalen, the colleges which caused most disruption (not all of it necessarily religious in nature) during Mary's reign, as they had done before and were to do later, were those with defective statutes, or no statutes at all, and which had been most disturbed and threatened by the Edwardian Visitation of 1549. These were Christ Church, which had no statutes, and All Souls whose statutes were in the hands of Cardinal Pole for revision.

The popular historical association of Oxford at this period is, of course, with the trials of Cranmer, Ridley and Latimer. Many Oxford men were involved in major or minor rôles in the disputations with these divines, the attempts to obtain their conversions, and so forth. But this impinges very little on the University records, which show rather the underpinnings, the sweeping of the floors, the erection of scaffolding.[17] For example, the incorporation of the Cambridge divines who were to take part in the disputations is recorded, as is a letter from Cambridge to Oxford and one from Oxford to Cambridge. The letter from Cambridge apologises for the heresy of members

---

[13] Reg. I.8. fo. 137v records that '*decretum est ex authoritate domus ob comitia et favorem Magdalensium qui insigniendi sunt Baccalaureorum titulo ut terminus prorogetur in xxviii Julii*' (1553). This would have enabled Magdalen men in a hurry to leave the University in the expectation of Mary's accession, to take their B.A. degrees before they left, though not to determine. The comitia was held on 17 July (Reg. I.8. fo. 138r) and acted irregularly in admitting to the B.A. degree, since it normally dealt only with inceptions. J. E. Booty, *John Jewel as Apologist of the Church of England*, 1963, 79–80, records that Jewel appears to have been asked to sign articles of religion, which may have been those on Transubstantiation which Ridley and Latimer refused to sign. See D. M. Loades, *The Oxford Martyrs*, 1970, 193 and n.4, and *Works of Thomas Cranmer – On the Lord's Supper*, ed. J. E. Coxe (Parker Society), Cambridge 1844, 393.

[14] *VCH Oxford* iii, 1954, 122 and n. Six members went into exile, resigned or were deprived for religion under Elizabeth, three suffered death for their Catholicism.

[15] *VCH Oxford* iii, 158, 178, 197.

[16] Oglethorpe was preferred to the deanery of St George's, Windsor, in 1554, which he vacated by November 1556. He became bishop of Carlisle in August 1557 and was deprived in June 1559. *BRUO 1501–40*, 423–4. See the ambivalent comments of William Allen on his willingness to crown Elizabeth, though he later refused the Oath of Supremacy, William Allen, *A True Sincere and Modest Defence of English Catholics*, ed. Robert M. Kingdon (Folger Shakespeare Library), Ithaca 1965, 109–11.

[17] Oxford University Archives, W. P. ß 21 (2) fo. 66, 'Item, for writing the book of Cranmers examination, iii *s* iiii *d*'.

of their University, to which Oxford politely replied by praising the sound doctrine and great learning of the Cambridge divines who were sent to dispute with their fallen brethren.[18]

On 1 October 1555, John White, bishop of Lincoln, was incorporated as a doctor of theology, having been dispensed from seeking first the more junior degrees required by statute. White presumably wanted to be an Oxford doctor of theology because he had, on 28 September 1555, been appointed a commissioner for the trials of Ridley and Latimer.[19] Two main points emerge from all this, however. The University was clearly under the watchful eyes of a number of Catholic dignitaries during this period, and it would never have been chosen as the suitable place for the trials had it been in any way too suspect. Mary in fact so much trusted the University's loyalty that she planned to hold a Parliament there also.

It was not only for participants in the trials of Cranmer, Ridley and Latimer that the University provided the necessary qualifications or robes. It did so also for Feckenham, chaplain to the queen, canon of St Paul's and Mary's future abbot of Westminster. He offered sixteen years' study in theology for his doctorate of divinity, and was given an unconditional grace. He was also allowed to receive his doctorate *in absentia* and without disputations, because he was involved in important business for the queen, provided that either Dr Chedsey, Dr Harpesfield or Dr Smith, all members of the faculty, inaugurated for him, and he paid the necessary fees.[20]

More surprisingly, perhaps, the University created John Boxall, B.D., the queen's secretary, a doctor of divinity on or about 8 July 1558, without any of the usual exercises, and, as Boxall himself said, in a letter to the University, without any request from him for the honour.[21] Oxford probably had recognised in Boxall a man of influence. It was the same sense of self-preservation which made them appoint Arundel their steward on the death of Bedford, accept the resignation of Mason as Chancellor and his replacement by Pole, and turn to Gardiner, Petre and Arundel when they felt their privileges were under threat.[22]

The religious record of the University, however, is not simply one of compliance, public disputations and the gracious rendering of services to the Crown. There is evidence of a revitalised canon law school in the University – a school which had officially been abolished under Edward. There is evidence of concern for the cure of souls where it was applicable, and increasing insistence that those seeking divinity degrees should give sermons,

---

[18] Reg. I.8. fo. 139r and fos. 142r–143r.

[19] Reg. I.8. fo. 155r. He was admitted and incorporated on the day he received his grace, without any fees mentioned.

[20] Reg. I.8. fo. 159r–v. See also fo. 145v, where Henry Cole D.C.L. was granted a doctorate of divinity without any of the usual exercises because he was engaged in weighty business for the queen, 20–25 June 1554. He was required to pay the usual fees.

[21] Reg. I.8. fos. 175v, 176v.

[22] Reg. I.8. fos. 150v–151v.

either in Latin or in English, in Oxford or at Paul's Cross, as part of their 'exercises' for their degrees. The University was not only grateful for Mary's gift in 1554, of three ex-monastic rectories, which trebled the University's annual income, but took some trouble to consult with her about the farming of the rectories, the repair of the churches and the stipend to be paid to the vicars.[23] Increasing stress was laid on the obligation on scholars to attend mass and University processions.[24] Masters were appointed to organise the sermons in the University. Money was collected to buy a new cross to be carried in University processions, and the Vice-Chancellor was authorised to spend as much money as seemed to him fitting on the repair of the divinity schools.[25] The money from Mary's gift was in part used for the repair of the arts and the divinity schools, and for a chantry priest to say mass for the queen and her progenitors.[26]

The accounts which contain these entries also record the sum of 9s 8d 'for the search for the benefices most convenient for the University to sue for',[27] and throughout the reign the University relentlessly pursued its ancient right (though it had lost the documents to establish it) to appoint to a canonry at Windsor. Such self interest should not be condemned out of hand. If the Crown wanted the University to provide preachers and teachers, it in turn had to provide the necessary patronage, and many Oxford men did indeed achieve high ecclesiastical office under Mary.

It is interesting that Pole never seems to have thought it necessary to impose on Oxford an oath of religious conformity such as Gardiner had thought necessary to impose on Cambridge.[28] As Jewel put it in May 1559, 'at Oxford there are scarcely two individuals who think with us, and even they are so dejected and broken in spirit that they can do nothing. The despicable friar Soto and another Spanish monk, I know not who, have so torn up by the roots all that Peter Martyr had so prosperously planted, that they have reduced the vineyard of the Lord into a wilderness.'[29]

The evidence from the college archives presents a similar picture of low-key Catholic conformity. Religion is rarely mentioned, though colleges such as Merton regularly record masses and exequies, and it seems unlikely that the colleges had any difficulty in finding their mass books and their

---

[23] Reg. I.8. fos. 150r, 145v, 147r. On canon law, see fos. 144v, 150r, 163v and other refs. On sermons and cure of souls, see fos. 162v, 163v, 168r and other refs.
[24] Reg. I.8. fos. 144r, 146v, 158r, 158v and other refs.
[25] Reg. I.8. fo. 166v.
[26] W.P.ß 21 (2) fos. 69, 67. For the gift see Mary's patent, Oxford University Archives, Hyp./L.13/xxiii, Long Box, xxiii, 1554. PRO, E318/41/2206 are the particulars for Mary's gift, dated 3 April 1554. I should like to thank Dr D. L. Thomas for this reference.
[27] W.P.ß 21 (2) fo. 66.
[28] The Letters of Stephen Gardiner, ed. J. A. Muller, Cambridge 1933, 474–6.
[29] The Zurich Letters, ed. Hastings Robinson (Parker Society), Cambridge 1984, i, 33, John Jewel to Henry Bullinger, 22 May 1559. Quoted in Henry Gee, The Elizabethan Clergy and the Settlement of Religion, 1558–64, Oxford 1898, 130–31.

ornaments, or were at all reluctant to do so.[30] The foundation of two new colleges, Trinity and St John's, in Mary's reign suggests that others besides the queen had faith in the University as a source of Catholic posterity, since Pope and White founded them to advance the old religion. The second foundation charter for St John's, issued on 5 March 1558, was confident enough of the future to include canon law among the subjects to be taught in the college.[31] Mary gave her support to both these foundations as she did to many other colleges that were in legal or financial difficulties.[32]

In June 1556, a date which suggests the influence of Pole's Visitors, the courses for M.A. and B.C.L. were, for one year only, made shorter than was demanded by the statutes. The intention was probably to increase the supply of clergy, much depleted by the Marian deprivations, though it is difficult to be sure whether the University took advantage of the alterations. It is likewise impossible to be sure if Pole's Injunctions were much heeded. The sources are too defective for a closer analysis to be possible, and the advent of the sweating sickness, often given by those supplicating for degrees as a reason why the statutes had not been complied with, makes interpretation difficult. The essentially conservative nature of Pole's Injunctions, combined with the University's permanent readiness to circumvent its own statutes when they were inconvenient, further complicates the picture. There are also supplications in the Marian grace book from people who had either studied abroad during much of the previous reign, migrated from theology to medicine, or deferred their supplications many years beyond the normal time. In such cases, which cover names such as John Boxall, William Lawly, Donald Riane, John Lynch, Arthur Cole, G. Cholwelly, John Harpesfield, Thomas Slythurst, William Wright, William Conden, Thomas Godwyn and others, this process may be due to Catholic religious sympathies, as the University's early letter to Mary had indicated.[33] By studying abroad, forsaking the dangers of theological study or avoiding the degree exercises, many who may have been doubtful Protestants could have avoided the embarrassment of exposure.

[30] Lincoln College Archives, Vetus Registrum, fo. 169r. This records the death and burial of Mary and Pole, concluding with a list of the Rector and all the Fellows. My thanks are due to the Archivist and the Librarian at Lincoln College.

[31] W. H. Stevenson and H. E. Salter, *The Early History of St. John's College, Oxford* (OHS n.s. 1), Oxford 1939, 119.

[32] See, for example, PRO, SP 46/8, fo. 36r and v, 28 January 1554/5, Waldegrave to the Lord Treasurer, confirming that New College had never been recompensed for land confiscated by Henry VIII.

[33] Reg. I.8. fo. 160r. Wood is surely wrong to argue that this was done to supplement the dearth of M.A.s caused by those leaving on account of the Visitors' arrival, see BL ms Lansdowne 96, fos. 25r–28v, endorsed 'An: 1554. Order to be moved with L. Cardinall for reformation of matters of religion.' fo. 25v, 'If anie be learned in the universities, they maye be (paper gone) to supplie where nede shalbe.' I owe this reference to R. H. Pogson's thesis, 86, n. 1. See above n. 10. For Oxford's letter to Mary, see above p. 214. The names of delayed supplicators are extracted from an analysis of the Marian Supplications in Reg. I.8. combined with a study of the previous academic careers of the supplicators.

It seems that, throughout Mary's reign, Oxford was a place of relative calm and tranquillity, free of the sort of turmoil the Edwardian Visitors had created, where men who had given up their divinity studies in Henry's or Edward's reign returned to their work, where heads of houses were, with few exceptions, left undisturbed in their offices, and the University's men pursued both their routine occupations and the search for preferment in much the way their predecessors had done for centuries. It remains to ask whether this calm and freedom from outward interference did more than produce a University which would support the queen and her religion during her lifetime, perhaps to do exactly the same for Elizabeth in her turn.

It is a singular fact that modern historians, who can find so few Catholics in England in Mary's reign, can yet find so many in the early years of Elizabeth's reign. Resistance to the Elizabethan settlement was not solely confined to the Marian bishops and other high ecclesiastics: it also appears at more humble levels. Either the country had taken a new Catholic imprint, or old habits had been successfully renewed at all levels, lay and clerical alike. Amongst those who resisted the Elizabethan settlement, Oxford men and, in particular, those who had been in Oxford during Mary's reign, or those closely influenced by them in the early years of Elizabeth's reign, are conspicuous. In 1559, Parkhurst wrote to Bullinger saying that Oxford was '. . . as yet a den of thieves, and of those that hate the light. There are but few gospellers there and many Papists.'[34]

Indeed, it can be argued that much of the social and administrative development at Oxford during the first thirty years of Elizabeth's reign was a direct consequence of the government's and the University authorities' determination to uproot Catholicism from the University.[35]

Anthony Wood remarked, 'It must be now known, that in the beginning of the reign of Queen Elizabeth, the university of Oxon was so empty (after the Roman Catholics had left it upon the alteration of religion) that there was very seldom a sermon preached in the University church called St. Mary'.[36] It should be also noted that Wood's own calculations of the number of Catholics involved in this exodus are not above suspicion. He was clearly a conservative at heart on religious matters. However, having tried to make the same calculations myself, I feel in no position to blame him. It would be valuable and interesting to know not only the number of Catholics who left Oxford for religious reasons early in Elizabeth's reign and who had attended or been closely involved with the Marian University and who were imprisoned for their recalcitrance or fled abroad, but also how these figures would compare with the number of Protestants who left Oxford for similar reasons early in Mary's reign and went into exile, and who had attended or been

---

[34] Claire Cross, *The Royal Supremacy in the Elizabethan Church*, 1969, 137.
[35] Elizabeth Russell, 'The Influx of Commoners into the University of Oxford before 1581: An Optical Illusion?', *EHR* xcii, 1977, 721–45.
[36] Wood. A. *Athenae Oxonienses*, ed. Philip Bliss, 1813, i, 374.

closely involved with the Edwardian University. But, granted the nature of the surviving records, the difficulty of identification and so forth, an exact figure is a pipe-dream. My own calculations lead me to be fairly certain that the two exoduses were at least of equal size, with a strong supposition that the Catholic exodus was somewhere between two and three times the size of the Protestant exodus. There are no figures for the number of Oxford Protestants who were simply deprived of their ecclesiastical livings by Mary, though the number was doubtless large. Some sixty-three Marian Oxfordians were deprived between 1558 and 1565, including sixteen heads of houses.[37]

To a large extent, of course, in comparing the Protestant with the Catholic exodus, one is not comparing like with like. In the first place, the time-scale is totally different. In the second place, the Elizabethan attempts to enforce religious legislation, and in particular the Oath of Supremacy, involved a policy of imprisonment for religious disaffection on a scale for which there is no Marian equivalent. Marian Protestants had no comparable encouragement to disaffection such as Catholics were to find in the Pope and in Phillip II in Elizabeth's reign. The Catholics were not, at least initially, facing any threat comparable to the Marian persecutions and burnings, though the Protestants were spared the need to subscribe to the Marian régime. By and large the Catholics did not flee into the arms of sympathetic communities abroad, but created their own communities in exile, similar to those that they had known in the Universities they had left behind. All these differences must make conclusions (drawn from such doubtful figures) about the comparative size and strength of Catholic and Protestant support in Oxford extremely tentative. What is clear from the exodus of Catholics is that a substantial portion of those who, under Elizabeth, went abroad or were imprisoned and persecuted for religion, or who simply melted discreetly into English Catholic households, had some previous record of either support for Protestantism, or at least of a sufficient conformity with Protestantism under Henry VIII and Edward VI. Men who had once found good and convincing reasons for conforming with the religion of their sovereign were no longer able to do so. This new steadfastness must go some way to validify the underlying assumptions of the Marian régime, that Catholicism was still very deep-rooted in the consciences and consciousness of many of the intellectual leaders in England, and that careful nurturing could make it once again a lively force to contend with.

Among those Oxford men who found that they could not give even a sufficient token support to Protestantism for a second time under Elizabeth was William Tresham, who was a canon of Christ Church until July 1560.

---

[37] These figures are extracted from the lists in Gee, *The Elizabethan Clergy*, 252–69. It is not possible to be sure if these lists are complete or wholly accurate. All figures arrived at on this subject involve an element of guesswork, and can be changed by a small alteration in the definition of the terms involved. See also Duncan, '*The Heads of Houses*', 234. For the Protestant exodus, see (with caution) C. H. Garrett, *The Marian Exiles*, Cambridge 1938.

He refused the Oath of Supremacy, was imprisoned and deprived of his benefices, and died in 1569. He had been in trouble with the Edwardian government in 1551, though this had not prevented him receiving a benefice in 1552, and his Oxford career was uninterrupted until he refused the Elizabethan subscription. William Chedsey who, like Tresham, had played a prominent part in the disputations with Cranmer, and had been appointed a canon of Christ Church in July 1557, was deprived of all his benefices on Elizabeth's accession and was imprisoned in the Fleet in 1562. In 1548 he had been made a canon of St Paul's, though in 1550 he had been imprisoned in the Marshalsea for 'seditious preaching' and had disputed with Peter Martyr in Oxford in 1549. Henry Cole, who was admitted D.D. in 1554, was made Provost of Eton in the same year, and Dean of St Paul's in 1556. He had, however, been Warden of New College continuously from 1542–51. He lost all his preferments for his refusal to take the Oath of Supremacy, was committed to the Tower in 1560, and then moved to the Fleet. Richard Marshall, who was Dean of Christ Church from 1553 till his resignation in May 1559, had been an active Protestant under Edward, changed his opinions under Mary, took an active part in the trial of Cranmer in 1555, and was responsible for disinterring the bones of Peter Martyr's wife on instructions from Pole. After his resignation, he retired to the north of England but was imprisoned in 1562, when he signed a recantation of some sort. He died in 1563, presumably while still in prison. These men, and others like them, such as James Dugdale, Thomas Atkynson, Ambrose Applebie, Thomas Ardene and others of less distinction, suffered close imprisonment or deprivation or were kept under close observation.[38] Their failure to serve Elizabeth was at the least a nuisance, frequently an embarrassment, and sometimes a cause of regret.

Other Marian members of the University escaped abroad, and some later became active and acute threats to the Elizabethan régime. Thomas Harding, Fellow of New College in Mary's reign and a doctor of theology in 1554, was imprisoned at Elizabeth's accession for refusing the Oath of Supremacy. On his release he fled to Louvain, where he became head of the English house of studies there, and famous for his subsequent controversies with Bishop Jewel. He also helped William Allen to found the English College at Douai.[39]

A list of recusants compiled, probably in 1561, by Grindal, Cox and four other commissioners notes the name of Thomas Harding and gives him the following 'character'. 'Learned in King Edward's time: preached the truth earnestly, and now stiff in Papistry, and thinketh very much good of himself.'[40] Harding had been chaplain to the marquis of Dorset and probably tutor to Lady Jane Grey. She is also reputed to have rebuked him for his

---

[38] *BRUO 1501–40*, 201–2, 576–7, 113–14, 128–9.
[39] *BRUO 1501–40*, 265–6.
[40] *CSP* Dom. 1601–1603, *Addenda, 1547–1565*, 521, no. 45.

lapse from Protestantism. He had been the Reader in Hebrew in Edwardian Oxford (perhaps why he thought so much good of himself) and he, in a sermon delivered before the whole University, probably in 1553, blamed his lapse into Protestantism on 'reading German commentators for the sake of the Hebrew'.[41] In 1554 he had vacated his fellowship at New College, where he had been sub-warden, to become chaplain and confessor to Stephen Gardiner, bishop of Winchester, and a canon and prebendary of Winchester Cathedral and treasurer of Salisbury Cathedral. He was there when Jewel was elected the Elizabethan bishop of Salisbury, and it was from there he went abroad to Louvain, after the new bishop had helped to deprive him.[42]

Bishop Horne found two of the three Oxford colleges for which he was the Visitor in 1561 were also 'stiff in papistry'. He dealt relatively easily with the problems at Magdalen, but encountered much more resistance at Corpus and New College. At Corpus the Fellows refused to complain against their President, William Chedsey, whom Horne wished to dislodge for religious reasons. In the end, Horne persuaded Chedsey to resign voluntarily. At New College, Horne found the Fellows were refusing to sign the Oath of Supremacy, and denied that he had any right to exact it. He told Cecil that he had examined two scholars who had refused to come to church, and had told him plainly, perhaps echoing Mary's own sentiments, that it was 'bicause by there Statutes thei ar bounde to have Masse, and ar generally probibit by the same to admitt and receyve nothing contrary or dyverse that therefore they ought not to allowe any other service'. Horne continued, 'and so in the rest is there meaning to be gathered, that albeit thei do in deed come to the service, yeat beinge against there othe and the observacion of there Statutes, they will not affirm it with the subscription of there handes'. Horne was reduced to handing over the two scholars to the Vice-Chancellor for punishment, and asking the Council to tell him what he should do about the others.[43]

Resistance at New College was deeper than perhaps Horne or the Council had realised. Wood claimed that as many as twenty-three fellows refused to subscribe to the Elizabethan Injunctions. This may be an under-estimate.[44] In all, nine of these deprived fellows ended up joining Harding and other former members of the Marian University, many of them highly distinguished, at Louvain, or joined the Jesuits. Some of those (not only from New College) who began their new careers in Louvain moved on to Douai soon after its foundation by William Allen and others in 1568. William Allen had been a

[41] *BRUO 1501–40*, 265–6.
[42] Booty, *John Jewel*, 68–81.
[43] PRO, SP 12/19 fos. 110r–111v, 26 September 1561. Horne to Cecil.
[44] Wood is cited in Gee, *The Elizabethan Clergy*, 233. See also 231–5. See also *VCH Oxford* iii, 158–9. John Bossy, *The English Catholic Community 1570–1850*, 1975, 12 and n. says New College lost twenty-seven fellows and other senior members between 1559 and 1566. He gives a total exodus from Oxford, between 1559 and 1569, of 'over a hundred fellows and other senior members'. Penry Williams, *The Tudor Regime*, Oxford 1979, 200, says twenty-one fellows were removed from New College by the Elizabethan Visitors.

fellow of Oriel and Principal of St Mary's Hall, from which he resigned in 1561. He was later to become a Cardinal.

The list of early members of the College at Douai, from its foundation to the first ordination list of 1573, gives names of fifty Englishmen. Of these, something like eighteen had been in Oxford during Mary's reign, or had some close association with Marian Oxford, such as belonging to the Marian foundations of Trinity and St John's.[45]

The continuity of personnel is equally marked in the lists of secular and seminary priests who were ordained outside England after 24 June 1559. Not less than thirty-three seminary priests had been in Oxford during Mary's reign. Some of them are found in Elizabeth's reign serving notable Catholic families. Martin Gregory became tutor to Philip Howard earl of Arundel. Thomas Stamp became chaplain to Sir George Peckham at his house in Holborn in 1579, where he was closely associated with the families of Vaux and Tresham. He was said to be at Lord Lumley's house in Greenwich after his release from Wisbech in 1594. Henry Stapper, an Oxford graduate in 1557, was still working as a recusant priest in Yorkshire in 1609.[46]

Jasper Haywood, admitted B.A. and elected Fellow of Merton in 1554, left the college in 1558 after three admonitions, and was elected a Fellow of All Souls. Under Elizabeth, Haywood went abroad and entered a Jesuit order in Rome. He spent seventeen years in a German university and returned to England in 1581, on a mission from the Pope, being the first Jesuit to arrive in Elizabethan England. In 1584 he was arrested on his way to France, but was soon released. He settled in Naples and died there in 1597.[47] His arrival in England had caused a considerable stir, for he represented a new and more aggressive Catholic attempt to uphold the body of the faithful in England.

The propaganda works of Marian Oxfordians such as Harding, Stapleton, Sanders, Allen, Oglethorpe and others, whether backed by work in the missionary field or not, were a thorn in the flesh of English Protestant divines and English Protestant councillors, for they needed lengthy and constant refutation. Such labour was necessary to guard both the dignity and the

---

[45] *Records of the English Catholics under the Penal Laws*, ed. T. F. Knox, 1878, i, 3–6. *Les Réfugiés Anglais dans les Pays-Bas*, R. Lechat, Louvain 1914, 33–6. It should be noted that only approximate figures of Oxford men in Mary's reign can be given in any context. It is also clear that Marian Oxfordians had a considerable influence on the first generations of scholars who took their degrees in Elizabeth's reign. The imposition of the Oath of Supremacy seems to have forced many Catholic students to avow themselves but, in 1558, this hurdle was, for many of them, still some way off in the future. See E. Russell, 'The Influx of Commoners', 732–5. See also C. J. Fordyce, 'Louvain and Oxford in the Sixteenth Century', *Révue Belge de Philologie et d'Histoire*, xii, 1933, 645–52.

[46] The numbers are extracted from G. Anstruther, *The Seminary Priests*, Durham 1968, i. See also H. Aveling, *Northern Catholics*, 1966, 43–4.

[47] G. C. Brodrick, *Memorials of Merton College* (OHS iv), Oxford 1885, 261–2. See also L. L. Martz, *The Poetry of Meditation*, New Haven 1954 and 1962, 33 and 182–3. Heywood was a minor poet, and related to John Donne.

integrity of the Elizabethan church, and also to prevent the Catholic polemic from making converts or confirming wavering Catholics. Men trained in Oxford under Mary were a continual threat to the stability and security of the Elizabethan settlement.

It is clear that Marian Oxford helped to produce two diverging strands of Elizabethan Catholics, the 'old religion' supporters, some of whom were imprisoned or went abroad or became private chaplains at the beginning of Elizabeth's reign, and, on the other hand, those who became increasingly associated with the both more defensive and more aggressive post-Tridentine Catholic church, largely through the work, if not the will of William Allen and his associates. Allen himself was, at least initially, part of the school of thought which supported the 'traditional' Catholicism of Mary's reign. The early propaganda works which reached England from Douai and Louvain were based not on Tridentine concepts of the church, but on a quasi-conciliar view of Catholicism that stressed the intrinsic and inescapable unity of a universal Catholic church that was at the heart of Marian Catholic thinking.

This view was, of necessity, eroded by the forces of Trent, and by its incongruity for exiled Catholic Englishmen. It was further eroded by the Papal attitude to England and to English Catholics from 1570 onwards, when Elizabeth was excommunicated. These changes made English Catholics at home and abroad traitors if they defended their religion, and provided spiritual and moral sanction for a war on Protestantism of a highly aggressive and missionary sort in the 'spirit of militant authority'.

While these developments made life extremely difficult for Catholics in England, it is not hard to see why some of the Marian Oxford exiles abroad eventually adopted this missionary stance. They did not do so with any uniformity. The young, not surprisingly, did so more readily than the old; they were also subject to greater temptation and pressure to do so. Stapleton never crossed the watershed between 'traditional' Catholicism and post-Tridentine Catholicism. Allen was near the point of divide, and Sanders was firmly committed to the post-Tridentine view. Marian Oxford had taught its graduates to be good Catholics. By the 1580s, the majority of the surviving exiles from Marian Oxford were, by force of circumstance (both English and Roman), counter-reformers, and far removed from the traditional outlook of Mary.[48]

There have been many and varied assessments made of the work of the English Catholic exiles in England in Elizabeth's reign. They have been regarded as martyrs for their faith, the saviours of a declining English Catholicism, or as those who, because of a too self-regarding neglect, helped

---

[48] Allen, *Modest Defence*, 130, 133, 145. On Stapleton, see Michael Richards, 'Thomas Stapleton', *JEH* xviii, 1967, 187–99. See Bossy, *Catholic Community*, 11–34, for a similar, though subtly different view from the one expressed here. See also A. D. Wright, 'The Significance of the Council of Trent', *JEH* xxvi, 1975, 353–62.

to diminish the chances of Catholic survival in England.[49] This debate is not, however, within the scope of this piece. Whatever the ultimate outcome of the English mission, nothing can diminish the significance of the fact that, on the death of Mary, large numbers of educated Englishmen refused to adjust again to a change in their religion, and went into exile to defend their faith in action and in writing and by waiting. That a large number of these exiled Englishmen were from Marian Oxford would seem to justify Mary's belief, by however random a route, in the power of discreet and sympathetic royal patronage in the Universities, that scholars might, 'as well by ther doings, as by there preachying instruct and confirm the rest . . .'.

---

[49] Christopher Haigh, 'From Monopoly to Minority: Catholicism in Early Modern England', *TRHS* 5th series xxxi, 1981, 129–47, 140–45, and 'The Continuity of Catholicism in the English Reformation', *P & P* xciii, 1981, 37–8 and n.

BIBLIOGRAPHY OF THE WRITINGS OF F. R. H. DU BOULAY

compiled by Ann Brown and Donald Desborough

1950 'A Note on the Rebuilding of Knole by Archbishop Bourgchier', *Arch. Cant.* lxiii, 135–9.
'Charitable Subsidies Granted to the Archbishop of Canterbury, 1300–1489', *BIHR* xxiii, 147–64.

1952 *Registrum Thome Bourgchier Cantuariensis Archiepiscopi, A.D. 1454–86, Pars Prima* (CYS liv).
Handlist of Medieval Ecclesiastical Terms
'Archbishop Cranmer and the Canterbury Temporalities', *EHR* lxvii, 19–36.

1953 'The Pagham Estates of the Archbishops of Canterbury during the Fifteenth Century', *History* n.s. xxxviii, 201–18.

1955 'The Quarrel between the Carmelite Friars and the Secular Clergy of London, 1464–1488', *JEH* vi, 156–74.
REVIEW
The Book of William Morton, Almoner of Peterborough Monastery, 1448–1467, ed. P. I. King, *JEH* vi, 237.

1956 REVIEW
The English Church in the Fourteenth Century by W. A. Pantin, *History* n.s. xli, 206–7.

1957 *Registrum Thome Bourgchier Cantuariensis Archiepiscopi, A.D. 1454–86, Pars Secunda* (CYS liv).
Various entries in *Lexikon für Theologie und Kirche*, Freiburg im Br.

1958 'Bexley Church: Some Early Documents', *Arch. Cant.* lxxiii, 41–53.
'The First English "Gentleman" ', *The Listener* lx, 30 October.
REVIEW
The Church in Chester, 1300–1540 by D. Jones, *History* n.s. xliii, 225.

1959 'Late-continued Demesne Farming at Otford', *Arch. Cant.* lxxiii.
REVIEW
A Biographical Register of the University of Oxford to A.D. 1500, vol. i, by A. B. Emden, *EHR* lxxiv, 104–6.

1960 REVIEWS
English Genealogy by A. R. Wagner, *History* n.s. xlv, 300–301.
A Biographical Register of the University of Oxford to A.D. 1500, vols. ii and iii, by A. B. Emden, *EHR* lxxv, 491–2.

VCH Cambridge and the Isle of Ely iii, *The City and University of Cambridge, EHR* lxxv, 681–3.

1961   *Medieval Bexley* (Bexley).
'Denns, Droving and Danger', *Arch. Cant.* lxxvi, 75–87.
REVIEWS
Diocesan Administration in Fifteenth Century England by R. L. Storey, *EHR* lxxvi, 136.
Register of Roger Martival, Bishop of Salisbury 1315–30 i, *Register of Presentations and Institutions*, ed. K. Edwards, *History* n.s. xlvi, 127–8.
The Stoneleigh Ledger Book, ed. R. H. Hilton, *JEH* xii, 125–6.

1962   'Gavelkind and Knights' Fees in Medieval Kent', *EHR* lxxvii, 504–11.
'The Archbishop as Territorial Magnate', *The Medieval Records of the Archbishops of Canterbury*, ed. J. E. Sayers, 50–70.
REVIEW
Thomas Langley and the Bishopric of Durham 1406–1437 by R. L. Storey, *History* n.s. xlvii, 61–2.

1963   REVIEW
Counsel and Consent by E. W. Kemp, *EHR* lxxvii, 765–6.

1964   *Documents Illustrative of Medieval Kentish History* (Kent Records xviii), ed.
'The Pipe Roll Account of the See of Canterbury during the Vacancy after the death of Archbishop Pecham', *Documents Illustrative of Medieval Kentish History*, 41–57.
'Calendar of Archbishopric Demesne Leases, 1503–1532', *Documents Illustrative of Medieval Kentish History*, 266–97.
'A Rentier Economy in the Later Middle Ages: The Archbishopric of Canterbury', *EcHR* 2nd series xvi, 427–38.
REVIEWS
Calendar of Inquisitions Miscellaneous (Chancery) v, *1387–1393, History* n.s. xlix, 58.
Calendar of Inquisitions Miscellaneous (Chancery) vi, *1392–1399*, History n.s. xlix, 344–5.
The Court Rolls of the Manor of Bromsgrove and King's Norton, 1494–1504, ed. A. F. C. Barber, *History* n.s. xlix, 64.

1965   'The Fifteenth Century', *The English Church and the Papacy in the Middle Ages*, ed. C. H. Lawrence, 197–242.
'Who were farming the English Demesnes at the end of the Middle Ages?', *EcHR* 2nd series xvii, 443–55.
'A Fifteenth Century Memorandum Book from the Diocese of Canterbury', *BIHR* xxxviii, 210–12.
REVIEW
A Biographical Register of the University of Cambridge to A.D. 1500 by A. B. Emden, EHR lxxx, 560–61.

1966   *The Lordship of Canterbury: An Essay on Medieval Society*
Foreword to *Land and Work in Medieval Europe: Selected Papers by Marc Bloch*, translated by J. E. Anderson, vii–xii.

1967 REVIEWS

Estate Documents at Lambeth Palace Library: A Short Catalogue by J. E. Sayers, *EHR*
lxxxii, 149.
Seventeenth-Century Kent by C. W. Chalklin, *EHR* lxxxii, 171–2.
Register of Roger Martival, Bishop of Salisbury 1315–30 iii, ed. S. Reynolds, *EHR*
lxxxii, 375.
Perpetual Chantries in Britain by K. L. Wood-Legh, *EHR* lxxxii, 376–7.

1968 REVIEWS

Canterbury under the Angevin Kings by W. Urry, *EcHR* 2nd series xxi, 169.
The Bishops of Bath and Wells, 1540–1640: Social and Economic Problems by
P. Hembry, *EHR* lxxxiii, 598.
William Courtenay, Archbishop of Canterbury 1381–1396 by J. Dahmus, *EHR* lxxxii,
827–8.
Medieval Society: the West Midlands at the End of the Thirteenth Century by R. H.
Hilton, *History* n.s. liii, 80–81.

1969 REVIEW

Thomas Arundel: a Study of Church Life in the Reign of Richard II by M. Aston, *EHR*
lxxxiv, 115–16.

1970 *An Age of Ambition: English Society in the Late Middle Ages.*

1971 *The Reign of Richard II: Essays in Honour of May McKisack*, ed. with Caroline M.
Barron.
'Henry of Derby's Expeditions to Prussia, 1390–91 and 1392', *The Reign of
Richard II*, 153–72.

1972 REVIEWS

Western Society and the Church in the Middle Ages by R. W. Southern, *EHR* lxxxvii,
107–11.
VCH Stafford iii, *EHR* lxxxvii, 865–6.

1973 REVIEW

Calendar of Scottish Supplications to Rome 1428–1432, ed. A. I. Dunlop and I. B.
Cowan, *EHR* lxxxviii, 422–3.

1974 'The Assembling of an Estate: Knole in Sevenoaks c. 1275 to c. 1525', *Arch.
Cant.* lxxix, 1–10.
'The Historical Chaucer', *Geoffrey Chaucer*, ed. D. Brewer, 33–57.
REVIEW
Register of Roger Martival, Bishop of Salisbury 1315–30 ii, *Register of Divers Letters*,
ed. C. R. Elrington, *EHR* lxxxix, 420.

1975 REVIEW

Canterbury Professions, ed. M. Richter, *EHR* xc, 879–80.

1976 REVIEW

*Itinerarium Italicum: The Profile of the Italian Renaissance in the Mirror of its European
Transformations*, ed. H. A. Oberman and T. A. Brady, *JEH* xxvii, 329–30.

1978 'Law Enforcement in Medieval Germany', *History* n.s. lxiii, 345–55.
REVIEW
Education in the West of England 1066–1548 by N. Orme, *EHR* xciii, 158–9.

1980 REVIEWS

Die Nurnberger Mittelschichten Im 15. Jahrhundert by M. Toch, *History* n.s. lxv, 292–3.

Rule and Conflict in Early Medieval Society: Ottonian Saxony by K. J. Leyser, *History* n.s. lxv, 461–2.

1981 'The German Town Chroniclers', *The Writing of History: Essays Presented to Richard William Southern*, ed. R. H. C. Davis and J. M. Wallace-Hadrill, Oxford, 455–69.

REVIEWS

The Northern Crusades: The Baltic and the Catholic Frontier 1100–1525 by E. Christiansen, *History* n.s. lxvi, 287–8.

The Limewood Sculptors of Renaissance Germany by M. Baxandall, *History* n.s. lxvi, 291–2.

1982 REVIEWS

VCH Stafford vi, *EHR* xcvii, 615.

For the Sake of Simple Folk: Popular Propaganda for the German Reformation by R. W. Scribner, *History* n.s. lxvii, 319–20.

1983 *Germany in the Later Middle Ages*

REVIEW

Profession, Vocation and Culture in Later Medieval England: Essays Dedicated to the Memory of A. R. Myers, JEH xxxiv, 649.

1984 REVIEW

Social Relations and Ideas: Essays in Honour of R. H. Hilton, ed. T. H. Aston *et al.*, *History* n.s. lxix, 125.

Other signed reviews have appeared in the following publications: *The Amateur Historian, History Today, Life of the Spirit, The Listener, The Month, The Ricardian, The Teacher, Theology*, the *Times Educational Supplement, Times Higher Educational Supplement* and *Times Literary Supplement*.

SUBSCRIBERS

Christopher Allmand
Derek Baker
Balliol College, Oxford – the Library
Melanie Barber
Caroline M. Barron
Geoffrey Barrow
Dr Michael J. Bennett
J. L. Bolton
Rosalind and Christopher Brooke
Dr Ann F. Brown
Christ's Hospital – the History Grecians
College of Ripon and York St John
Dr P. J. Corfield
Anne Crawford
Prof. J. Mordaunt Crook
Prof. C. M. D. Crowder
Mrs M. M. Darby
Richard G. Davies
R. R. Davies
R. H. C. Davis
Barrie Dobson
Robert W. Dunning
Rev. Prof. G. R. Dunstan
C. R. Elrington
Prof. G. R. Elton
John Gillingham
Dr Joan Greatrex
Ralph A. Griffiths
Dr DeLloyd J. Guth
John Hare
Christopher Harper-Bill
Barbara F. Harvey
Dr M. M. Harvey
Prof. P. D. A. Harvey
Peter Heath
R. H. Helmholz
Dr Michael Hicks

J. R. L. Highfield
Rosalind Hill
Christopher Holdsworth
G. A. Holmes
Anne Hudson
Prof. R. Ian Jack
Michael Jones
Maurice Keen
Mrs Gillian Keir
William Kellaway
Ann J. Kettle
Dr T. Kido
C. H. Lawrence
F. Donald Logan
Dr K. G. T. McDonnell
A. K. McHardy
Kathleen Major
Rev. Prof. F. X. Martin, osa
Dr Emma Mason
Prof. D. J. A. Matthew
David Morgan
Douglas Moss
Mrs D. M. Owen
Rosl Philpot
Dr Martyn C. Rady
Hilary Roper-Lowe
Joel T. Rosenthal
Conrad and Elizabeth Russell
Dr J. E. Sayers
R. W. Scribner
Sir Richard Southern
Dr Pamela Taylor
Keith Thomas
Dr J. A. F. Thomson
J. A. Turner
D. E. R. Watt
Diana M. Webb
Michael Wilks